WOMEN'S PROFESSIONAL LIVES IN RHETORIC AND COMPOSITION

Women's Professional Lives in Rhetoric and Composition

Choice, Chance, and Serendipity

EDITED BY

Elizabeth A. Flynn

AND

Tiffany Bourelle

THE OHIO STATE UNIVERSITY PRESS | COLUMBUS

Copyright © 2018 by The Ohio State University.
All rights reserved.

Library of Congress Cataloging-in-Publication Data
Names: Flynn, Elizabeth A., 1944– editor. | Bourelle, Tiffany, 1977– editor.
Title: Women's professional lives in rhetoric and composition : choice, chance, and serendipity / edited by Elizabeth A. Flynn and Tiffany Bourelle.
Description: Columbus : The Ohio State University Press, [2018] | Includes bibliographical references and index.
Identifiers: LCCN 2017032630 | ISBN 9780814213568 (cloth ; alk. paper) | ISBN 0814213561 (cloth ; alk. paper)
Subjects: LCSH: Rhetoric—Social aspects. | Composition (Language arts) | Women professional employees—Communication. | Women and literature. | Academic writing. | Serendipity.
Classification: LCC PN175.W66 2018 | DDC 808/.0082—dc23
LC record available at https://lccn.loc.gov/2017032630

Cover design by Lisa Force
Text design by Juliet Williams
Type set in Adobe Minion Pro

♾ The paper used in this publication meets the minimum requirements of the American National Standard for Information Sciences—Permanence of Paper for Printed Library Materials. ANSI Z39.48-1992.

9 8 7 6 5 4 3 2 1

CONTENTS

ACKNOWLEDGMENTS		vii
FOREWORD		
	M. ANN BRADY	ix
INTRODUCTION		
	ELIZABETH A. FLYNN AND TIFFANY BOURELLE	1
CHAPTER 1	How to Get a Nonacademic Position: An Essay on Serendipity—Personal, Professional, and Intellectual	
	LISA EDE	18
CHAPTER 2	Becoming a Feminist Teacher, Researcher, and Administrator	
	ELIZABETH A. FLYNN	30
CHAPTER 3	My Kairotic Career	
	ANNE RUGGLES GERE	49
CHAPTER 4	Choice and Serendipity, Supple Synergy	
	LYNN Z. BLOOM	58
CHAPTER 5	Composing a Poetic Life	
	LIBBY FALK JONES	74

CONTENTS

CHAPTER 6   Choreography: Running Away, Moving Toward, Living In
SUELLYNN DUFFEY   89

CHAPTER 7   Embracing Scrappiness: Troublesome Knowledge and Serendipity
LINDA ADLER-KASSNER   108

CHAPTER 8   Word by Word, Bead by Bead: Making a Scholarly Life
MALEA POWELL   124

CHAPTER 9   When Depression and Resilience Collide: Might as Well Get Up
JACQUELINE RHODES   142

CHAPTER 10   The Camino: A Pilgrim's Journey of Choice
BETH L. HEWETT   154

CHAPTER 11   Southern Girl Seeks Wide-Open Spaces: My Journey through Academia
TIFFANY BOURELLE   173

CHAPTER 12   My Kismet in the Making: Navigating the Profession "alla Turca"
IKLIM GOKSEL   191

CHAPTER 13   My Life in Composition Studies: Serendipity, Shame, Status Anxiety, and Trusting My Instincts
IRENE PAPOULIS   203

CHAPTER 14   Empowerment through Change and Resilience: A Technical Communicator's Tale
NATASHA N. JONES   218

CHAPTER 15   What I Learned about Teaching, Administration, and Scholarship from Singing with the Scottsdale Chorus
SHIRLEY ROSE   235

LIST OF CONTRIBUTORS   245

INDEX   249

ACKNOWLEDGMENTS

Beth and Tiffany would like to thank each other for maintaining a wonderful collegial and collaborative spirit throughout this long, multiyear process. We would also like to thank the contributors to the volume for doing the same. Once, when we were requesting one form or another, Linda Adler-Kassner joked that it was like herding cats. But it really wasn't. Everyone always came through on time while maintaining a cheerful demeanor (or at least the appearance of one). It was fun rereading the essays in preparation for writing the introduction and noticing the many coincidences, serendipitous, of course, which never made it into the introduction. Did Linda Adler-Kassner know that Irene Papoulis had also taught at the University of California, Santa Barbara for a time? Did Libby Jones know that Tiffany had spent her undergraduate years at the University of Tennessee? Did Beth Hewett know that Suellynn Duffey and Beth Flynn also lived in Germany at one point? Tiffany did know that Lynn Bloom had also taught at the University of New Mexico. Lynn Bloom did know that Anne Ruggles Gere had also gotten her PhD at the University of Michigan. There's also the Ohio State contingent—Lisa Ede, Beth, Suellynn Duffey—and Taralee Cyphers! How amazing to be publishing a book at our doctoral institution after being away for so many years.

Speaking of Tara, she has done an outstanding job pulling this project together. She has been enthusiastic—and patient—all along. We found her by way of Wendy Hesford, coeditor of the New Directions in Rhetoric and Materiality series published by Ohio State. While the book was not in alignment with that series, we were put in touch with Tara. As it turns out, Tara already knew about the project because she had attended Feminisms and Rhetorics in 2015 where Beth mentioned it in her keynote presentation. Good fortune all around. Staff at the Press has also been impressively helpful, competent, and enthusiastic, especially Michelle Hoffmann, who oversaw the production of the book, Kelly Clody, who did the copy editing, and Laurie Avery and her assistant Meredith Nini, who handled marketing. Thanks, too, to Scott Smiley, for preparing the index.

We'd also like to thank the anonymous reviewers of the manuscript at two stages of the process and Andrea Lunsford, who chose to make her identity known in the first review. The collection definitely reflects their values and judgments, and their reviews prompted more revisions of essays than we care to count.

Beth would like thank her daughter Kate Flynn for housing her in January of 2017 while she worked on a revision of the introduction and for pointing out the many DC coffee houses where work of this kind is possible. She'd also like to thank her sister Alice Hayes and friends Christa Walck, Melinda Quivik, and Bonnie Peterson for providing feedback on possible cover images. In addition, she'd like to thank her colleague in the Department of Humanities at Michigan Tech, Marcelino Vieira-Ramos, who invited his mentor at the University of Michigan, Gareth Williams, for a talk, hence the serendipitous awareness of his work and chance theory.

Tiffany would like to thank Thomas Turner, Associate Dean of Research at the University of New Mexico, for generously providing subvention funds. She would also like to thank her husband, Andy Bourelle, for being so supportive throughout the process.

FOREWORD

M. ANN BRADY

"If we do something over and over again, it becomes normal. If we see the same thing over and over again, it becomes normal" (13). Chimamanda Ngozi Adichie uses these words to comment on ongoing gender inequalities persisting in Nigeria. But, they could also be used to describe certain stories we hear, over and over again, about women's professional lives.

Regardless of where they work—in academic or nonacademic settings—such stories encourage women to view the challenges they face as "normal," promising them an uncomplicated path to professional success if only they remain single-minded, self-sufficient, and determined. The strategies women use to negotiate these challenges are also normalized. Regardless, that is, of their race, class, ethnicity, ability, gender expression, or age, women are admonished to adopt the right mindset, know their value, and lean in. These narratives sidestep the details of the lives women lead, blur the particulars of the challenges they negotiate, and disregard the social and relational contexts in which they live and work. Because they lack detail and context, they easily reinforce familiar binaries, setting the private against the public, the personal against the professional, the communal against the individual, the intuitive against the rational, the body against the mind.

The fifteen contributors to this volume locate themselves as "valuable strangers" (Harding 124) to the normalizing narrative I have described and as it is told in universities, community colleges, writing centers, classrooms, and academic offices. In doing so, they reclaim and retell it, offering "more adequate, richer, better accounts of [the] world in order to live in it well and in critical, reflexive relation" to their own practices and those of others (Haraway 187).

The fifteen focus their narrative essays on the collaborative nature of choice, the kairos of chance, and the ephemerality of serendipity, thus challenging what might be considered "normal" in the lives of academic women, specifically those working in the field of rhetoric and composition. Because context nourishes choice, chance, and serendipity, it is no surprise that the women focus on places, people, and conversations. Expanding and complicating the normalizing narrative's core metaphor—the professional path—the writers liken their experiences to those such as beading a peyote-stitched standalone, choreographing a dance, taking a *dolmuş* ride, singing a barbershop "uptune," preparing a meal.

Each writer contextualizes her images in ways that make clear how they emerge from personal interactions with others. The interactions are serendipitous, taking place on a car ride with a father and grandmother, or in a meeting with an advisor, or during a job review with a supervisor. The exchanges vary. Some are exhilarating, making it clear that the opportune moment is now and can be seized. Others are withering, calling into question the very likelihood of such a moment. Regardless, the writers turn these chance encounters to their advantage, using them to imagine possibilities for future actions, all of which require movement.

For some women, the movement is geographic: they leave behind familiar places and people to seek advanced degrees or promising employment in new locations. More, however, describe themselves as moving across, within, and among disciplines. So, while they may all be grounded in rhetoric and composition, they also write, carry out research, produce scholarship, and teach in far-ranging, but interconnected fields, such as global rhetorics, women's studies, diverse literatures, poetry, writing center administration, technical communication, and basic writing. By thus "recirculating, recreating, reforming, reshaping, and engaging" (Flynn, Sotirin, Brady 12) the field as they inhabit it, the writers collapse conventional knowledge frames that separate disciplines, one from the other, to create richer, more complex and dynamic academic spaces. In this way, the women who contribute to this collection help us to understand the materiality and humanity of interdisciplinary exchange. Perhaps more importantly, their work, struggle, and achievements in these new spaces reclaim the story of what is expected of women, retelling it as what women choose, and chance, for themselves.

WORKS CITED

Adichie, Chimamanda Ngozi. *We Should All Be Feminists*. New York: Anchor Books, 2014. Print.

Flynn, Elizabeth A., Patricia Sotirin, and Ann Brady, eds. *Feminist Rhetorical Resilience*. Logan: Utah State UP, 2012. Print.

Haraway, Donna. *Simians, Cyborgs, and Women: The Reinvention of Nature*. New York: Routledge, 1991. Print.

Harding, Sandra. *Whose Science? Whose Knowledge?* Ithaca, NY: Cornell UP, 1991. Print.

INTRODUCTION

ELIZABETH A. FLYNN AND TIFFANY BOURELLE

At a dinner of women academics in rhetoric and composition a few years ago, stories of career paths began to emerge that had overlapping themes: ones of agency, resilience, opportune timing, good fortune, and occasionally not the fortune that one would have asked or wished for. We realized that our collective paths were circuitous rather than linear, our successes as often as not tainted by failures or at least false starts. Advice about how to be a successful academic—set goals and stick to them—didn't seem to match up with the serendipitous routes we all seemed to have taken. Tiffany was not at the dinner, but she and Beth had already been talking about unexpected developments in their careers and had already decided to write about them. Tiffany suggested a book, Beth told her about the dinner, and the project was born. Most of the dinner partiers agreed to contribute a chapter, and others were added based on increasing the diversity of the perspectives. When the responses to our invitations were mostly positive, it became clear that we were onto something big.

We note that the "women" of our title should be seen as having quotation marks around it. For one thing, "women" clearly encompasses females of diverse ages, races, sexual orientations, class backgrounds, geographical locations, abilities, disabilities, and privilege or lack thereof. For another, the term can be seen as including men as our authors write about the numerous women as well as men who enabled their careers. Also, within any one individual, there are multiple identities. As Roxane Gay, the self-proclaimed "bad feminist" who has become a spokesperson for feminism in numerous venues of late, explains in an exchange with Erica Jong at the Decatur Book Festival in Georgia, "Feminism has to realize it's really about intersectionality . . . but that word tends to be off-putting. That just means that we inhabit more than one identity. I'm not just a woman. I'm Haitian American. I'm Catholic. I'm from Nebraska. I have a body. I have tattoos. I mean not all these identity markers matter as much as others." The women in this collection inhabit various identities, including teacher, scholar, poet, administrator, mother, dancer, beader, and many more. In addition, each woman inhabits multiple identities: many combine teaching, administrating, conducting research, attending to family matters, contributing to their communities, and participating in one or more extracurricular activities. Racial, ethnic, familial, and class identities are often mixed. Each contributor has changed locations one or more times as she has become a specialist in rhetoric and composition, often working far from where she was raised. The identities discussed in the chapters abound and are not described by the use of one simple word.

Some of the scholarship upon which this book builds and from which it departs includes *Women/Writing/Teaching*, edited by Jan Zlotnik Schmidt; *Women's Ways of Making It in Rhetoric and Composition*, coedited by Michelle Ballif, Diane Davis, and Roxanne Mountford; and *Rewriting Success in Rhetoric and Composition Careers*, coedited by Amy Goodburn, Donna LeCourt, and Carrie Leverenz. Schmidt's book, published in the 1990s, emphasizes that for the twenty contributors to her volume, writing and teaching are represented as intertwined, essential ways to construct meaning in life. The book includes stories by women in rhetoric and composition as well as women in other fields such as education and women's studies—bell hooks, Mary Gordon, and Adrienne Rich, for instance—who see themselves as writing teachers. The more recent Ballif, Davis, and Mountford volume focuses on eight very successful women in rhetoric and composition selected as a result of a survey—Andrea Lunsford, Patricia Bizzell, Shirley Wilson Logan, and Jacqueline Jones Royster, for instance—and relates the stories of their successes to serve as models for other women in the profession. The book is a kind of handbook on how to make it in rhetoric and composition. Goodburn, LeCourt, and Leverenz's collection was written as a response to the Ballif, Davis, and Mountford book. If *Women's Ways of Making It in Rhetoric and Composition* focuses on successful, research-oriented women, *Rewriting Success in Rhetoric and Composition Careers* recounts stories of women and men who are closer to the periphery of the profession. They are part-time adjuncts, teachers at two-year colleges, professionals outside the academy in a variety of careers, professionals who have taken time out from the academy only to return to an improved situation, and teachers and administrators in full-time, non-tenure-track positions within the academy.

Our collection differs from these in that it places emphasis on the convergences of choice, chance, and serendipity in the professional lives of women with diverse backgrounds and situated in diverse locations within the field of rhetoric and composition. Like the Ballif, Davis, and Mountford collection, we include essays by very successful and highly visible senior members of the rhetoric and composition community who have published widely and held leadership positions within the field, and like the Goodburn, LeCourt, and Leverenz collection, we include an essay by a woman who has held a non-tenure-track position for a number of years, by one with a temporary non-tenure-track position, and by an independent scholar with no university affiliation at present. Unlike either of these books, though, we focus on the circuitous ways professional and personal commitments have evolved and on the intersectionality of identities regardless of position on a continuum from greater to lesser privilege or marginalization. Contributors come from diverse kinds of institutions—small liberal arts colleges, Big Ten universities, technological universities, and large state universities on the East and West Coasts, in the South, the Midwest, and the Southwest. They also have a range of experience—well-established professors emeritae, endowed chairs, full professors, advanced associate professors, untenured assistant professors, a long-time lecturer, an independent scholar, and a part-time faculty member. Contributors self-identify as African American, American Indian, Turkish American, white, lesbian, and disabled. Some come from working-class backgrounds or married into the working class, while others identify as middle class or do not directly address the issue of class. Almost all have directed writing programs, and all have taught writing. All have professional lives with personal intersections—mothers, primary breadwinners, spouses of professionals of equal status, single mothers, a caregiver of an aging parent (or, in one case, caregiver of a grandchild), and single women.

All of our contributors made choices within the constraints necessarily imposed by chance and serendipity involving changes in direction that seemed risky at first but that usually resulted in productive work involving teaching, administration, and research within rhetoric and composition. While our themes revolve around choice, chance, and serendipity within the contexts of kairos and resilience, these terms call to mind other concepts such as agency, control (or lack thereof) over one's path, and a general openness to various experiences. The intention of these narratives is not only to illustrate how scholarship and outside influences have impacted careers and lives but also to provide guidance for women and men who find themselves in similar situations—searching for academic jobs and sometimes failing, and striving for "success" as it is often defined in our field. The book is addressed primarily to scholars and graduate students in rhetoric and composition, though it should appeal to scholars and students in other humanistic fields as well. It is especially well suited to graduate students attempting to find their way into professional positions and ways of thinking. In her chapter in this collection, Suellynn Duffey accurately describes how all of the contributors "create stories that seem much more coherent than the lived experiences they narrate, and from that coherence we create advice for others to follow" (90).

CHOICE, CHANCE, SERENDIPITY, KAIROS, AND RESILIENCE

A recurring theme in the narratives is resilience. Flynn, Sotirin, and Brady in *Feminist Rhetorical Resilience* argue in their introduction that a feminist conception of resilience is best seen not as fundamentally psychological but as rhetorical, relational, and contextual. They see resilience as resulting from the agency or choices of the rhetor as well as relationality or an ability to form relationships with others, and *mêtis*, or an ability to shape shift in challenging circumstances. They also suggest, and the essays in their collection suggest, that feminist resilient communicative action can include multiple and sometimes contradictory strategies that need to be worked out in relation to specific situations and within a number of contexts (1).

The idea of agency intersects with our themes in that the authors of these essays have made difficult choices in their lives at certain unforeseen opportune or even inopportune moments and in response to chance occurrences that comprise everyone's lived experiences. In speaking within the context of resilience, Flynn, Sotirin, and Brady define rhetorical agency as "vested in a strategic rhetor marshaling the available means of public action and responding efficaciously to the demands of the circumstances and larger historical-structural forces" (7). Their definition of agency implies that the agent is actively responding to the world around her.

Other modern and postmodern approaches extend while interrogating this idea of agency, suggesting that the choices made by agents are not always conscious decisions, and often chance plays as large a role as choice. Philosophers Bernard Williams and Thomas Nagel in 1976, for instance, developed a concept they called "moral luck." Morality, they argued, is not entirely a matter of an agent making a deliberate choice, the consequences of which are clear at the time of the decision. Luck plays a role as well, and as a result, future outcomes cannot be fully known. Jacques Derrida in *Politics of Friendship* (1997) says, "There would be no future without chance" (50). Gareth Williams in *The Mexican Exception* (2011), drawing on Derrida's approach to decision-making in *Politics of Friendship*, says, "It is the relation between chance and the decision that determines the action" (128). Emphasizing that decisions are not always deliberate, in her article "Rhetorical Agency as Emergent and Enacted," Marilyn Cooper claims that while a rhetorical agent may not recognize her intentions, her choices are influenced by past and current experiences within natural and social environments (420). Gesa Kirsch and Liz Rohan, in their coedited book *Beyond the Archives*, explain that consciously or subconsciously, a rhetorical agent can call upon lived experiences, letting the past guide intuition and creativity (4).

Here lies the intersection of agency and accidental sagacity: if the circumstances are right, we begin to learn from our past and trust our intuitions. Accidental sagacity or serendipity, then, is not solely coincidence or luck but the willingness to act on hunches or trust one's own intuition—to learn from one's experience. In *Making and Unmaking the Prospects for Rhetoric: Selected Papers from the 1996 Rhetoric Society of America Conference* (1997), Patricia Bizzell notes the importance of learning from one's past, suggesting to us that historical consciousness and accidental sagacity combined define rhetorical agency (40). Direction and meaning emerge from the convergence of histories—in the right situations, we become aware of ourselves and our paths from insight, clues, hunches, and the general ability to connect with this intuition—these are what give us some agency over our own lives.

As Lynn Bloom notes in her chapter in this collection, the origin of the word *serendipity* can be traced as far back as 1754 to Horace Walpole in a letter to Sir Horace Mann. In the letter, Walpole observes that the word comes from a fairy tale he once read, "Three Princes of Serendip." In the story, the princes made discoveries, "by accidents and sagacity, of things in which they were not in quest of." It is significant that Walpole merges both accident and sagacity in defining serendipity, calling it "*accidental sagacity*" (his emphasis). In "Serendipity and Scientific Discovery," Martin Rosenmann sees the word "sagacity" as pertaining to "penetrating intelligence, keen perception and sound judgment," making the term "a key element of serendipity" (132). As he notes, sagacity has been omitted from more recent definitions of serendipity, which most often place greater emphasis on accident or chance. Rosenmann also mentions the story of the princes, comparing it with the scientific world, specifically that of Alexander Fleming's discovery of penicillin, suggesting that Fleming followed up on a promising lead with a *prepared mind* (his emphasis), leading the scientist to make one of the most important discoveries of our time. Rosenmann notes the serendipitous nature of this event, suggesting that researchers have questioning minds, causing them to challenge assumptions while recognizing and appreciating the unexpected. The researchers Rosenmann describes are similar to the women in this collection—all have listened to their intuition, made choices based on their past that sometimes challenged the status quo, and learned from or embraced events not necessarily within their control or even within their conscious awareness.

Responses to circumstances or larger forces may cause the agent to recognize the opportune time—the kairotic moment—that presents itself when making these decisions. In *Rhetoric and Kairos: Essays in History, Theory, and Practice* (2002), James Kinneavy defined kairos as the "right or opportune moment to do something, or right measure in doing something" (80). Erwin Panofsky's definition of kairos in *Studies in Iconology: Humanistic Themes in the Art of the Renaissance* (1972) is perhaps more applicable to the stories told in this book; he describes the concept as "the brief, decisive moment which marks a turning-point in the life of human beings or in the development of the universe" (71). The narratives in this collection often point to times in the writers' lives where opportune moments to act changed the course of their careers, their personal lives, and at times, their research.

In the foreword of *Rhetoric and Kairos* (2002), Carolyn Miller suggests there are two approaches to the definition of kairos. One view approaches the concept as "the principle of adaptation and accommodation to convention, expectation, predictability," and the other calls upon us to challenge the expected and "be creative in responding to the unforeseen, the lack of human order in life" (xiii). Miller notes that the challenge in the latter view of kairos is to act in a way that is "uniquely meaningful" within the circumstances (xiii). The actions or responses to unexpected circumstances encourage rhetorical agency, existing at the intersection of a network of semiotic, material, and intentional elements and rational practices (8). Kairos, or the exact moment these elements and practices come together, influences agency and authority, causing one to act on her intuitions and call upon her lived experiences. When these intuitions are ignored, an agent may miss out on leads that enrich her understandings of past, present, virtual, and historical experiences. Indeed, kairotic opportunities may not present themselves, not because they do not exist, but because we are not aware of them. Kairos, serendipity, and resilience together encourage us to call upon our intuitions, our learned histories to make decisions at the time when chance makes decision-making possible; when faced with the unexpected, many of the authors illustrate actions that were also unexpected.

CHALLENGING CIRCUMSTANCES IN RHETORIC AND COMPOSITION

As discussions of women's careers in rhetoric and composition demonstrate, women, regardless of background, have encountered unforeseen challenges as they forged their careers. The academy is an institution that was structured by and for men, so some degree of difficulty and conflict is inevitable. Senior women scholars struggled to establish themselves and find positions when the field was in its early stages and had not yet developed graduate programs. If they were raising children, they did not have the benefit of maternity leave or childcare centers common now at colleges and universities. On the other hand, the newness of the field sometimes afforded freedom from strict disciplinary boundaries and opportunities to help develop the emerging field and subfields within it. Some women in the collection also faced familial challenges such as attempting to develop careers in tandem with partners. Others raised children either by themselves or with partners, attempted to manage disabilities, were first-generation professionals, had difficulties establishing themselves early on, or were raised in a different country and culture from the one in which they find themselves.

Foremothers in the field often had even greater challenges to contend with. Win Horner did not begin her career until age 54 and did not obtain her endowed chair at Texas Christian University, the position that enabled her to publish nine scholarly books, until age 62. Before obtaining the PhD and the endowed chair, while she and her husband raised four children, she had non-tenure-track positions. Maxine Hairston wrote textbooks as scholarship against the advice of tenured professors. Susan Miller had difficulties at the three institutions where she worked—Ohio State, where she was denied tenure, the University of Wisconsin-Milwaukee, and the University of Utah. She died of cancer at age 70. It is no wonder hers is a dark view of the profession. In *Textual Carnivals*, she speaks of compositionists as sad women in the basement, victims of hierarchical structures that place them at the bottom in terms of status as well as pay and working conditions. Theresa Enos in *Gender Roles and Faculty Lives in Rhetoric and Composition* speaks of writing programs in their relatively early days as having a "classic patriarchal construction" with its large groups of underpaid and undervalued teachers, mostly female, whose supervisors are mostly male (freshman writing directors, department chairs, directors of advanced writing programs, deans, provosts, chancellors, presidents; vii). She says, "The pattern of well-rewarded, male supervision of under-rewarded, female workers is entrenched in our whole culture" (vii).

Sue Ellen Holbrook and others speak of women in the field and the field as a whole as feminized.

Focusing specifically on problems that result from their contingent status within the academy, Eileen Schell in *Gypsy Academics and Mother-Teachers: Gender, Contingent Labor, and Writing Instruction* argues that although a significant number of women have earned PhDs and attained tenure-track positions in English studies as well as rhetoric and composition, "many still function as a reserve army of labor, a 'disposable' and/or 'recyclable' work force composed of part-time and temporary non-tenure-track teachers" (8). Schell, though, perhaps because she was a contingent laborer herself, is careful not to portray them as victims or martyrs.

CHALLENGING CIRCUMSTANCES IN OTHER FIELDS

Accounts of academic women in larger, better-established fields make evident that it has historically not been any easier for them. Women mainstream and nonmainstream academics have faced resistance to feminism; invisible and subtle discrimination; racial, ethnic, and class prejudice; and family challenges that are not always balanced by successful assimilation. VèVè Clark, Shirley Nelson Garner, Margaret Higonnet, and Ketu H. Katrak's *Antifeminism in the Academy* grew out of discussions in the late '80s when the Modern Language Association's Commission on the Status of Women in the Profession met to share ideas for future collaborative projects. One of the women told a story that resonated with the experiences of others in the group—antifeminism with overlays of racism and violence (xi). A result of the discussion was an "open hearing" at the 1989 Modern Language Association (MLA) Convention in which a number of women told their stories. Writing in a similar vein, but with considerably more emphasis on positive action needed to bring about change, Jane Roland Martin in *Coming of Age in Academe* likens the struggles of feminist scholars within the academy to the struggles for women's suffrage at the beginning of the twentieth century. Virginia Valian in her classic *Why So Slow?* takes a more fine-grained look at what she calls the invisible factors that retard women's progress in the academy, largely within the contexts of academic careers in engineering and the sciences. Her central thesis is that "a set of implicit, or nonconscious, hypotheses about sex differences plays a central role in shaping men's and women's professional lives" (2). Suggesting that success comes from creating and consolidating small gains (4), she insists that fairness demands that there be "no consistent advantage for members of one group relative to another" (7).

Works that illustrate graphically some of the problems discussed in these books include Gloria Anzaldúa's *Borderlands: La Frontera: The New Mestiza* and Nadya Aisenberg and Mona Harrington's *Women of Academe: Outsiders in the Sacred Grove*. Chicana writer and writing teacher Gloria Anzaldúa recounts, in both English and Spanish, her struggles amidst adversity and violation in her community on the border between Mexico and Texas. She speaks of herself as writing in the shadows and as the book having saved her sanity (i). Anzaldúa had a relatively short life, dying at age 62, probably from diabetes-related complications. Despite the widespread influence of *Borderlands*, her PhD was awarded posthumously as she had not quite finished her dissertation when she died.

Nadya Aisenberg and Mona Harrington in *Women of Academe* recount the difficulties of women professionals outside the mainstream academy. A common pattern emerges: "social norms that are constructed to cast women in subordinate, supportive roles in both their private and their public lives" (xii). Shirley Geok-Lin Lim and María Herrera-Sobek in their edited collection *Power, Race, and Gender in Academe: Strangers in the Tower* speak of the considerable challenges faced by gays, lesbians, and people of color within the academy, focusing on the question: "How do we understand strangeness or alterity in the context of pedagogy, departmental collegiality, and university administration?" (2). In a follow-up volume, *"Strangers" of the Academy: Asian Women Scholars in Higher Education* (2006) edited by Li and Beckett, Lim problematizes the concepts of "Asian," "female," and "scholarship," emphasizing that "within the fascinating multiple layers of self-narrating and scholarly interpretations of 'teacher stories' resides a core of ambivalence, contradiction, and paradox" (xiii). She nevertheless sees the stories included in the volume as tracing successful assimilation and as cause for celebration (viii).

Deborah Gray White in *Telling Stories: Black Women Historians in the Ivory Tower* also sees positive developments, suggesting that the very presence of African American historians in the academy is an indication of revisionism and change (2). White proceeds to chart the entry of black women into the professional world of historians beginning with their entry into the field in the early '70s. She calls the seventeen contributors to her volume "brave" (20). They had to overcome what she calls "raw unmitigated discrimination" that marginalized most black people and left them struggling for survival (6). She reminds the reader that black women endured both racism and sexism (11). Some black women who did write history in the twentieth century did so as amateurs according to White (9) with only a few in the pre–civil rights era joining the ranks of academically trained professional historians (11).

The collection *Our Studies, Ourselves: Sociologists' Lives and Work* edited by Glassner and Hertz, which focuses, as does our book, on the intersection of the personal and the professional, includes a section on gender. They speak of the authors of the pieces in the section, all women, as illustrating how several generations of women sociologists "learned how to push the structure of the workplace and navigate the constraints imposed upon her because of her sex" (6). They say, "The older generations pushed the structure of the academy enough to finally change it, and younger women with doctorates could imagine having careers similar to their male counterparts" (6).

Two collections focus on women's struggles trying to balance work and family either in the academy (*The Balancing Act: Gendered Perspectives in Faculty Roles and Work Lives,* eds. Bracken, Allen, and Dean) or in the workplace more generally (*Work, Life, and Family Imbalance,* eds. Paludi and Neidermeyer). The first collection grew out of the work of the women's caucus of the American Association for Higher Education and discusses the field of women's studies in the academy. They conclude their introduction by suggesting that women faculty design gender research that questions what is normal, that they embrace the philosophy that "the personal is political" in one's work life, and that they reenvision themselves as adult learners in addition to experts (7). In the introduction to their collection, Paludi and Neidermeyer emphasize the incompatibility between work and family roles, stressing that women still do more of the work at home including care of children and elderly parents, lack fringe benefits and job flexibility, suffer from salary inequities (especially women of color), and that very few childcare centers have provisions for sick children so parents can work (xv). A more recent collection, *Women in the Academy,* coedited by Gutgold and Linse, suggests that women still face inequities in the workplace and are unfairly represented in our culture. They call for women to provide greater support for one another and advocate against the injustices they see (xii).

CHOICE, CHANCE, AND SERENDIPITY: AN OVERVIEW OF COLLECTION ESSAYS

Our authors, too, describe considerable institutional and familial challenges. They have made choices, been resilient, and benefitted from good fortune and good timing, or not, especially in relation to the areas of 1) jobs, including looking for jobs and obtaining them, often in tandem with a partner, changing jobs, and working at a job, especially in conducting research; 2) background, including academic, family, and cultural background; and 3) nonacademic activities, especially as an enhancement to one's career or one's family situation.

Lisa Ede charts the role that both serendipity and kairos have played during her long career as she searched, at first unsuccessfully, for a tenure-track position, changed positions, struggled to obtain tenure in an institution inhospitable to her extensive collaborative work with Andrea Lunsford, and found very satisfying administrative work as director of a writing center. Ede mentions that she has been the primary breadwinner in her family as her husband is a professional artist. Elizabeth A. Flynn describes choices enabled and constrained by chance and decisions that illustrate kairos, serendipity, and resilience. Job-related challenges include attempting to find a job in a tight market, working against institutional expectations that, early on, proscribed doing research in the area of her dissertation—feminist studies—and attempting to investigate feminist approaches to both reader-response criticism within literary studies and rhetoric and composition at a time when little work had been done on these topics. A parallel theme is the challenge she faced in a marriage in which her husband was a part-time faculty member in the same department in which she held a number of administrative positions, including department chair. For her, non-work-related experiences such as raising a child, buying a farm and renovating an old farmhouse, and establishing long-term friendships with people outside the department were healing.

Explaining how the personal and professional have overlapped in her career, Anne Ruggles Gere speaks of the "opportune moment"—or kairos shaping these intersections. She met the challenge of finding positions in tandem with her husband's ministries in several different locations by attending graduate school in one, finding a tenure-track position in a second, having a commuting relationship in a third, and finally finding a very satisfying position back at the first location. Like Ede, Flynn, Bloom, Libby Jones, and Papoulis, her graduate education did not include formal training in rhetoric and composition, though she was able to become familiar with the field through study of cognate fields including education and literacy studies, and through her work with the National Writing Project. She speaks, too, of the importance of care and support—her mother helping with her children and care of a granddaughter whose mother suffers from fetal alcohol syndrome. On top of these responsibilities, she has held several important leadership positions at the national level as have many of the other contributors to the volume. Lynn Bloom walks her readers through the choices she made in her life, both seemingly insignificant and others monumental. Like Gere, she needed to find positions as her husband changed jobs while they cared for two children, and like Gere, she spent a time commuting some distance for a time. Focusing on two risky decisions in her career, Libby Falk Jones speaks of having to practice—and learn—resilience. Like Gere and Bloom, she and her husband managed two careers while raising two children. Like Ede and Flynn, they have settled on an arrangement whereby she is the primary breadwinner. Similar in some ways to many contributors in this volume, she has remade herself several times by changing jobs or changing positions within an institution.

Suellynn Duffey illustrates how forces beyond her control have often structured her steps, and how the paths she has followed "were often jagged instead of smooth, patched together out of missteps rather than elegantly choreographed, evolved from a combination of opportunity, improvisation, desperation, and resilience rather than consciously designed." Duffey describes non-tenure-track administrative positions and then positions at other institutions, only the last three of which were tenure-track. These stories are intertwined with stories of the birth of a child, a divorce, and primary custody of her son as well as care of her mother who was terminally ill and eventually died. Unlike contributors who studied literature in graduate school, since there were no programs in rhetoric and composition at the time, Duffey had substantial formal training in rhetoric in the communication department at Ohio State. She also speaks of being a first-generation college student and of the challenges her working-class background presented in deciding to get a PhD and in moving into professorial positions. Linda Adler-Kassner, like Duffey, describes holding a number of very responsible administrative positions, and, like Duffey, had formal training in communication before switching to rhetoric and composition, which had by then developed graduate programs in the area. She has raised a daughter and moved three times after obtaining the PhD.

Malea Powell compares her composing process to that of Native beadwork, which involves stringing gemstones together to make one continuous thread. She speaks of a scholarly life focused on resilience, serendipity, agency, and relationships. Like Duffey and Rhodes, Powell comes from the working class and like Adler-Kassner, she entered graduate school after there were established programs in rhetoric and composition. Unlike them, she is part Native and so has had challenges specific to this identity. She struggled in graduate school, for instance, with feelings of isolation and with the essentialized conception of race held by her fellow graduate students. At every stage of her career she made choices that moved her toward greater freedom, independence, and connection with her ancestors. Jacqueline Rhodes questions who she might be without the history that has defined her. Like Duffey and

Powell, she comes from the working class, though unlike them, she seems to have been more obviously scarred by her past, which manifested in the form of struggles with depression. While telling the story of her path through academia, Rhodes interweaves stories of difficulties finding both her scholarly identity and her queer identity.

Beth Hewett illustrates her remarkable resilience in the face of an unusually challenged and challenging life and career. She speaks of the homelessness of being a military spouse and the placelessness of life as an independent scholar. Like other contributors, she has faced grief—but she writes of "working with grief" by both becoming a grief counselor and using it as a subject of her writing. Tiffany Bourelle talks through difficult decisions she made early on in her academic career, discussing the kairotic nature of her choices, from attending graduate school based on a trip she took out West, to leaving a tenure-track job for a contingent one, to deciding to start a family before being tenured. Like Flynn, Gere, Bloom, and Libby Jones, she and her husband have struggled to find positions at the same institution. Iklim Goksel describes very well the ways in which kismet, which she associates with resilience, choice, chance, and serendipity, has allowed her to become a successful student and now academic in ways that reflect her non-Western, Turkish culture.

Irene Papoulis attends to failure in addition to success. She writes about her feelings of shame because she has remained a lecturer for her entire career, because she has felt the effects of the low status of rhetoric and composition within the academy, and because she has felt the effects of adhering to expressivism, which has low status within rhetoric and composition. Like Flynn, Gere, Bloom, and Libby Jones, she has had to negotiate dual career issues, like Flynn and Natasha Jones, she has been a single mother, and like many of the contributors, but especially Flynn, Rhodes, Powell, and Hewett, she speaks of having to deal with considerable psychological stress. Natasha N. Jones explores the power of agency in both her personal and professional life in meeting the challenges of going to graduate school and obtaining a tenure-track job as an African American in a field, technical communication, in which African Americans are a distinct minority, and as a single mother. She equates agency with empowerment, defining the term as "resilience and transformation—a movement toward a goal or an ideal" (218).

The narrative Shirley Rose provides differs from the others in that she talks through the "last quarter" in her life—the time in which her academic career is slowly winding down before retirement. She discusses the unique opportunity to learn more about her role as the Writing Program Administrator at Arizona State University through the serendipity of her participation in an all-female chorus, an activity that is clearly satisfying and healing as are Flynn's farm and Powell's beading.

SOME CLOSING THOUGHTS

What we have collectively created here is an intervention that asks that we reconsider what the field of rhetoric and composition is and how it emerged in the way that it did. Importantly, it demonstrates that narrative is a significant form of knowledge. In his review of Eli Goldblatt's *Writing Home: A Literacy Autobiography,* Steve Parks observes that the book shows how literacy narratives can provide alternative ways to produce "knowledge" in our academic-discourse-laden discipline (491). Several contributors, especially Libby Jones and Malea Powell, make evident in their pieces that narratives are constructed and could be told in any number of ways. The stories are not the Truth about lived experience but contingent truths. Irene Papoulis makes clear that contexts shift as does resilience, and so stories recount moving states rather than static ones. Resilience cannot be achieved once and for all.

Like Goldblatt, we, too, are contributing to alternative ways of producing knowledge in the field since our narratives integrate personal and professional lives. These are not stories, though, of rational decision-making or carefully planned out goals and strategies. Choice, chance, and serendipity converge, resulting, usually, in unforeseen accomplishments despite setbacks and frustrations along the way. Several contributors, for instance, speak of bearing children without paid maternity leave and raising them without adequate childcare and describe the challenges of raising a child or children while developing a professional career, sometimes with the added challenge of caring for an elderly parent. One contributor speaks of dealing with workaholism.

The narratives are, in many ways, particular to women in rhetoric and composition. They are stories of careers as writing program administrators and as teachers of writing. Many contributors mention collaboration, an activity that is especially valued in the field. Several describe holding non-tenure-track positions as do many women in rhetoric and composition. When they did not obtain or retain tenure-track positions, however, they did not become what Susan Miller refers to as sad women in the basement. Rather, they seized opportunities when they arose and re-created themselves and their careers on the basis of circumstances in which they were unable to have complete control.

The collection captures an important historical moment within rhetoric and composition, a time in which women have achieved substantial inroads within the academy and have had considerable success in overcoming resistance and discrimination. A number of the contributors have participated in very high-level leadership positions both within their institutions and within the field, and many of the publications of contributors have been cited frequently and reprinted a number of times. Entering a relatively undeveloped field might seem to be a disadvantage, especially as, early on, there were no graduate programs, as was the case for Ede, Flynn, Gere, Bloom, Libby Jones, and Papoulis. Helping create a field can be energizing, though, and can provide opportunities that might not be available in more mature fields. Several contributors were able to participate in more than one field or subfield, for instance, often resulting in rich, interdisciplinary work. The field also seems to have provided several contributors more than the usual opportunities for mobility. Being able to teach writing or administer writing programs would seem to be good preparation for any number of jobs in any number of contexts. Hewett describes finding work on military bases and changing positions every few years, sometimes more frequently, early in her career, as she followed her husband who was in the military. Duffey describes moving from institution to institution until she finally found a congenial academic home. Rhetoric and composition also seems to be a field that is especially welcoming to women and to newcomers from diverse backgrounds. Gere and Flynn taught at the high school level before going to graduate school and entering the field. Powell, Rhodes, Adler-Kassner, and Natasha Jones arrived via especially circuitous routes that involved employment that does not usually lead to an academic career. Flynn, Duffey, and Adler-Kassner began their academic careers working with basic writers. Goksel's entry into the profession required entry into a new culture and use of a new language and, in turn, provides a valuable non-Western perspective to the collection. If our collection is any indication, women in rhetoric and composition have been unusually resilient, have exhibited considerable agency, especially in taking risks, and have made decisions in serendipitous ways and at kairotic moments.

WORKS CITED

Aisenberg, Nadya, and Mona Harrington. *Women of Academe: Outsiders in the Sacred Grove.* Amherst: U of Massachusetts P, 1988. Print.

Anzaldúa, Gloria. *Borderlands: La Frontera: The New Mestiza.* San Francisco: Aunt Lute Books, 1987. Print.

Ballif, Michelle, D. Diane Davis, and Roxanne Mountford. *Women's Ways of Making It in Rhetoric and Composition*. New York: Routledge, 2008. Print.

Bizzell, Patricia. "The Prospect of Rhetorical Agency." *Making and Unmaking the Prospects for Rhetoric: Selected Papers from the 1996 Rhetoric Society of America Conference*. Vol. 7. Mahwah, NJ: Lawrence Erlbaum Associates, 1997. 37–48. Print.

Bracken, Susan J., Jeanie K. Allen, and Diane R. Dean, eds. *The Balancing Act: Gendered Perspectives in Faculty Roles and Work Lives*. Sterling, VA: Stylus, 2006. Print.

Clark, VèVè, Shirley Nelson Garner, Margaret Higonnet, and Ketu H. Katrak, eds. *Antifeminism in the Academy*. New York: Routledge, 1996. Print.

Cooper, Marilyn M. "Rhetorical Agency as Emergent and Enacted." *College Composition and Communication* 62.3 (February 2011): 420–49. Print.

Derrida, Jacques. *Politics of Friendship*. Trans. George Collins. New York: Verso, 1997. Print.

Enos, Theresa. *Gender Roles and Faculty Lives in Rhetoric and Composition*. Carbondale: Southern Illinois UP, 1996. Print.

Flynn, Elizabeth A., Patricia Sotirin, and Ann Brady, eds. *Feminist Rhetorical Resilience*. Logan: Utah State UP, 2012. Print.

Glassner, Barry, and Rosana Hertz, eds. *Our Studies, Ourselves: Sociologists' Lives and Work*. New York: Oxford UP, 2003. Print.

Goldblatt, Eli. *Writing Home: A Literacy Autobiography*. Carbondale: Southern Illinois UP, 2012.

Goodburn, Amy, Donna LeCourt, and Carrie Leverenz, eds. *Rewriting Success in Rhetoric and Composition Careers*. Anderson, SC: Parlor P, 2013. Print.

Gutgold, Nichola D., and Angela R. Linse. *Women in the Academy: Learning From Our Diverse Career Pathways*. Lanham, MD: Lexington Books, 2016. Print.

Hodges, Elizabeth Jamison. *The Three Princes of Serendip*. New York: Atheneum, 1964. Print.

Holbrook, Sue Ellen. "Women's Work: The Feminizing of Composition." *Rhetoric Review* 9 (1991): 201–29. Print.

hooks, bell. *Teaching to Transgress*. New York: Routledge, 2014. Print.

Kinneavy, James L. "*Kairos* in Classical and Modern Rhetorical Theory." *Rhetoric and Kairos: Essays in History, Theory, and Practice*. Ed. Philip Sipiora and James S. Baumlin. Albany: State U of New York P, 2002. 58–76. Print.

Kirsch, Gesa E., and Liz Rohan, eds. *Beyond the Archives: Research as a Lived Process*. Carbondale: Southern Illinois UP, 2008. Print.

Li, Guofang, and Gulbahar H. Beckett, eds. *"Strangers" of the Academy: Asian Women Scholars in Higher Education*. Sterling, VA: Stylus, 2006. Print.

Lim, Shirley Geok-Lin. "Foreword." *"Strangers" of the Academy: Asian Women Scholars in Higher Education*. Eds. Guofang Li and Gulbanar H. Beckett. Sterling, VA: Stylus, 2006. xiii–xviii. Print.

Lim, Shirley Geok-Lin, and María Herrera-Sobek, eds. *Power, Race, and Gender in Academe: Strangers in the Tower?* New York: Modern Language Association, 2000. Print.

Martin, Jane Roland. *Coming of Age in Academe: Rekindling Women's Hopes and Reforming the Academy*. New York: Routledge. 2000. Print.

Miller, Carolyn. "Foreword." *Rhetoric and Kairos: Essays in History, Theory, and Praxis*. Eds. Phillip Sipiora and James S. Baumlin. Albany: State U of New York P, 2002. xi–1. Print.

Miller, Susan. *Textual Carnivals: The Politics of Composition*. Carbondale: Southern Illinois UP, 1991. Print.

Nagel, Thomas. "Moral Luck, II." *Proceedings of the Aristotelian Society*. Supplementary. Vol. 50: 137–51, 1976. Print.

Paludi, Michele A., and Presha E. Neidermeyer, eds. *Work, Life, and Family Imbalance: How to Level the Playing Field*. Westport, CT: Praeger, 2007.

Panofsky, Erwin. *Studies in Iconology: Humanistic Themes in the Art of the Renaissance*. New York: Harper and Row, 1972. Print.

Parks, Steve. "Sponsors and Activists: Deborah Brandt, Sponsorship, and the Work to Come" (Review Essay). *College Composition and Communication* 66.3 (February 2015): 483–99. Print.

Rosenmann, Martin F. "Serendipity and Scientific Discovery." *Journal of Creative Behavior* 22.2 (1988): 132–38. Print.

Schachner, Anna. "Roxane Gay and Erica Jong Discuss Feminism and It Instantly Gets Awkward." *The Guardian*. September 7, 2015. September 15, 2015. Web.

Schell, Eileen. *Gypsy Academics and Mother-Teachers: Gender, Contingent Labor, and Writing Instruction*. Portsmouth, NH: Boynton/Cook. 1998. Print.

Schmidt, Jan Zlotnik. *Women/Writing/Teaching*. Albany: State U of New York P, 1998. Print.

Valian, Virginia. *Why So Slow? The Advancement of Women*. Cambridge, MA: MIT P, 1998. Print.

Walpole, Horace. "To Horace Mann." January 28, 1754. Horace Walpole Correspondence. Yale Edition. The Lewis Walpole Library. August 28, 2015. Web.

White, Deborah Gray. *Telling Histories: Black Women Historians in the Ivory Tower*. Chapel Hill: U of North Carolina P, 2008.

Williams, Bernard. "Moral Luck, I." *Proceedings of the Aristotelian Society*. Supplementary. Vol. 50: 115–36, 1976. Print.

Williams, Gareth. *The Mexican Exception: Sovereignty, Police, and Democracy*. New York: Palgrave Macmillan, 2011. Print.

CHAPTER 1

How to Get a Nonacademic Position

An Essay on Serendipity—Personal, Professional, and Intellectual

LISA EDE

The title of my first Conference on College Composition and Communication (CCCC) presentation is there on my vita for anyone to see. But I expect that few who look at my vita, if anyone does other than to count up numbers of talks, article, books, and so on, have noticed that my first CCCC conference talk was on the subject of "How to Get a Non-Academic Position."

There's a story behind that talk, which when I gave it I assumed would be both my first and last CCCC presentation. Here it is in brief: I entered the PhD program in English at Ohio State University in the fall of 1970 not even knowing that it was possible to undertake study in the field that we have come to call rhetoric and composition (or some related title). My area was Victorian literature, and by the time that Susan Miller and Andrea Lunsford came to Ohio State (Susan to direct the writing program and Andrea to cobble together the first PhD program of study in rhet/comp in the English department), I was well underway on a dissertation on the Victorian nonsense literature of Edward Lear and Lewis Carroll.

I was also quite involved with the writing program—not only through my own teaching but also as a result of my participation in the teaching assistant (TA) council that advised the Director of Writing. To say that Susan Miller brought energy and intellectual excitement to the writing program is an understatement. Susan brought in outside speakers (David Bartholomae! Rick Coe! Erika Lindemann!), and she spoke of the development of a new field. (Later I would learn that depending on your perspective the field wasn't so new. I would also learn of the important role that OSU Professor Edward P. J. Corbett played in the field's contemporary formation. At the time, I knew Professor Corbett primarily as a scholar of eighteenth-century literature.)

I still remember the moment when, in the spring term of my final year of grad school, I was sitting in Susan's office discussing some matter related to the TA advisory council that I then chaired. "Lisa," Susan said to me, "you are going to have to make some decisions about your future career. You're going to have to decide how seriously you want to take the teaching of writing as a profession." Given the job market at the time—reportedly the worst for PhDs in the humanities since the depression—the notion of a "future career" in the academy was hard to imagine. By the time Susan and I had that conversation, I had already gone on the job market once (earlier that year) with no luck, and I was getting ready to put myself out there a second time. I would support myself during what I hoped would be a transitional year by working as an editor at a sociology research center on campus, and I was grateful to have that opportunity for full-time employment.

The year that I completed my dissertation is a blur now, and it probably was then too. But at some point in 1975, I realized that the upcoming 1976 CCCC would be in Philadelphia. My good friends and graduate school colleagues Andrea Lunsford and Suellynn Duffey were planning to go to the conference and would share a university van. I could travel with them if I proposed a talk and had it accepted. Attending the conference would give me a chance to learn more about the emerging field of rhet/comp, and giving a talk there would look good on my vita. I had already decided that when I went on the job market the following year I would apply both for Victorian literature and (newly created) rhet/comp positions and see what happened.

Like many of my peers, I was at a crossroads, and my future looked uncertain. My immediate challenge was to determine a topic and write a proposal. Why not draw upon my good fortune in finding what we would now call an alt-academic position? Others might benefit from my experience of turning part-time work that supplemented my TA stipend into a full-time editing position. Hence my topic: How to Get a Non-Academic Position. Given the job market, I knew this would be a useful presentation for others whose situation resembled mine. And indeed the panel on which I participated was well attended.

By the time I gave that talk in the spring of 1976, I thought that my future was clear—and that it would not follow a traditional academic path. I had interviewed for two or three positions (a pitiful but at the time not unusual number) at the MLA the previous December in San Francisco. No job offers came my way. I did get a letter from the State University of New York (SUNY) Brockport saying that they were interested in my candidacy, but their position was frozen. I had been in my editing position for several terms by this point, and I liked it. I had already decided not to put myself through the job market process again. Why humiliate myself a third time?

So I gave that talk. I was energized by the conference, but I thought that my future was set: I would be an editor of scholarly publications—and I was grateful to have work that I enjoyed and that was meaningful to me. Then in the summer of 1976 SUNY Brockport called. Their position was unfrozen. They wanted to interview me on campus. Could I come? I did, and I was offered a tenure-line position of Director of Composition at that university.

Serendipity indeed.

I will have more to say about the role that serendipity has played in my career later in this essay. For now, I want to note the important role that certain key preferences and predilections have played in my life and career. I should perhaps be embarrassed to admit this, but I knew as early as middle school that I wanted to be a teacher, and looking back I can easily identify teachers who made a huge difference in my life. Mrs. Ryan in middle school, who taught me to love history and affirmed my identity as a serious student who cared enough to get my own subscription to my first scholarly (or semi-scholarly) journal: the hard-bound *American Heritage*. Mrs. Falk in high school (AP English junior and senior years) who required students to write an essay (some more formal than others) every day of the school year, and who developed what I later realized was an early form of portfolio evaluation.

I also knew as early as grade school that I loved reading and writing and that they were central to my sense of myself, though of course I couldn't have articulated that at this point. By the time I was in high school I knew what I wanted to be: a high school English teacher. I loved teaching, and I loved literature—and teachers consistently praised my writing. What I discovered when I did my student teaching for my undergraduate English education degree at Ohio State was that I didn't love the public school system—at least not the crowded inner city school where I taught. So I did what seemed natural to many students of my age and temperament at that turbulent but exciting time: I applied to grad school.

I barely knew what I was doing. I applied to only two universities—Cornell and the University of Wisconsin, Madison. I have no idea how I chose them other than that they were outside of Ohio, where my family lived, but not too far away. I ended up in Madison with an out-of-state tuition remission scholarship. The English department had just abolished the first-year writing requirement in retaliation against teaching assistants who had spearheaded a failed move toward unionization, so TA positions were available only to a limited number of PhD students. I supported myself during my one-year MA program by working at the Wisconsin State Department of Education, even as I marched with others in massive campus protests against the Vietnam War.

My time in Madison was difficult. I did well in my courses, but the MA program was huge: some of my MA classes that year were larger than my undergrad English classes had been at Ohio State. While some courses and professors were excellent, the goal of the program—to pass a test that included multiple-choice questions (example: Upon what does the worm sit in Blake's *Book of Thel?*) at the end of the year—was uninspiring. So I applied to the PhD program at Ohio State. I did so not as a result of serious research about PhD programs or careful career planning but rather to reconnect with my then boyfriend. When I counsel students who are making decisions about grad school applications, I am astonished at the knowledge and professionalism they bring to this task. I had neither.

It was at Ohio State that I had my first experiences teaching undergraduates and my first involvement with the rhet/comp field. My interest in audience also developed in grad school. A chance conversation with a fellow TA about an assignment that he was experimenting with, one that required students to write to real or hypothetical audiences, piqued my curiosity. I began to experiment with nontraditional assignments—assignments that one way or another encouraged students to engage in writing tasks that at least offered the possibility of something resembling an authentic experience. My first publication, a brief essay entitled "Oral History," which appeared in *CCC* in 1977, explored one such assignment. (Ed Corbett, who by this time was a mentor and also the editor of *CCC*, encouraged me every step of the way in this, my first publication.) My second publication, also in *CCC*, attempted to formalize some of the questions that I had begun to ask myself about the role of audience in discourse and in the teaching of writing. This essay, "On Audience and Composition," appeared in 1979.

As I transitioned from the field of Victorian literature to that of rhet/comp, I experienced a satisfying sense of coming full circle. My earliest aspiration had been to become an English teacher, which I knew meant being a teacher not only of literature but also of writing. When I entered grad school, that goal shifted, and I focused on the scholarly work of English studies—at least in my coursework. But my teaching drew me back to my aspirations as a teacher. With my "conversion" to rhet/comp, I felt a renewed sense of pedagogical commitment and purpose, one that was strengthened with my position directing the writing program at SUNY Brockport.

In my early years at SUNY Brockport, I had a very steep learning curve: I was the sole "expert" on the teaching of writing on my campus, even as I was attempting to educate myself about my new field. In hindsight, I see that serendipity played a role here too. While some of my contemporaries entered the field in the late 1970s and early 1980s as graduate students in rhet/comp, many others "converted" to the field after completing PhDs in literary studies. (For a discussion of this phenomenon, see chapter three of my *Situating Composition: Composition Studies and the Politics of Location*). The timing was fortuitous. In the wake of a purported literacy crisis (one that ultimately was more about a new generation of students entering college than a real decline of literacy), funding was available to "solve" the problem of illiteracy. Definitions of expertise in the field of rhet/comp were evolving, and commitment and pedagogical/administrative experience in many instances counted as much as a traditional graduate education—particularly given the tiny number of rhet/comp grad programs at the time.

The more I learned about writing and rhetoric, the more engaged I became in questions about the role of audience in writing and the teaching of writing. This quest for understanding led to additional serendipitous moments in my career. The first was when I was accepted into Richard Young's 1978–79 yearlong NEH seminar at Carnegie Mellon. My proposed topic? To explore the concept of identification in classical rhetoric, Burke's dramatistics, and Pike's tagmemics. At the heart of this study was my continued interest in audience. In the years since I "converted" from Victorian literature to rhet/comp, I had gained a much richer understanding of both the classical and contemporary rhetorical traditions, an understanding that was dramatically enriched by my year of study with Richard Young and with fellow seminarians Jim Berlin, Victor Vitanza, Sam Watson, Charles Kneupper, and others.

The NEH seminar was an intellectual and professional boost, and it gave me the confidence to go back on the job market. I valued my work at SUNY Brockport and enjoyed my colleagues—and I continued to marvel at the serendipity that led to my first tenure-line appointment—but in the late 1970s, the college was in the midst of a serious financial crisis. Even my colleagues encouraged me to consider other options, grimly citing the possibility of what one referred to with dark humor as tenure on the Titanic. The time seemed right for a change. I interviewed for the position of Director of Writing at Oregon State and was offered it.

OSU looked like a good professional opportunity, but I have to admit that for my husband and me the thought of living in the Pacific Northwest played an important role in my decision to accept the position. Avid hikers and backpackers, we loved the thought of living in a place where we could be in the mountains in two hours and at the coast in one hour. Our friends Andrea and Steve Lunsford also were living in the Northwest—Andrea's first job was at the University of British Columbia—and told wonderful stories of life there.

Once we moved to Oregon, the four of us took advantage of every opportunity we could to be together, traveling the eight hours up and down the I-5 corridor at least once a term, and more often in the summer. Andrea's and my collaboration, which has played such an important role in my career, could not have taken off—especially given the technological limitations of the time (no email, no word processing, etc.) without that physical proximity. Even so, Andrea and I first collaborated almost by accident. With our friend Robert Connors, we were coediting *Essays on Classical Rhetoric and Modern Discourse,* a collection in honor of our mentor Edward P. J. Corbett. We were vacationing on the Oregon coast, and while on a long walk it suddenly occurred to us that it might be rewarding to write a collaborative essay for that collection. We had each planned on contributing an individual essay. Our memories of our motivation differ somewhat. I remember thinking that it would please Ed Corbett. Andrea remembers thinking that it might be practical and efficient to write together, given our other responsibilities as coeditors. We both agree that serendipity played a role in our decision to write together. Without that chance conversation, our long collaboration might never have happened.

Andrea's and my essay "On Distinctions between Classical and Modern Rhetoric" was published in *Essays on Classical Rhetoric and Modern Discourse* in 1984. We were surprised by how much we enjoyed writing together and, especially, how productive our collaboration was. It was clear to us that working together encouraged us to be particularly ambitious and to challenge ourselves in ways that we might not have done if we were writing alone. So to us, it felt natural to continue to undertake significant collaborations—even as we each engaged in individual projects. However, what felt natural and productive to us was anything but to our colleagues. In fact, we quickly realized that many of our colleagues (including Ed Corbett) viewed our collaboration as shocking—even dangerous. "You will never get tenure if you insist on writing together," Andrea and I remember Ed fretfully warning us. And his concerns were justified. When Andrea prepared her materials for promotion and tenure at UBC she was told by her chair that "of course her collaborative work couldn't be considered." Anticipating similar difficulties, my chair invited Andrea to "spontaneously" send him a letter noting that all of our collaborations were equal. Nevertheless, my college's promotion and tenure committee requested that Andrea and I go through all of our coauthored essays and use colored markers to indicate who had written which sentence. Needless to say, we refused—and fortunately I was promoted and tenured despite this refusal.[1]

Earlier in this essay, I commented on the importance of key preferences and predilections, and in the case of Andrea's and my collaboration I would have to call attention to our stubbornness. The more people challenged our desire to write together, the more persistent we were in attempting to understand—and critique—the preference for single authorship in the humanities. This led to our 1990 *Singular Texts/Plural Authors: Perspectives on Collaborative Writing*, and to much additional work. But our very close friendship also played a central role in our collaboration.

In 2012 Andrea and I published *Writing Together: Collaboration in Theory and Practice*, a collection of previously published and new work. The collection gives a good sense of the range of topics we have explored over thirty-plus years of collaboration. In the first section, we address the question "Why Write Together?" The second section includes several chapters from our 1990 *Singular Texts/Plural Authors: Perspectives on Collaborative Writing*, as well as more recent thoughts on this topic. The third section focuses on our research on audience and includes our essay "Audience Addressed/Audience Invoked: The Role of Audience in Composition Theory and Practice," our most anthologized work; the fourth, on rhetorics and feminisms, and the final section on writing centers. Each section concluded with a new essay written especially for this collection.

Putting this collection together was a joyful act; however, I do not want to romanticize our collaboration. In the introduction and in various new essays, Andrea and I attempt to dispel some potential myths about our collaboration. No, we have not always been "together" and not always been in accord. Yes, we have experienced some painful personal and professional moments as a result of our collaboration. But yes, despite the complexities that are part of any human experience, we are grateful for the journey that we have taken together.

One powerful insight that we slowly came to recognize in recent years is the extent to which developments in new literacies and technologies have caused what we always viewed as two more or less separate strands of research—our work on audience and on collaborative writing—to merge. As we note in "'Among the Audience': On Audience in an Age of New Literacies," another of the new essays in *Writing Together*, we have come to understand that

> as writers and audiences merge and shift places in online environments, participating in both brief and extended collaborations, it is increasingly obvious that writers seldom, if ever, write alone. In short, when receivers or

consumers of information become creators of content as well, it is increasingly difficult to tell when writers are collaborative writers or authors and when they are members of audiences. (238)

This insight has played an important role in our recent research—and also in a relatively new textbook that we have undertaken with coauthors Michal Brody, Beverly Moss, Carole Clark Papper, and Keith Walters. (Our editor Marilyn Moller has also played an essential role in this project.) *Everyone's an Author* attempts to respond to the exigencies described in this statement and to present rhetorical strategies appropriate to twenty-first-century readers and writers.

I mentioned earlier that one of the sections in *Writing Together* focuses on Andrea's and my research on feminisms and rhetorics. I would like to say a bit more about my (and Andrea's and my) engagement with feminist research in our field. I have already noted how rewarding it felt when I transitioned from Victorian literature to rhet/comp to reaffirm my strong commitment to teaching and to find a way formally to express that commitment. I felt a similar sense of satisfaction in the 1990s as my research increasingly engaged feminist theories and practices. A strong feminist since my undergraduate days, I did not originally see how to make connections between my personal and scholarly commitments.[2] My friend Beth Flynn emphasized the importance of making these connections in her pathbreaking 1988 *CCC* article "Composing as a Woman." In my case, that meant making a transition from research that focused primarily on classical and contemporary rhetorical theory to explicitly feminist research. In that regard, I view the article that Cheryl Glenn, Andrea, and I coauthored, "Border Crossings: Intersections of Rhetoric and Feminism," which was published in *Rhetorica: A Journal of the History of Rhetoric* in 1995, as a particularly important turning point.

When we published this piece, Cheryl, Andrea, and I knew that it was important work: we believe that our article was the first feminist article published in *Rhetorica*, a journal that until that point had focused on traditional rhetorical historiography and analysis. That article also planted a seed in Cheryl's and my minds. In the fall of 1995, our chair invited us to cocoordinate a one-time conference on any topic that we thought might draw interest. (At that time, Cheryl was still teaching at Oregon State and had not yet moved to Penn State.) Cheryl and I pinned our hopes and dreams on the then-still-nascent topic of rhetorics and feminisms. In August 1997 the conference "From Boundaries to Borderlands: Rhetoric(s) and Feminism(s)" was held at OSU. Just as I assumed that my 1976 CCCC presentation on how to get a nonacademic position would be my first and last appearance at the CCCC, so too did Cheryl and I assume that "From Boundaries to Borderlands" would be a one-time phenomenon. However, near the end of the conference Lillian Bridwell-Bowles and Lisa Albrecht announced that the conference was so powerful as a site of feminist research, inquiry, and networking that it had to continue, and that the University of Minnesota would sponsor it in two years. Thus was the first of what has come to be an ongoing succession of conferences exploring the intersections of feminisms and rhetorics. (For more on the history of the feminisms and rhetorics conference series, which is now sponsored by the Coalition of Women Scholars in the History of Rhetoric and Composition, see the chapter on that topic in *Writing Together*.)

Sometimes we recognize a serendipitous occurrence the moment it happens: that was definitely the case when I was offered my first tenure-line position at SUNY Brockport (which I am happy to report has weathered its earlier financial storm nicely). Sometimes we can only recognize serendipity in action in hindsight, as was the case with the chance conversation that caused Andrea and me to undertake our first collaborative project.

I certainly didn't recognize it as a serendipitous moment when during my interview in 1980 at Oregon State the chair nonchalantly mentioned, "We wondered if in addition to directing the writing program you'd also agree to head up the writing center . . ."—but it was. Even though this meant that I would direct two writing programs as an untenured assistant professor, my thirty-plus years of directing OSU's Writing Center, and thus of being able to interact with colleagues like Lex Runciman, Jon Olson, Wayne Robertson, and Dennis Bennett and literally hundreds of writing assistants, has been a highlight of my career. My work with the writing assistants and with student writers at the Center also played an important role in my decision to write a first-year writing textbook. That book has gone through ten editions since it was first published in 1989. The first six editions came out under the title *Work in Progress: A Guide to Academic Writing and Revising*. After a radical revisioning of the text, it reappeared in 2008 as *The Academic Writer: A Brief Guide for Students*. This text is now in its fourth edition.

I am grateful for the opportunity that writing this essay has given me to take a long view of my scholarly work, and of the personal, intellectual, and professional commitments and predilections that, in hindsight, have proven to be constant (if not always visible, and certainly not always conscious) threads. In that regard, I would like to turn again to the dissertation I wrote on the Victorian nonsense of Edward Lear and Lewis Carroll. Imagine my surprise when Patrick Bizzaro contacted me in the late 1990s wanting to interview me about possible connections between my dissertation topic and my subsequent work in composition, especially my interest in audience. Up to this point, I had viewed these two research interests as completely disconnected. As Bizzaro persuasively argues in his 1999 *CCC* essay, "What I Learned in Grad School, or Literary Training and the Theorizing of Composition," the connections that I originally couldn't see were nevertheless there. Bizzaro cites frequent statements of concern about miscommunication, a predilection for ranging broadly in terms of sources and disciplines, and a preference for what Bizzaro terms "a tactic of complication" as connections between my dissertation and my work on audience. (In case you're interested, Bizzaro also looks at connections between the dissertations of other scholars of my generation who "converted" to composition after completing PhDs in literature, including William Irmscher, Linda Flower, Art Young, David Bartholomae, Erika Lindemann, Toby Fulwiler, and Peter Elbow.)

Bizzaro's essay was published in part two of a special issue of *CCC*, "A Usable Past: *CCC* at 50." In the introduction to this issue, editor Joseph Harris writes of the importance of uncovering "a people's history of our field" (559). This and other essays in this collection contribute, I hope, to this project. It goes without saying that a true people's history of any field requires diverse contributions from diversely situated participants. A colleague fresh out of grad school or in the first ten years of his or her postgraduate career would necessarily (and refreshingly) have a different story to tell than I have.

In my own narrative, I have tried to emphasize the central role that serendipity has played in my career, while also emphasizing that key preferences and predilections can also be relevant. But I should also acknowledge that what the editors of this volume refer to as accidental sagacity played a role as well. After all, my long-time commitment to teaching encouraged me to take advantage of the kairotic opportunities that I had as a graduate student at Ohio State when Susan Miller took over the writing program. Mentors also played an important role. Some mentors were inspirational intellectually; Susan surely was that. But other equally important mentors intervened in practical ways in my career. When I came to Oregon State, for instance, my contract stated that I would teach eight courses out of a usual nine-course load (over three quarters). When my chair Robert Frank realized how much I was up against directing two writing programs as an untenured assistant professor (no one in the English department knew anything about the writing center, which had been connected with another unit and was radically underfunded), he rearranged my schedule so that I taught one course that entire year. He was also an advocate for rhet/comp at a time when most members of my department saw it as a new and questionable area—an assumption that I am happy to say has changed considerably over the years.

In turning toward my conclusion, I should acknowledge that as I worked on this essay I found myself troubled by a persistent question: how do I avoid the potential narcissism inherent in a focus on *my* research, *my* career? What do I have to say, I found myself asking over and over as I sat fretting at my computer, that might be of some use to those who are earlier in their scholarly and professional paths? At a minimum, I hope that I have documented, however sketchily, a particular moment in the development of the field of rhetoric and composition—a moment when a PhD student could begin writing a dissertation thinking that (if lucky) she was embarking on a career teaching literature only to discover that a (to her) new field would issue her an invitation in the form of mentors and colleagues like Susan Miller, Ed Corbett, Andrea Lunsford, Beth Flynn, Suellynn Duffey, Robert Connors, Jim Berlin, Victor Vitanza, and others.

I hope that this essay reminds readers that ethical questions are always present for any member of any field, including our own. In *Situating Composition: Composition Studies and the Politics of Location*, I attempted to raise some questions about the costs as well as the benefits of composition's professionalization. My goal in this study is not to challenge the value of theory but rather to remind scholars in our field of our responsibilities given academic hierarchies of knowledge, which value the practice of theory over the practice of teaching. In so doing, I call attention to the importance of considering what philosopher Linda Alcoff refers to in her much cited essay "The Problem of Speaking for Others." I appreciate the ongoing efforts of younger scholars to continue this conversation and to find powerful and persuasive ways to act upon it.

Throughout this essay, I have attempted to call attention to the role that serendipity plays in (I would argue) any career in any field—but especially in the academy, where individual success is both highly valorized and (in research universities, at least) narrowly defined in terms of scholarly productivity. Over the years, I have looked for any and every opportunity to share the story of my first CCCC talk with graduate students and colleagues. So often it can be tempting to think that someone who has managed to secure a tenure-line position and to publish was somehow destined for success. I like to think that in our current climate—where many are advocating for contingent faculty members and exploring alt-academic careers—this assumption has been vigorously challenged. If my narrative can help further dislodge this assumption, I would be pleased.

NOTES

1. In rejecting this request, we were not being brave. As we explained to the committee, the practice of revising each other's writing is central to our collaboration, so even in the earliest stages of a project it is impossible for us to know who wrote which words and sentences.

2. I would be remiss not to acknowledge the important role that my husband's and my shared commitment to feminism has played in my career. We decided early in our marriage that given our fields—the teaching of writing for me and art for my husband Greg Pfarr, who has an MFA in printmaking and painting—that my career would take precedence in terms of positions accepted, places lived, and so on should I be so lucky as to have opportunities. As a result, though my husband is a successful artist, I have been the primary wage earner over the course of our forty-two-year marriage. It has not always been easy for Greg, who has had to deal with patriarchal assumptions that at times position him as a "trailing spouse." But it has been worth it, and it is a road we have traveled together.

WORKS CITED

Alcoff, Linda. "The Problem of Speaking for Others." *Cultural Critique* 37 (1991): 5–32. Print.

Bizzaro, Patrick. "What I Learned in Grad School, or Literary Training and the Theorizing of Composition." *CCC* 50 (1999): 722–42. Print.

Connors, Robert J., Lisa Ede, and Andrea Lunsford, eds. *Essays on Classical Rhetoric and Modern Discourse*. Carbondale: Southern Illinois UP, 1984. Print.

Ede, Lisa. *The Academic Writer: A Brief Guide for Students*. New York: Bedford/St. Martin's P, 1989. (2nd ed., 1992; 3rd ed., 2014; 4th ed., 2017). Print.

———. "On Audience and Composition." *CCC* 30 (1979): 291–95. Print.

———. "Oral History." *CCC* 28 (1977): 380–83. Print.

———. *Situating Composition: Composition Studies and the Politics of Location*. Carbondale: Southern Illinois UP, 2004. Print.

———. *Work in Progress: A Guide to Academic Writing and Revising*. New York: Bedford/St. Martin's P, 1989. (2nd ed., 1992; 3rd ed., 1995; 4th ed., 1998; 5th ed., 2001; 6th ed., 2004). Print.

Ede, Lisa, and Andrea Lunsford. "Audience Addressed/Audience Invoked: The Role of Audience in Composition Theory and Pedagogy." *CCC* 35.2 (May 1984): 155–71. Print.

———. *Singular Texts/Plural Authors: Perspectives on Collaborative Writing*. Carbondale: Southern Illinois UP, 1990. (Paperback ed., 1992). Print.

Ede, Lisa, Cheryl Glenn, and Andrea Lunsford. "Border Crossings: Intersections of Rhetoric and Feminism." *Rhetorica* 13 (1995): 285–325. Print.

Flynn, Elizabeth A. "Composing as a Woman." *CCC* 39 (1988): 423–35. Print.

Lunsford, Andrea, Michal Brody, Lisa Ede, Beverly Moss, Carole Clark Papper, and Keith Walters. *Everyone's an Author*. New York: W. W. Norton, 2013. (2nd ed., 2017). Print.

Lunsford, Andrea, and Lisa Ede. *Writing Together: Collaboration in Theory and Practice*. Bedford/St. Martin's P, 2012. Print.

CHAPTER 2

Becoming a Feminist Teacher, Researcher, and Administrator

ELIZABETH A. FLYNN

Where I grew up—in the suburbs of northern New Jersey, about twenty-five miles from New York City—and when I grew up—in the '40s, '50s, and early '60s—women were expected to become housewives and mothers just as their mothers were.[1] Feminism was nowhere to be seen. In high school, I had had a few dates with a young man from a nearby town who was going to Dartmouth and later became a local physician with some affiliation with Columbia University. Over the years, my mother would, from time to time, send me newspaper clippings about his achievements. These clippings always made reference to his wife and children and seemed always to be a reminder that I had somehow missed the boat. What was in the cards for me was marriage to someone similar, children, and a life of golf and bridge at the country club. Never mind that such a life made my mother miserable and depressed. What she perhaps thought was that I'd be happier than she was because if I married well I'd have more money. Although her father had been vice president of a corporation, and she had spent her college junior year abroad in Paris during the Depression, my father's background and income were considerably more modest. The oldest of six children, his father worked in the Jersey City, New Jersey, bureaucracy. My father would work his way out of his family situation by going to college, getting an MA, becoming a college professor at Pace College (now University), and later getting a PhD (we all went to his graduation when I was in sixth grade). He never made a lot of money, though we did live in the suburbs near a golf course and a clubhouse. Perhaps my mother's inheritance helped. My father was able to put all four of us all through college at Pace because we got free tuition and sometimes even free books from his colleagues.

The story I tell here describes the unlikely outcome, given my background, of helping create the emerging fields of feminist reader-response criticism within literary studies and feminist rhetoric and composition. I did so by making some good choices (and some not so good), in some cases rather blindly, by having very good luck (and in some cases not such good luck), and by being open to the forces of serendipity. My path has been circuitous rather than straight, unexpected rather than predictable. In college I studied to be a high school English teacher and did teach high school English for a year but soon found myself, in the late '60s and early '70s, studying rhetoric at Ohio State with Edward P. J. Corbett, writing a long seminar paper on Sylvia Plath with Murray Beja, and doing a dissertation on feminist literary criticism with James Kincaid. Graduate school prepared me for a position as a literature specialist, but I found myself, instead, in a position at Michigan Tech in reading and composition. Such a position might have stifled my development as a feminist professional had I not found a way, in the '80s, to explore feminist reading and feminist composition at a time when few were doing so. I became a feminist professional by creating my own paths at every stage of my career.

MOVING AWAY

In college, which I started in 1962 and completed in 1966, I was influenced by my exposure to Betty Friedan's *The Feminine Mystique* in a speech class the year it came out, 1963. It was especially powerful for me because it helped provide an explanation for my mother's unhappiness. I was also influenced by countercultural movements that made evident social and racial injustices, as well as student protests against the Vietnam War. I taught myself to play the guitar and tried to imitate heroes such as Joan Baez and Bob Dylan. Although there was little in the English curriculum to point toward feminism, extracurricular visits to Greenwich Village with college friends provided a glimpse of an alternative lifestyle.

An early choice that defied expectations, and that surely suggested a move away from the choices available to me as a middle-class woman, was my marriage to John Flynn in 1966 immediately after I graduated from college. We also defied expectations by resisting what his mother called "settling down" for several decades. John, though two years ahead of me, also went to Pace, also majored in the liberal arts (Pace, at the time, was largely an accounting school), and was also raised Irish Catholic. But he was from working-class Brooklyn, the son of immigrants from Newfoundland who had not finished elementary school. His father supported the family of six children as an iron worker, a job in which he had little job security, but thanks to ever stronger unions, he did have good wages and benefits. His mother was a traditional housewife—cooking, cleaning, handling the money, and making sure that the children did well in school. The four girls were strong students at their Catholic high school, married neighborhood young men, and moved to the suburbs to raise their families. John's brother, who never finished high school, spent four years in the Navy, became an iron worker like his father, got married, and had six boys. We were also expected to start a family shortly after getting married, but I was forty-three and interim chair of my department at Michigan Tech before we did so. The pattern in John's family had already been broken right from the start since I was not from the neighborhood and was in college when we met. The pattern in my family was also broken because I married outside the middle class. A high school friend I've reconnected with recently observed that I was ahead of my time. Women these days are much more likely to do what I did, that is, establish themselves professionally before starting a family, whereas many of my high school classmates had multiple children in their early twenties.

After college, John got an MA in history from West Virginia University and then a job teaching at New York Military Academy (NYMA) in Cornwall-on-Hudson, about fifty miles north of New York City. One of its more famous alums is Donald Trump, though they missed each other by a year. When we were first married, we lived on the NYMA campus, and I taught English at Newburgh Free Academy. Teaching high school didn't suit me, though, because I was not enough of a disciplinarian. Without thinking through the consequences, for example, that he would lose his draft deferment, John took a job in industry, which took us to Columbus, Ohio, in the summer of 1967.

LEARNING TO BECOME AN ACADEMIC

Uncertain about what I would do in Columbus, I decided to inquire in the English Department at Ohio State and had an interview with Edward P. J. Corbett, who was then director of first-year writing (freshman composition, as it was called). As chance would have it, at the time there were about 10,000 first-year students, and they were required to take three first-year courses.

Staffing those courses was a huge challenge, and when Corbett heard that I had trained as an English teacher and had a year of experience teaching on the high school level, I was effectively hired on the spot, even before I had applied to the graduate program. I was admitted and found myself in September teaching two sections of first-year writing and taking a graduate seminar and the required course for those students who were teaching, a course Corbett taught. It focused mainly on rhetorical theory, and within the context of the first-year course we were then teaching, pedagogy pretty much amounted to exploring ways to impart rhetorical theory to our first-year students. Ohio State was an open admissions university at the time, so this was sometimes quite a challenge.

How serendipitous to have stumbled into Corbett's class and to have an excellent introduction to the field that would eventually become mine! As an undergraduate at Pace, we were introduced to cutting-edge concepts in literary studies because our professors were graduate students at universities such as Columbia and NYU, but there was never mention of rhetoric or composition. In Corbett's course, we read his *Classical Rhetoric for the Modern Student* and a collection of essays on rhetorical theory called *The Province of Rhetoric* edited by Joseph Schwartz and John A. Rycenga. Some of the authors included in the collection were: Walter Ong, Albert Duhamel, Richard Weaver, I. A. Richards, Kenneth Burke, Rosemond Tuve, and Wayne Booth. We had quizzes at the beginning of every class session because Corbett had found the previous year, the first time he taught the course, that the students were not doing the reading. The textbook required of the approximately 10,000 students taking the first term of the composition course was Harold C. Martin and Richard Ohmann's *The Logic and Rhetoric of Exposition*. Corbett boasted from time to time that this was the textbook being used in the first-year writing course at Harvard. We, however, struggled to bridge the gap between the book and our students. Corbett paid a mandatory visit to my class, and I had the ill fortune of having to teach the syllogism that day (we had a common syllabus). I thought of a way to engage the students in conversation on a topic that I thought would no doubt otherwise be uninteresting and difficult, but Corbett suggested after the class that I should have lectured instead. He was asked to step down from the directorship of the program the following year perhaps because it was clear that what was needed was an approach to composition better suited to Ohio State students. What I loved about his course, though, was the stylistic analysis that was the final assignment: we had to analyze the style of a professional writer and compare it to our own. I can't remember what professional essay I selected, but I do remember enjoying identifying periodic and loose sentences and explaining why the emphases they provided were appropriate in particular contexts, and I had great fun analyzing my own style.

Teaching in the late '60s and early '70s at Ohio State as an MA candidate, then later, for several years, as a lecturer, and then as a PhD candidate, was exciting. The approaches we experimented with, though not overtly feminist, were radically egalitarian. Peter Elbow was telling us we could teach teacherless classes (*Writing without Teachers*), and Ken Macrorie was laying the blame for routinized education on the faculty (*Uptaught*). We had to decide if we were going to teach our classes when the Ohio National Guard occupied campus after the attempted takeover of the administration building (I did). Kent State would soon follow. We found creative ways to teach writing. I remember a fellow graduate student getting on the elevator with a tray full of orange slices—she was heading to teach her composition class.

In graduate school I was fortunate to have encountered a favorite teacher and course early on, Joan Webber's Renaissance Prose. Here I could continue to do the fascinating stylistic analyses I had learned to do in Corbett's class. Joan's class was different from the other graduate courses I had taken, perhaps because she had a more feminine style and was more tentative in her pronouncements and open to our opinions. I also thought her interpretations of the texts we were reading were brilliant. I credit her with recognizing my potential and encouraging me to do strong work. Joan was in the process of preparing one of the first women's studies courses, focusing on women's poetry, which she subsequently taught for the department. It was after I had taken her Renaissance Prose course and my writing became more focused and confident that professors began saying I should consider revising and publishing the papers I was submitting. Publication wasn't something I understood at all, though, so I let these opportunities go by. Although I did not study women's writing or feminism with Joan, I see now that she was my first feminist mentor.

PURSUING FEMINISM

I was definitely moving in the direction of feminism when I began working on the PhD, and my long seminar paper, written under the direction of Murray Beja, was on Sylvia Plath. Not surprisingly, I saw her suicide as stemming, at least in part, in addition to her estrangement from Ted Hughes and her having to endure the coldest London winter on record, from having to raise small children by herself. I remember Beja commenting that I seemed to be suggesting she would have been okay had she only had day care. Who knows how it would have impacted her life, but it probably wouldn't have hurt.

I would perhaps not have made the decision to do a dissertation on feminism had it not been for the encouragement of my advisor, James Kincaid. It was a stretch, though, because I had never had a women's studies course. Indeed, in the mid-70s no women's studies courses were offered in the English Department at Ohio State, and few were offered at any university in the country. I had had only two women professors (the same number I had had as an undergraduate), and they were teaching work by male authors. Feminism, though, like rhetoric and composition, was definitely on the horizon. Kincaid, I'm sure, considered himself to be a feminist and even made the claim at a women's studies conference in the mid-70s that men may be even better than women in understanding women's issues because they can see women with greater detachment. This claim did not go over well with the feminists in the room, as might be imagined.

I effectively came out as a feminist in my dissertation, "Feminist Critical Theory: Three Models," completed in 1977. It aimed to explore what feminist literary criticism might be. I had originally intended to examine three novels from a feminist perspective, but I went into Kincaid's office one day, early on in the process, and said I thought it would make more sense to develop three theoretical models and apply them to a single novel—Woolf's *Mrs. Dalloway*. He explained that making this change had consequences because I would be presenting myself on the job market as a literary theorist, and, as he gently reminded me, I had never had a course in literary theory. Indeed, although literary theory, like feminism, was on the horizon at Ohio State and at universities across the country, the Department of English in the late '60s and early '70s did not then have a single course on the topic. I said I was willing to take that chance and proceeded to develop feminist approaches to Marxist criticism, archetypal criticism, and neo-Aristotelian criticism. I had to educate myself about these forms of criticism, though I was able, late in the process, to sit in on the first course in literary theory to be offered in the department, a course that had a neo-Aristotelian emphasis rather than a Marxist one. The decision to shift the emphasis in my dissertation from practical feminist literary criticism to feminist literary theory was an example of a willingness to step off the not-so-beaten path (not many, after all, were studying feminist literary criticism in the mid-70s) and create my own.

In defining my project, I was also influenced by John who, no doubt because of his working-class background, was deep into Marxist theory as a graduate student. His dissertation research, which he undertook in an archive located in a castle outside Düsseldorf, focused on the French occupation of the Ruhr Valley in 1923 during the Weimar Republic, the period that immediately preceded the rise of Adolph Hitler. As my mother liked to point out, this was the same time period in which *Mrs. Dalloway* was set, an example of serendipity.

In the dissertation, I was well aware that the three approaches I was exploring were not obviously compatible. Archetypal and neo-Aristotelian criticism, after all, were formalist and sometimes considered politically reactionary whereas Marxist criticism was, obviously, all about politics. Fredric Jameson's *Marxism and Form*, published in 1971, helped me make the case that formalism and Marxism could be usefully juxtaposed. His book was my introduction to the work of Theodor Adorno, Herbert Marcuse, and others, as well as the work of the Czech and Russian formalists. I followed Jameson's lead in attempting to integrate Marxism and formalism. In a footnote toward the end of *Marxism and Form*, Jameson says, "This is perhaps the moment to say that I do not regard Formalism—either Czech or Russian—as being at all irreconcilable with Marxism" (409). I made much of this idea since I was suggesting that the assumptions underpinning formalism, Marxism, and feminism had commonalities. This was another example of my creating my own path since Jameson presented the idea in a footnote whereas I was making it central to my argument.

SHIFTING DIRECTIONS

It is typical in the academy that one's career is launched as a result of one's dissertation. This was not the situation in my case, though, because there were few positions in literature, and the jobs that were opening up were in the newly emerging field of rhetoric and composition. Once again, I found myself creating a new path. I might easily have become another literature specialist unable to find a position had I not had the foresight to take advantage of opportunities to become more familiar with the field of rhetoric and composition. In addition to Corbett's class and the training I received in teaching composition, toward the end of my coursework for the PhD, I attended a study group conducted by Susan Miller, who, several years after Corbett stepped down, had become director of first-year writing. The group focused on theories of reading and included the work of K–12 educators such as Kenneth and Yetta Goodman and Frank Smith along with some reader-response criticism. This study group positioned me well for the job I would ultimately obtain, assistant professor of reading and composition at Michigan Tech. Few graduate programs in English at the time were attending to reading, though this was soon to change. Susan was also influential in helping set up the Writing Workshop directed by Sara Garnes, and after I completed the PhD, I worked there and gained very useful experience conducting composition research and teaching basic writers. At the same time, I sat in on a class taught by visiting professor James Britton of the University of London in the College of Education at Ohio State. As it turned out, Britton was the inspiration for the Writing Across the Curriculum (WAC) Program at Michigan Tech, which I was hired to help develop. I guess you could say I had the equivalent of a postdoctorate in rhetoric and composition, foresight in terms of preparing myself for positions outside literature, and considerable good luck.

Before John and I graduated together in 1977, we decided we would both go on the job market and see who ended up with a job. John came close to getting one at a university in Virginia but couldn't promise he'd be finished by the following fall. He also had a possibility at a university in Northern Iowa where a friend of ours was the provost, but, after a campus visit, we learned that there would be no position for me so we didn't pursue it. I came up with a non-tenure-track position in the Writing Workshop at Ohio State and then with a non-tenure-track position at Antioch College in literature and women's studies the first year I was on the market. In getting these positions, it no doubt helped that when I was a graduate student at Ohio State, I received a teaching award from the English Department. In the Writing Workshop, we did research as well as taught, and we prepared a report of our findings. I remember some of our work involved counting t-units, defined by Kellogg Hunt as a dominant clause and its dependent clause.

Women's studies had arrived at Antioch, and the experience I had there definitely advanced my understanding of feminism. I encountered many openly lesbian and gay students and many feminist faculty in areas other than literary studies. I also participated in discussions of women's studies curricula at meetings of the Great Lakes College Association of which Antioch was a member. The Antioch students prepared me well for teaching graduate seminars after the Department of Humanities at Michigan Tech developed graduate programs in the late 1980s. At Antioch, I also taught courses in women's literature and was given considerable latitude when it came to teaching other literature courses such as romantic and Victorian literature as well as twentieth-century literature and literary theory. Classes were generally small seminars, though an introductory Women in Literature course had at least thirty students. I also taught a course in feminist argument there.

My second year on the job market I cast a wider net, which included applying to Michigan Tech, a school I had overlooked the previous year. A friend from graduate school, however, had applied to Tech that year and gotten a preliminary interview at the Modern Language Association (MLA) conference. After her interview, I so vividly remember, a group of us sat on the floor of our living room, looked at a map, and wondered how she could possibly consider moving to such a place. Being more open and more flexible resulted in a preliminary interview, an on-campus interview, and ultimately an offer for a tenure-track position at Michigan Tech. I interviewed on Valentine's Day of 1979, the day the snowfall record was broken—356 inches. I had fond memories of northern New Jersey winters when I was young—sledding and skiing with skis that we strapped to our rubber boots—but 356 inches of snow did seem rather daunting. There were flags on fire hydrants so they would not be hit by snowplows, and Art Young gave me a tour of the area in his car, which, he boasted, had no snow tires.

BECOMING A FEMINIST PROFESSIONAL

I was hired into a humanities department rather than an English department to teach undergraduate courses since there was then no graduate program. The department, while including a number of humanistic fields, did not include history so John inquired about teaching possibilities in the Department of Social Sciences and did teach a course for them on the nearby Native reservation. He was resilient, though, and an excellent teacher and was just as glad to be free of the pressures of a tenure-track job so he willingly taught first-year writing and later specialized in the philosophy of technology. The department prided itself at the time on not erecting strong disciplinary barriers so he was happily able to contribute as a generalist rather than a specialist.

Although it was unusual then for the woman to have the tenure-track job and her partner or spouse to have a part-time position, it was happening more and more in the '80s and '90s within the academy, perhaps a response to affirmative action initiatives. Nevertheless, studies focusing on academic dual career couples make clear that when I was hired in 1979 it was more typical that the woman PhD followed her husband. In their essay "Babies Matter," for instance, Mason, Goulden, and Wolfinger observe that "married women PhDs are more likely than their male counterparts to indicate that their spouse's career limited their search for a faculty position" (14). The assumption implicit in the remaining essays in the book *The Balancing Act* edited by Bracken, Allen, and Dean is that it is the woman who has to make accommodations rather than the reverse.

We were fortunate that there were other faculty in the department with relationships such as ours. Carol Berkenkotter, who had been hired a year before me, for instance, had the tenure-track job while her partner, Jim Hefling, had a non-tenure-track position, and the four of us naturally became friends. These arrangements were not without tensions, however. Jim and John, for instance, would suggest from time to time that we were taking our careers entirely too seriously by intoning "a girl and her career," and we would reply "a boy and his truck" since Jim had one and John would get one eventually. After about a decade of teaching part-time, Jim left the department entirely and obtained a position as a social worker until Carol took a position at the University of Minnesota and left the department in 2001. John remained but took the line, as the department was developing graduate programs and becoming increasingly more research-oriented, that this was the wrong direction and greater emphasis should be placed on excellent undergraduate teaching rather than research. This led to tensions at home since I was the department chair encouraging the shift. He also was quite critical of the emphasis within the department on rhetoric and composition since it did not seem to him a rigorous field. He could not see how traveling across the country doing WAC workshops, as we did in those early days, was the life of a scholar as he envisioned it.[2]

It helped that I had developed an important coping mechanism, right from the start of my career at Michigan Tech, in the form of resisting a narrow definition of my job and my career. John was critical of workshopping and workshoppers, and I was certainly one of them, but I had never given up my commitment to the study of literature, though it morphed into an emphasis on reader-response criticism, a move I thought was justified by the word "reading" in my title. There was a split in the department early on between the compositionists, who dominated by virtue of their numbers and positions of authority, and faculty in the other humanistic fields, which included John. In important ways, though, I was really in both. Actually the compositionists in those early years, twenty in all hired in the late '70s and early '80s (they called it redundant hiring), had for the most part also specialized in literature in their graduate work since there were no graduate programs in rhetoric and composition at the time. Many changed their emphasis to rhetoric and composition as they were expected to do and had titles to demonstrate it—my title "reading and composition" is typical—though a few continued as literature specialists. I tried to do both, a move, I can now see, that was both resistant and resilient.

What was not clear when I was hired, though, was what role my commitment to feminism would play as my career developed. During my first few weeks on campus, I had a meeting with the dean, and he emphasized that I had not been hired for a position in women's studies. Characteristically, I resisted his warning and started working with a group of women from diverse areas of campus developing a project, "Discovering Copper Country Women's Heritage." We put together a grant proposal for the Michigan Council for the Humanities, and a colleague from the department and I became codirectors of the project, which was funded quite generously. The committee included Department of Humanities faculty and students as well as faculty and staff from areas such as the library, the School of Business, the Department of Social Sciences, the nearby two-year college (Suomi College, now Finlandia University), and the community. One of the students was openly lesbian, and one of the community members was African American (she would later become Dean of Students at Tech). We also involved the Ojibwa tribal community, located forty-five minutes away. The only trained historian on the committee was my husband John who was a non-tenure-track faculty member.

The women's heritage project was a dramatic and public form of resistance to a narrow definition of my position. "Discovering Copper Country Women's Heritage" was far more successful than we ever imagined it would be, due, certainly, to a convergence of choice, chance, and serendipity. Our timing was perfect as nothing similar had ever been done in our area, and there was considerable community interest. We also had good fortune in involving a very diverse committee. In addition, we had excellent promotion provided by local newspapers and radio stations and were able to attract outstanding speakers from elsewhere and from the local community. Program sessions were attended by hundreds of participants from the local community, Suomi College, Michigan Tech, and the Ojibwa Native community. The project won a Certificate of Commendation awarded by the American Association for State and Local History in 1982, and in 2004 it was named by the Michigan Humanities Council (the Council changed its name from the Michigan Council for the Humanities some years after we received our grant), one of thirty outstanding humanities projects in the Council's thirty-year history.

Central to the project were three evening sessions designed to explore diverse perspectives of women in the community. Held the week of March 16–20, 1981, the first session was a keynote address by Professor Bea Medicine of the University of Wisconsin, Madison, on "What Is Women's History and Why Should It Be Studied?"; the second session focused on oral histories in the form of slide/tape presentations of local women, each representing an occupation that typified the work of women of their era; and a third session included lectures by professionals on important Copper Country women. In this third session, for instance, Gladys Beckwith of Michigan State University spoke on Annie Clemenc, "Big Annie," supporter of the 1913 strike. The selection of Beckwith was timely because she had recently become president of the newly founded Michigan Women's Studies Association, which had just inducted Annie Clemenc into the newly created Michigan Women's Hall of Fame. At a time when feminism within the academy was just emerging, and when the emphasis was too often on the situations of white middle-class women, we had the foresight to recognize that race and class were as important as gender in these women's lives. In so doing, we anticipated the concept, so important in discussions of feminism today, of intersectionality, the idea that identities are composed of multiple intersecting strands rather than singular totalities and that power plays an important role in these intersections.

I paid a price for this coming out as a feminist, however, in that the project set back my progress toward tenure. In those days, before Michigan Tech became a full-fledged research university, faculty came up for tenure in their fourth year rather than their sixth year, as recommended by the American Association of University Professors. I had spent a year and a half of those first three years working on the women's heritage project, which resulted in no publications. I tend to have good luck when it comes to professional matters, though, and it definitely helped that I had spent six weeks during the summer of 1981 at the School of Criticism and Theory at Northwestern University where I studied with Bulgarian/French literary theorist Tveztan Todorov and wrote a draft of what would become "Gender and Reading," published in March 1983 in *College English*. Untenured faculty in composition at MTU were told that we needed at least one article in a major journal in a related area, *CCC* or *College English*, for instance, so we aimed high. "Gender and Reading" would, in turn, become the beginnings of *Gender and Reading*, coedited with Patsy Schweickart, whom I met, by chance, at the School. She, too, had graduated with a PhD in English from Ohio State, though we did not meet there, no doubt because I did coursework for the PhD in record time and spent two years in Germany while Patsy was busy raising two daughters. At Ohio State, though, we kept hearing about each other as we had common interests. *Gender and Reading* would be published by Johns Hopkins University Press in 1986.

By the beginning of my fourth year, the fall of 1982, I had an acceptance of an article in *The New Orleans Review* on women reader-response critics Louise Rosenblatt, Susan Suleiman, and Jane Tompkins (the editor was someone I met at the School), a revision of a paper I had delivered at the Midwest Modern Language Association (MMLA) conference in the fall of 1981. This paper had found its way to Jane Tompkins because MMLA made papers available to conference participants, and one of the participants sent it to her. I also had an article accepted on composing responses to literary texts in *College Composition and Communication* and an encouraging letter from Hopkins for *Gender and Reading*. It also didn't hurt that the person who became Hopkins's reader was Jane Tompkins. These acceptances were plenty for a little over three years of work in a department that had no graduate program, and my tenure went through. I would go on to write about Rosenblatt at greater length in a chapter of my book, *Feminism Beyond Modernism*, published in 2002, and in a "Reconsiderations" piece in *College English* in 2007.

In spending a year and a half on the women's heritage project, in addition to paying a price when it came to publishing, I also paid a price because I was inadvertently signaling to administrators that I had administrative capabilities. One of the things I liked about the position I originally obtained at Tech was that it involved no administrative responsibilities, though many of my Ohio State classmates were getting jobs as directors of writing programs or writing centers. This freedom, though, didn't last long. After I was tenured, I was asked to be assistant head of the Department of Humanities (and served on ten departmental, college, or university committees that year). Then I became interim head, then codirector of phase two of the Tech WAC Program, then director of the undergraduate Liberal Arts Program, then director of the graduate program in Rhetoric and Technical Communication (RTC). I went into phased retirement in 2010, shortly after stepping down as director of the RTC Program, and retired fully in May 2013. So much for trying to avoid administration.[3] Since I never saw myself as a career administrator, though, I continued to do research. Often this meant working entirely too hard, especially since I was a single mother from the time my daughter Kate was in middle school.[4]

BECOMING A MOTHER AND THEN A WIDOW

Kate's birth in 1988 after twenty-two years of marriage was an event that challenged all of our preconceptions of just about everything and certainly forced us to focus on life beyond the department and beyond work. Although there was no formal maternity leave policy, I was able to take time off or work halftime in Kate's early weeks, and we had the very good fortune, when Kate was six weeks old, of finding an excellent caregiver, a neighbor who lived around the corner who had raised four children.

I was pregnant when I worked on "Composing as a Woman" and a new mother when it was published. I was also interim chair of my department. Why did I think I could do it all? I was drawn, while writing the essay, to works such as Chodorow's *The Reproduction of Mothering* (1978), Gilligan's *In a Different Voice* (1982), and Belenky, Clinchy, Goldberger, and Tarule's *Women's Ways of Knowing* (1986), no doubt because I was experiencing the ultimate difference between women and men—childbirth. The essay actually originated, though, in a conference paper in the early '80s and so coincided with work I was doing on the essay "Gender and Reading," and with Patsy Schweickart on *Gender and Reading*. Literary studies had not yet attended to ways in which gender impacted reading, just as composition studies had not yet attended to the ways in which it impacted writing. It was the kairotic moment to introduce gender into both fields.

My life changed quite dramatically, though, when John died of a rare form of cancer in 2000, when Kate was just starting sixth grade. He had been treated by world-class oncologists at the Mayo Clinic, but they told us in late fall of 1999 that they could do nothing more for him. He returned home, became a hospice patient, and stopped teaching. He continued, though, to lead a fairly normal life until his death the following September. He cooked dinner for us and guests on a Sunday and died on Thursday.

Suddenly Kate and I were on our own, and just as suddenly my work day ended at 3:00 p.m. since Kate's middle school had no after-school program. It was even more challenging because, despite a disability (see the discussion of his hip surgeries in note 2 below), John had done virtually all of the cooking and shopping, managed the finances, and tended to our vehicles and to our 160-acre farm, which we purchased in 1988 and moved to in 1993. I had a lot to learn. Eventually, in high school, Kate learned to drive and bought a car so her final year she drove herself to school and home. Then she went off to Beloit College and graduate school at American University in Washington, DC. She is now a writer at the National Trust for Historic Preservation in DC.

CONTINUING AS A FEMINIST SCHOLAR AND PROFESSIONAL

My scholarship continued, though at a slower pace. I had written much of *Feminism Beyond Modernism* (2002) before John died. It departed from the approach to gender I had taken in "Composing as a Woman," which, I will admit, flirted with essentialized approaches to gender. The book provided me an opportunity to explore feminism in considerably more depth and to identify several strands—modern, postmodern, and antimodern. I came to the defense of postmodern feminism by arguing that it arises out of modern feminism, with its Enlightenment commitments to equality for women, but is skeptical rather than optimistic, as modern feminism is, about the possibility of achieving this goal. Antimodern feminism, in contrast, opposes modernist scientific and rationalist projects and is associated with romantic interests in spirituality, emotion, and irrationality. John was interested in modernism and antimodernism, and several of the books in his library were very helpful in developing my argument. I'm glad that in the book I defended truth (with a small "t") and accuracy, and argued against "anything goes" relativism since it is easy, as we have recently seen, to slide into public discourse in which lies and fake news become normalized. *Reading Sites* (2004), coedited with Patsy Schweickart, continued the project of *Gender and Reading* by expanding the frame of reference to include other factors such as race, class, ethnicity, and sexual orientation, a decidedly intersectional approach. *Feminist Rhetorical Resilience* (2012), coedited with Michigan Tech colleagues Patty Sotirin and Ann Brady, made clear that resilience is a valuable concept that, though heretofore ignored within feminist rhetoric and rhetoric as a whole, helps explain the persistence and accomplishments of women in a variety of contexts. Central concepts are relationality, agency, and *mêtis*. Evidence of increasing national recognition as a feminist professional includes the Elizabeth A. Flynn Award for the Most Outstanding Article in Feminist Rhetoric and Composition, first awarded by The Association of Teachers of Advanced Composition in 2003. It has been given to excellent scholars ever since. Over the years, I also participated actively in the Conference on College Composition and Communication (CCCC) and MLA. I served two terms on the Executive Committee of CCCC, on the Delegate Assembly of MLA, on executive committees of the MLA, and was president of the Women's Caucus for the Modern Languages, an affiliate of MLA.

As I've indicated, coming out as a feminist was challenging at first at Michigan Tech, but as the profession began to embrace it, so did the institution. The dean who warned me about doing research in the area of women's studies did not complain when *Gender and Reading* came out. The Department of Humanities continued to hire feminists over the years, and some of us have formed a gender group that has sometimes served as a reading and writing group, sometimes a support group, and continues as a social group despite my retirement. Every March we celebrate Women's History Month by having a public reading of our favorite passages from feminist texts. The feminisms and rhetorics conference held at Michigan Tech in 2005 was a product of collaboration among three members of the group—myself, Patty Sotirin, and Ann Brady—as was the collection that resulted from it, *Feminist Rhetorical Resilience*. Our graduate program provided me many opportunities to teach courses in gender studies, and recently a graduate student wrote a dissertation which had its beginnings in the last graduate seminar I taught, Rhetorical Witnessing, which included discussion of Kelly Oliver's *Witnessing* and Judith Butler's *Frames of War*, works we had read in the course. I was considerably more reluctant to come out as a feminist in undergraduate courses, though, and sometimes addressed the subject less directly by including readings by feminists such as Virginia Woolf and Adrienne Rich along with male writers. A former student whom I had in first-year English in 1984, and whom I encountered by chance recently, reminded me that we read the Belenky et al. book *Women's Ways of Knowing* in the class, and I occasionally taught literature courses in which all of the readings were by women.

FINAL REFLECTIONS

The farm was John's dream, but I'm realizing it's an alternative to the suburban home that caused my mother unhappiness and has become a creative outlet. I designed our house around the old log cabin that was its origin. Together a group of friends and I created a communal garden in 2004, and I continue to garden, something that was always John's interest. I've done some landscaping, entertain frequently, and enjoy the company of squirrels, chipmunks, deer, and occasionally bear, fox, and (in the pond we created), beaver, muskrats, and otter. Shortly after I retired, in the summer of 2013, I took a photography course at Tech. My final project was a series of pictures of an abandoned one-hundred-year-old threshing machine that sits under a collapsing shed in one of our fields. At the suggestion of my instructor (a graduate student whom I had had in class and who grew up in the house in town that we departed when we moved to the farm), I mounted the pictures on a board from the shed. I've also joined or created a number of groups; at last count, there were at least ten. One group, which includes friends with Michigan Tech affiliations outside the Department of Humanities, meets once a week for dinner. The core group has been together since before Kate was born. I've also joined two hiking groups recently. Another group dates from the time Kate was in middle school and includes mothers of children around her age. We continue to meet at a local coffee shop every Friday afternoon and have collectively gotten our children, now adults, through middle school, high school, college, and sometimes professional school. I have worked at managing stress, which has been a perennial problem since I gave birth to Kate while I was department chair, by doing yoga and meditating.[5]

Presumably one's career follows a relatively straight trajectory. At least that seemed to be the case at Ohio State when I entered graduate school. There were Victorianists, Romanticists, Medievalists, and so on, and they generally remained in the positions for which they were hired. I remember a controversy over a faculty member who wanted to switch periods. I can't remember if she pulled it off, but I do remember that there was resistance. It was typical that one studied a subject in graduate school, proceeded to get a job in the field, and continued to teach and do research in a fairly continuous way. My career, though, has been nothing like that. I focused in graduate school on twentieth-century literature and did obtain a temporary position at Antioch in the field, and I taught quite a bit of literature at Michigan Tech, but the areas in which I've done most of my publishing—rhetoric and composition, reading, and gender studies—were areas in which I had little or no preparation in my coursework in graduate school. I had the good fortune of entering the profession at a time when there were opportunities for those of us willing to take a chance and venture beyond the boundaries of what was comfortable and familiar. I realize in writing this essay that I did the same in my personal life. Marrying into the working class, moving to the remote Upper Peninsula, and starting a family after many years of marriage were certainly not usual. Becoming a feminist professional has meant choosing not one different path but a number of them all along the way and being open to serendipitous opportunities as they presented themselves in my career and my life.

NOTES

1. I wish to thank Lisa Ede, Suellynn Duffey, Tiffany Bourelle, Libby Jones, my sister Alice Hayes, Andrea Lunsford, two anonymous reviewers, and our editor, Tara Cyphers, for their very useful feedback on drafts of this essay. A recently published interview with Tiffany Bourelle complements this essay.
2. These challenges were compounded by John's four surgeries to repair a broken femur as a result of a cross-country skiing accident in the early 1980s. The first three, the second and third of which were done at the Mayo Clinic, were unsuccessful in that they left him with chronic pain. It wasn't until the last one in the mid-1990s, also done at the Mayo Clinic, that he could walk pain free. When he was at the Mayo Clinic for the second of these surgeries, he was diagnosed with and treated for testicular cancer which, luckily, never returned. Early in our relationship, we discussed the concept of stoicism, one of us thinking the adjective was "stoic" and the other thinking it was "stoical." Little did we know this concept would help define our married life.
3. In "Why Women's Voices Matter," Gutgold and Linse speak of the longer hours of administration and the need to be "on call" at all times as reasons why women may be discouraged from moving from teaching to administration.
4. For an in-depth examination of the invisibility of the labor of service in the field of language and literature within the academy, see Massé's edited collection, *Over Ten Million Served: Gendered Service in Language and Literature Workplaces*.

5. Paludi, Vaccariello, Graham, Smith, Allen-Dicker, Kasprzak, and White in "Work/Life Integration" discuss research on the impact on women of juggling multiple roles.

WORKS CITED

Adorno, Theodor. *The Authoritarian Personality.* New York: Harper and Row, 1950. Print.

Belenky, Mary Field, Blythe McVicker Clinchy, Nancy Rule Goldberger, and Jill Mattuck Tarule. *Women's Ways of Knowing: The Development of Self, Voice, and Mind.* New York: Basic Books, 1986. Print.

Bourelle, Tiffany. "Kairos, Resilience, and Serendipity: An Interview with Elizabeth Flynn." *Composition Forum* 35 (Spring 2017). Web. June 4, 2017.

Bracken, Susan J., Jeanie K. Allen, and Diane R. Dean, eds. *The Balancing Act: Gendered Perspectives in Faculty Roles and Work Lives.* Sterling, VA: Stylus, 2006. Print.

Britton, James, Tony Burgess, Nancy Martin, Alex McLeod, and Harold Rosen. *The Development of Writing Abilities (11–18).* London: Macmillan, 1975. Print.

Butler, Judith. *Frames of War: When Is Life Grievable?* London: Verso, 2009. Print.

Chodorow, Nancy. *The Reproduction of Mothering.* Berkeley: U of California P, 1978. Print.

Corbett, Edward P. J. *Classical Rhetoric for the Modern Student.* New York: Oxford UP, 1965. Print.

Elbow, Peter. *Writing without Teachers.* New York: Oxford UP, 1973. Print.

Flynn, Elizabeth A. "Composing as a Woman." *CCC* 39 (1988): 423–35. Print.

———. *Feminism Beyond Modernism.* Carbondale: Southern Illinois UP, 2002. Print.

———. "Feminist Critical Theory: Three Models." Diss. The Ohio State University, 1977. Print.

———. "Louise Rosenblatt and the Ethical Turn in Literary Theory." *College English* 70 (September 2007): 52–69. Print.

———. "Women as Reader-Response Critics." *New Orleans Review* 10.2.3 (Summer–Fall 1983): 20–25. Print.

Flynn, Elizabeth A., and Patrocinio P. Schweickart, eds. *Gender and Reading: Essays on Readers, Texts, and Contexts.* Baltimore: Johns Hopkins UP, 1986. Print.

Flynn, Elizabeth A., Patricia Sotirin, and Ann Brady, eds. *Feminist Rhetorical Resilience.* Logan: Utah State UP, 2012. Print.

Gilligan, Carol. *In a Different Voice: Psychological Theory and Women's Development.* Cambridge, MA: Harvard UP, 1982. Print.

Goodman, Kenneth. *What's Whole in Whole Language?* Portsmouth, NH: Heinemann, 1986. Print.

Goodman, Yetta. *How Children Construct Literacy: Piagetian Perspectives.* Newark, DE: International Reading Association, 1990. Print.

Gutgold, Nicola D., and Angela R. Linse. "Why Women's Voices Matter." *Women in the Academy: Learning from Our Diverse Career Pathways.* Ed. Nichola D. Gutgold and Angela R. Linse. Lanham, MA: Lexington Books, 2016. 137. Print.

Hunt, Kellogg. *Grammatical Structures Written at Three Grade Levels.* Research Report No. 3. Urbana, IL: NCTE, 1965. Print.

Jameson, Fredric. *Marxism and Form: Twentieth-Century Dialectical Theories of Literature.* Princeton: Princeton UP, 1971. Print.

Kincaid, James R. "There Are No Women in Literature—Only Words." Paper presented at the Pioneers for Century II Convention, Cincinnati, Ohio, April 1976. Print.

Macrorie, Ken. *Uptaught*. New York: Hayden, 1970. Print.

Martin, Harold C., and Richard M. Ohmann. *The Logic and Rhetoric of Exposition*. New York: Holt, Rinehart, and Winston, 1963. Print.

Mason, Mary Ann, Marc Goulden, and Nicholas H. Wolfinger. "Babies Matter: Pushing the Gender Equity Revolution Forward." *The Balancing Act: Gendered Perspectives in Faculty Roles and Work Lives*. Ed. Susan J. Bracken, Jeanie K. Allen, and Diane R. Dean. Sterling, VA: Stylus, 2006. 9–29. Print.

Massé, Michelle A., and Katie J. Hogan, eds. *Over Ten Million Served: Gendered Service in Language and Literature Workplaces*. Albany: State U of New York P, 2010. Print.

Oliver, Kelly. *Witnessing: Beyond Recognition*. Minneapolis: U of Minnesota P, 2001. Print.

Paludi, Michele A., Rebecca Vaccariello, Traci Graham, Melissa Smith, Kelsey Allen-Dicker, Hilary Kasprzak, and Christa White. "Work/Life Integration: Impact on Women's Careers, Employment, and Family." *Work, Life, and Family Imbalance: How to Level the Playing Field*. Ed. Michele A. Paludi and Presha E. Neidermeyer. Westport, CT: Praeger, 2007. 21–36. Print.

Rich, Adrienne. *The Dream of a Common Language: Poems 1974–1977*. New York: Norton, 1978. Print.

Rosenblatt, Louise M. *Literature as Exploration*. 5th ed. New York: Modern Language Association, 1938, 1995. Print.

——. *The Reader, the Text, the Poem: The Transactional Theory of the Literary Work*. Carbondale: Southern Illinois UP, 1978. Print.

Schwartz, Joseph, and John A. Rycenga, eds. *The Province of Rhetoric*. New York: Ronald P, 1965. Print.

Schweickart, Patrocinio, and Elizabeth A. Flynn, eds. *Reading Sites: Social Difference and Reader Response*. New York: Modern Language Association, 2004. Print.

Smith, Frank. *Psycholinguistics and Reading*. New York: Holt, Rinehart and Winston, 1973. Print.

Woolf, Virginia. *Mrs. Dalloway*. New York: Harcourt, Brace, and World, Inc., 1925. Print.

CHAPTER 3

My Kairotic Career

ANNE RUGGLES GERE

I went to graduate school because I wanted to learn how to do a better job of teaching writing to my high school students . . . that sounds like a clear and informed choice, but the full story is more complicated. I had been teaching English at Princeton High School for three years, and my husband's work was going to take us to Ann Arbor, Michigan, in the fall of 1970, so I started looking for a teaching job there. I figured I would be an attractive candidate since I had an MA and three years of experience at a very good school. However, 1970 was when the high school teaching market began to lose its momentum. In 1967, when I looked for my first job, one superintendent told me that he had just hired a teacher, whom he had never met, on the basis of a postcard inquiry, because it was so hard to find enough teachers. But in 1970, there was exactly one opening for an English teacher in the Ann Arbor area, and they hired a BA with no experience because "she was cheaper," as the HR person explained.

Back at Princeton High, I happened to mention my disappointment to a colleague with whom I shared my classroom, and she volunteered that the chair of the English Department at the University of Michigan was a good friend. "I'll write to him about you," she said. A few weeks later, I received a letter from the chair, offering me either one semester of teaching introduction to poetry or a position as receptionist in the main office. Poetry was the instant winner, and during that fall semester I discovered that Michigan had a program called the Joint PhD in English and Education. It seemed like an excellent fit, and since I really did want to know how to do a better job of teaching writing, I applied and began taking courses the next semester.

As I learned more about the program, it became clear that there were no courses where I could learn about writing instruction. So I began looking for alternatives. Rich Enos was a faculty member in what is now the Department of Communications, and I had several very helpful conversations with him about rhetoric. Even though I couldn't take courses with him, he guided me toward readings that helped me understand more about how rhetoric could help me think about writing instruction. In addition to rhetoric via Rich, I found my way into literacy studies. Ruth Finnegan, a British anthropologist who had written a book about African literature, came to campus at just the right moment to help me understand a much broader view of literacy. Shortly after that my husband and I led a mission trip to West Africa, and as I prepared by reading Chinua Achebe's novels, I began to think that I could write a dissertation about the rhetoric of West African fiction, focusing on the relationship between oral and written literacies. This was, after all, before Brian Street blew apart the Goody/Olson/Ong dichotomous perspective on literacy.

The series of chance encounters and serendipitous meetings continued as I began looking for a job after graduate school. As had been true for high school jobs in 1970, the mid-1970s were not a good time to be on the academic job market. My chief memory of my first MLA in 1973 is sitting under a fake palm tree drinking from a flask in the lobby of the Palmer House in Chicago. My friend John Hollowell and I went to the convention because driving there and staying at the nearby YMCA was affordable. We were still finishing our dissertations but thought it was time to see what the job market looked like. The highlight of that conference was meeting Ed White, who was serving as an MLA job counselor. I don't remember what advice he gave me, but he became and remains a friend. I had no interviews in Chicago, but I brought home images of nervous looking peers dressed in suits swarming in the lobby of the Palmer House. Miraculously I had three interviews at MLA the next year, one of them for a position at the University of Washington. Back on campus, Joseph Blotner, an English professor whom I knew because his daughter was in our church youth group, asked how the search was going, and I mentioned my University of Washington interview. Blotner, a Faulkner scholar, immediately responded that he would call his friend Robert Heilman, who had chaired the UW English Department for the past twenty years. As I later learned, Heilman put in a good word with the search committee, and my application rose to the top.

On the strength of the UW offer, my husband—always a feminist—left his position, and we sold our house and moved all our worldly goods to Seattle, a city we had never seen. There were no campus visits in 1975. During my final year of graduate school, we had adopted a three-year-old daughter. For us, products of the 1960s who had worked with children in marginal communities of New York City and Los Angeles, adoption was a first choice. Although we were prepared for the challenges of incorporating an older and racially different child into our family, we had specified that our choice did not mean we were prepared for dealing with handicaps. Cindy, an American Indian, was a very lively—I later realized, too lively—child who had been born in Yukon Territory, Canada. That August, we three drove over Snoqualmie Pass, gasped at an unimaginably beautiful Mount Rainer looming over the city, and I began two parallel tracks of learning, one focused on Fetal Alcohol Syndrome and one on writing instruction.

I had a PhD and had some background in rhetoric and literacy, but I still didn't know much about teaching writing. "Theories of Writing Instruction," a course I was regularly assigned to teach, made me feel particularly inadequate. Likewise, in my work with prospective high school English teachers, I felt almost fraudulent offering advice about how to teach writing. As I began looking for resources, I heard about the Bay Area Writing Project (BAWP), a program that had begun at UC Berkeley a couple of years earlier. When I got in touch with Jim Gray, the director, he expressed interest in the possibility of establishing a BAWP site in Seattle. Jim came to visit, and I began developing the Puget Sound Writing Project as BAWP morphed into the National Writing Project. The NWP model, with its emphasis on teacher expertise and one's own writing, helped me understand writing instruction in an entirely new way. Watching an excellent teacher of first graders show how she had her students create narratives, seeing a middle school teacher's demonstration of strategies for drafting, and being captivated by a high school teacher's display of seventeen versions of one of his poems to emphasize the importance of revision—these and many other presentations by highly effective teachers stimulated my thinking about writing. This, combined with joining a writing group and embarking on a program of self-study to read authors like Janet Emig, Ed Corbett, and Donald Murray along with a host of writers in the journals *College Composition and Communication* and *College English* who had not been part of my graduate education helped me feel more confident about writing instruction. The convergence of BAWP/NWP with my teaching needs and the emergence of research and scholarship on composition made an impact on the rest of my career. It also reinforced the developing theme that I would find academic sustenance in many different places, like a trip to West Africa or an elementary school classroom or an article in the most recent *CCC*.

My own experiences in a writing group, my observations of NWP teachers who blossomed as they shared their writing with others, and my work with UW students whom I assigned to writing groups heightened my interest in what I would now call the social dimension of writing. With a colleague in the College of Education, I conducted research on how students talked about one another's writing, and I began reading explanations of the origins of these groups. The more I read, the more I became convinced that there was more to the story than what appeared in the existing literature, so I began my own investigation. *Writing Groups: History, Theory, and Implications* was the result of that work, and I'm certain I never would have written that book if I hadn't chosen to be involved with the National Writing Project.

Another choice, to adopt children, led to a very different kind of learning. At the same time that I was learning about teaching writing, I was learning about Fetal Alcohol Syndrome. As it became clear that Cindy, even with lots of support, was not learning to read and had difficulty with many kinds of learning, we began seeking help. Our pediatrician referred us to Dr. David Smith, a UW researcher who did ground-breaking research in Fetal Alcohol Syndrome (FAS). The diagnosis of FAS was heartbreaking. Because of her birth mother's alcoholism, Cindy's brain was permanently damaged. Her disability was largely invisible, but it carried devastating consequences, and no amount of intervention could improve her mental capacities. What made this situation especially challenging was my realization that we had a name for Cindy's difficulties, but we had no models to follow since hers was the first generation of FAS children to be identified. I would have to rely on chance and serendipity while I reinvented myself as the mother of a disabled child.

When I joined the English Department, I was the only woman who was married and had a small child. I had several female colleagues who were married and a few older women colleagues who had grown children, but no one who was trying to juggle a career and a family as I was. Desperate for a peer group, I looked outside the department and found a few women in other fields who were doing the same juggling act. Together we created the Other Moms group and met regularly at the faculty club to share ideas about departmental politics, the tenure process, and childcare. When the Seattle public schools were closed by a teachers' strike, it was the Other Moms who organized a rotating play group that incorporated all our children until schools opened. It was also the Other Moms who suggested schooling options for Cindy and encouraged me with stories of special-needs children who found success. One of the Other Moms was a pediatrician who helped me navigate the medical-ized language surrounding FAS. Another was a specialist in social work who alerted me to resources to support Cindy's learning. It was another instance of serendipity to find this expertise among the Other Moms.

The years flew by as I made my way into the tenured ranks. In the year I was coming up for tenure, my husband and I adopted a second child. Sam never used "dissertation" as a curse word the way Cindy had, but he surely felt the growing tension as my tenure vote came closer. Fortunately the vote was positive, but the journey wasn't always easy. One day as I walked toward my late afternoon class, a male colleague smiled knowingly and said, "Going home to cook, dear?" The day after my tenure vote, I encountered another male colleague who had never spoken to me during my entire tenure as an assistant professor. As we met in the stairwell, he intoned, "Welcome to the senior faculty."

One of the things that made my juggling act possible was the fact that my mother chose to move to Seattle at the same time we did. A retired school teacher, she relished spending time with her grandchildren, and I knew that when one of the children was sick and all other emergency systems failed, I could call my mother to rescue me. My mother and I had always been very close. My father died when I was twelve, and as the oldest of two sisters I became my mother's helper; then she, in turn, became mine. Her choice to move to Seattle made many other choices possible for me.

There were many wonderful things about living in Seattle. The diverse population provided strong cultural support for our children. My husband and I joined the Mountaineers, learned that what we had called climbing in New England was really just hiking, and prepared to summit Mount Rainer. We learned to sail in Puget Sound and became frequent visitors to the San Juan Islands. We made lifelong friendships and became involved in many community activities. On my own, I might have stayed at the University of Washington for my entire career, but my husband's work as a Presbyterian minister took us in another direction.

Ministers are inherently nomadic, and after I had gained tenure it was time for him to think about his next move. Finding positions for two mid-career professionals was not easy. We each turned down several attractive opportunities because there wasn't a nearby position for the other person. This was not an easy process. One search committee for a church in a very affluent community backed my husband into a corner (literally) and told him that "the little lady" should just come along. "She can get a job at the community college," one of them said. An East Coast university offered me a position and held it for a year because my husband and I were sure that an evolving position would come his way. It didn't, and I had to turn down a position that seemed very attractive. After several years of near misses, we finally found a match in Michigan. I was hired to return to Ann Arbor to become a cochair of the program where I had taken my PhD, and my husband accepted a call at a church in suburban Detroit. This convergence of positions for both of us within reasonable driving distance was both serendipitous and kairotic; it was clearly the right time to leave Seattle.

One of the saddest things about leaving Seattle was my mother's decision to move to Salt Lake City (rather than Michigan) to be near my sister. I understood her fair-minded intention to spend more time with her other daughter and to get to know her younger grandchildren, but it was still painful. That pain became much greater in subsequent years as my mother was diagnosed with Parkinson's disease and eventually succumbed to dementia. I confronted this loss directly one morning when she was visiting us in Michigan. As I entered the room, she smiled brightly at me and said, "Good morning. Who are you, dear?"

When I'm asked about the research agenda that has shaped my career, I often explain that my work on writing groups led me to think further about the extracurricular, and that, in turn, led me to study women's clubs because they were the site of so much self-sponsored writing. The full story is more complicated. As my mother became someone with whom I could no longer communicate, someone I could hardly recognize, I felt as if she had already died even though she was still alive. I needed a way to connect with the mother I had known. When I was growing up, she had been very active in the local and state women's club, and her scrapbooks and club records reminded me of a time when she had been a highly competent leader, as did photographs of her younger self. Writing *Intimate Practices: Literacy and Cultural Work in U.S. Women's Clubs, 1880–1920* gave me a way to build a different connection with my mother; it got me through the deeply sad process of watching her decline and ultimately die.

As my mother was fading, my parenting responsibilities became more challenging. I had one child in special education and the other in the gifted and talented program. Cindy, always a very hard-working student, struggled with every class, and helping her with homework absorbed several hours every day. After failing the required math test multiple times, she finally graduated from high school at age twenty. Sam, on the other hand, grasped almost everything with no apparent effort, and I had to find ways to keep him engaged in learning. Parenting two such different children taught me a lot about variations in learning that made me a better and more understanding teacher.

Graduate students took up increasing amounts of time as I began serving on more exam and dissertation committees. As my children moved on with their lives, I took increasing pleasure in mentoring the next generation of professionals. Then my husband decided it was time for his next move, and I exchanged my forty-five-minute daily drive for weekly plane trips to and from St. Louis and Ann Arbor. In addition to accruing a huge number of frequent flyer points, I could tell students exactly when I would get a paper or a dissertation chapter back to them because I could count on uninterrupted hours in the air. The chance to travel by plane rather than car actually gave me more time to focus on my teaching and research.

During the first years of this new commute, my husband and I described ourselves as a "'90s couple" since for the first time we had no children living at home. This period was short-lived because Cindy became a single mother who was not able to take up the responsibilities of parenting. So my husband and I became do-over parents for infant Denali. Once again, I made play dough, sewed Halloween costumes, and trekked to Disneyland. As it became clear that our family would do better living in one place, serendipity intervened once again, and my husband found a position in Ann Arbor. For the first time in seventeen years, I could bike to work.

As I moved from leading Denali's Brownie troop to heading a group of Girl Scouts, my professional life took another turn, and I was given the choice of becoming the director of the Sweetland Center for Writing in 2008. This endowed center provided resources to take up many new projects. A modified Directed Self-Placement process, a minor in writing, a series of courses focused on writing in new media, an electronic portfolio requirement, and courses for international/multilingual students have all given me opportunities to do research, including a longitudinal study of the development of undergraduate writers. Perhaps most exciting is the work we have begun in order to integrate writing into gateway science courses.

Like many women, I went to college planning to major in science, and after a terrible semester in biology, I retreated to English. Looking back, I realize that it was the pedagogy more than the content that drove me away from science. Answering multiple choice questions on tests didn't help me engage with biology. Although many aspects of higher education have changed since I went to college, the pedagogy in many science, technology, engineering, and math (STEM) courses remains pretty much the same, and an appalling number of women and students of color leave, as I did, after a semester or two. A colleague in chemistry and I are currently developing ways of building regular content-focused writing into large-enrollment gateway courses by using automated peer review systems. Our preliminary results indicate that women who participate in this writing do better in the course and are more likely to remain in the natural sciences.

Serendipity in the form of a mutual friend brought Ginger, the chemist, and me together. Her interest in chemical education and mine in integrating writing into STEM courses led to a very productive collaboration. Ginger and I have received several large grants to integrate writing-to-learn pedagogies into multiple gateway STEM courses, and at a time when I might otherwise be looking toward retirement, I am involved in more projects than I can count. As if that weren't enough, I was recently elected incoming president of the Modern Language Association. When the representative of the nominating committee called to ask if I would be willing to run, my first thought was that my plate was already too full, but my husband reminded me that he had recently retired and could give me even more support. I also reminded myself that the last time someone from rhetoric and composition led the MLA was 1907, when Fred Newton Scott served as president. When the University of Michigan awarded me a collegiate chair, I had chosen Gertrude Buck as my chair name because I wanted a constant reminder of Scott's student, the first woman to receive a PhD in rhetoric. I couldn't turn my back on Buck's pioneering spirit by saying I was too busy.

As I negotiate the rolling eyes and inevitable moodiness of the now adolescent Denali, I imagine for her a future very different from the one my adolescent self could envision. Teacher and nurse were the career options that seemed open to me, and women were always supposed to follow and support a husband's career. Growing up poor in a very small town, graduating in a class of twenty-seven, and having limited access to the larger world, I could not envision entering the professorate and taking part in national conversations. But serendipity or fortunate chances gave me a rich array of choices. Several of these serendipitous moments can best be described as kairotic because they came at exactly the right time and led to permanent transformations in my life and career. Coming of age in the early 1970s, I benefited enormously from the kairos of beginning my career as more opportunities emerged for women as well as from many kairotic moments like the intervention of Joe Blotner, the development of the NWP, the two positions in Michigan, and the opportunity to lead the Sweetland Center for Writing. These, interwoven with choosing to spend my life with a supportive feminist, parenting in an interracial and variously abled family, and having the freedom to move across the country and back, made my career both possible and joyous. I didn't have a career plan when I began because I didn't know that was something women could do. Whatever choices she makes in the future, Denali already knows that she can do anything.

WORKS CITED

Achebe, Chinua. *No Longer at Ease*. Portsmouth, NH: Heinemann, 1960. Print.

———. *Things Fall Apart*. Portsmouth, NH: Heinemann, 1958. Print.

Finnegan, Ruth. *Oral Literature in Africa*. Oxford: Clarendon, 1970. Print.

Gere, Anne Ruggles. *Intimate Practices: Literacy and Cultural Work in U.S. Women's Clubs, 1880–1920*. Carbondale: U of Illinois P, 1997. Print.

———. *Writing Groups: History, Theory and Implications*. Carbondale: Southern Illinois UP, 1987. Print.

Goody, Jack. *The Domestication of the Savage Mind*. New York: Cambridge UP, 1977. Print.

———. *The Logic of Writing and the Organization of Society*. New York: Cambridge UP, 1986. Print.

Olson, David R. *Literacy, Language and Learning: The Nature and Consequences of Reading and Writing*. New York: Cambridge UP, 1985. Print.

Olson, David R., and Nancy Torrance. *Literacy and Orality*. New York: Cambridge UP, 1991. Print.

Ong, Walter J. *Orality and Literacy: The Technologizing of the Word*. New York: Metheun, 1982. Print.

Street, Brian. *Literacy in Theory and Practice*. New York: Cambridge UP, 1985. Print.

CHAPTER 4

Choice and Serendipity, Supple Synergy

LYNN Z. BLOOM

THE PLAN

> I had rehearsed my first line and my second line [preparing for the phone call to ask for my first date]. I planned to say, "Hello, can I please speak to Eileen?" Then, when she came to the phone, I planned to say, "Hello, Eileen, this is Elwyn White." From there on, I figured I could ad-lib it.
> —E. B. White, "Afternoon of an American Boy"

I had rehearsed my first line. I would earn a PhD in English and become a writer and college professor. Although my real passion was for writing, and for what would come to be called "composition studies," that field didn't exist when I was at Michigan in the '60s. English with its wealth of wonderful works (not *texts!*) to read and ponder was a close second, so English it was.

I had rehearsed my second line as well. I would marry a fellow grad student, also aiming for a professorial career; who but another professor could understand a professor's work life? He could be in any field except English, to eliminate competition. He would be a feminist, not easy to find in midcentury, even in academia; our careers would be equivalent; we would share childcare and housework. Reader, I married Martin, a social psychology doctoral student, and from there on I figured I could ad-lib it.

Making good choices positions you to take advantage of serendipity.

From early childhood, I have had the happy faculty of ignoring advice I didn't want to hear. My career choices—to earn a PhD, to become a college professor in three nonexistent fields—defied the 1950s expectations of what a woman college graduate should do. Get married (check), have children (check), and "Get a teaching certificate, so you'll have something to fall back on" (never!)—the implication of that sentence was "in case your husband leaves you for another woman and you have to go to work" (not on your life!). My marriage itself defied my parents' expectations. "As Martin's wife, you'll be the victim of anti-Semitism for the rest of your life. If you marry him we will have nothing to do with you, or your husband, or any children you may have," they said as I was leaving for England to marry Martin, in exile, and travel around Europe for two months before beginning doctoral work. "Sorry I have to choose," I thought, though I had already learned you cannot argue with bigots, "but it's their life or mine." My parents never relented. Having chosen at the beginning of my career to do what I loved with the man that I loved—and still do to this day, fifty-eight years later—toughened me up. Having made these major life-sustaining choices, of marriage, motherhood, and disciplinary specialties by the time I earned my PhD, I was willing to risk everything to act on congenial serendipitous opportunities that came along in order to do work that was original, exciting, and fun.

But until I started to write this essay I had never thought of my life as a garden of serendipities, but so it has been, full of, as Annie Dillard says, the natural world, "unwrapped gifts and free surprises," there to be selected and savored. If I'd had a mentor, I might have had a plan and followed it step-by-step to a foreordained goal. Still, in midcentury America, married women with children were written off as lost to the profession, so I had to invent a professional life as I went along, a life full of improvisation and surprises. Although I took these serendipities for granted when they occurred, it is startling to discover in retrospect their number, variety, and profound importance in a career whose choices have often defied both logic and prudence.

SERENDIPITY, A DEFINITION HAPPY AND EXPANSIVE

Serendipity is universally acknowledged to be the unexpected discovery of a good thing, or the faculty someone has for making such happy and surprising discoveries. In *The Travels and Adventures of Serendipity,* sociologists Robert Merton and Elinor Barber devote 303 sprightly pages to tracing the term's meanings and implications—scientific, social, humanistic, and moral. Coined by Horace Walpole in 1754,[1] the word itself is as pleasant to utter (how many words can claim such metrical dips and skips?) as the concept is to experience. Fortune favors prepared minds, say Merton and Barber, tracing its use to people who "come from social milieux where happy unanticipated discoveries" are frequent and common (123). The authors distinguish between luck and serendipity. "In the world of science . . . to be considered lucky is undesirable," for when luck is "coupled with such qualities as passivity, irresponsibility, pretension, and unreliability," it is accidental and undeserved rather than earned and very likely a one-time occurrence for which the individual "has no right to take credit." In contrast, "When serendipity is used to enhance the reputation of an individual, the component of luck is made dependent on qualities that are unambiguously admired. Luck or chance . . . does not favor people at random; rather, it is prepared minds who are able to benefit from luck," especially when associated with "alertness, flexibility, courage, and assiduity. Only the able and virtuous are lucky in the field of discovery, just as on the battlefield fortune favors only the brave" (171).

Merton and Barber cite two prominent analysts of serendipity. Walter Cannon, MD, who restricts the word's meaning to accidents that lead to "fresh insights," observes, for instance, that when the culture Alexander Fleming was working with "underwent dissolution by accidental contamination with a mold—'A careless worker might have thrown the culture away,'" but Fleming, "an appropriate, intelligent observer" recognized the potential implicit in this unusual occurrence, and consequently discovered penicillin (171–72). In order to exploit the possibilities for making serendipitous discoveries, medical educator David Seegal, recommends cultivating a "capacity for free association, . . . self-confidence, dedication, and 'pride of work performed.'" These qualities can be enhanced by the mentorship of a "trained investigator" who can abet creative thinking outside the box, and sufficient leisure for imaginative reflection (174–75).

Much of what follows in this essay is an analysis of the conditions under which I have chosen to take advantage of serendipitous opportunities that have occurred in my professional life (intertwined, invariably, with the personal) in a climate that has prepared me not only for creative discoveries but provided the opportunity to interpret, understand, and act on them. My existential definition of serendipity is latitudinarian because of the unplanned consequences of decisions, geography, and personal temperament. I secretly (so as not to sound hubristic, but virtue is always perfumed with a soupçon of smugness) identify with "the able and virtuous" who have made their discoveries through meticulous preparation and hard work; as a feminist, I try not to throw away earned success by attributing it to luck. I'm eager to try new research areas and thus willing to take risks, and sometimes to fail.[2] Rather than repeat what I already know how to do, I'd rather spend thought, time, money, and unlimited energy on worthwhile, generative projects that open into new areas. The humility that makes me recognize and confront my limitations is balanced with the optimism (or naiveté) that tells me most problems can be solved, difficulties overcome.

A bonus. I am blessed with the happy temperament that William James identifies in *Varieties of Religious Experience* as bestowed on the "once-born," happy souls from their earliest years, "people who, when unhappiness is offered or proposed to them, positively refuse to feel it," who "seem to have started in life with a bottle or two of champagne inscribed to them" (104).[3] If all else fails, I'm resilient enough to cut my losses and move on. *Advantages beyond measure.* Moreover, hugely important, for nearly sixty years, from the first day of graduate school to the present, I have dwelt in a supportive research environment—with time, money, spouse, and helpers on board the research express, and consistent good health and energy to sustain the momentum.

RESEARCH AREAS AND SERENDIPITOUS BOOKS

Our two children, I hasten to say, were defiant rebuttals to the standard advice for '60s women, which equated maternity with professional suicide. In the absence of maternity leaves, they arrived during summer vacations, right on cue, in June and August. Research priorities were, to an extent, pragmatic. Any project had to be do-able in a limited amount of time because that's all I had to spend in a busy life. Consequently, a research subject had to be new, cutting-edge, so there wouldn't be a centuries-old backlog of research to plow through. It had to be generative, full of interesting primary materials that would open up possibilities for future research. And I had to love it. Three areas that scarcely existed when I was in graduate school—biography and autobiography, writing and composition studies, women's literature—looked exciting. They were so new that it was possible to work in three left fields at once, though I've always seen them as interwoven by means of the inextricable interrelationship among the writer's life (actual and constructed), the creative process(es), and the resulting literary works. I realize in retrospect that I had anticipated contemporary autobiographical theory (as epitomized through Sidonie Smith and Julia Watson's overview of the field in *Autobiography* and many of their more specialized works), the precepts of Donald

Murray in *A Writer Teaches Writing* ("Teach process, not product"), and the philosophy of Robert Scholes's *Textual Power* ("Write a text in response to a text").

So although I am not a gambling woman, not with money, not with men, I am always game for intellectual adventure and professional risks, the bigger the better.[4] Because any job can get boring, any area of research is mundane unless it is shaken and stirred with regularity, I pick huge, generative research topics, intending to discover brave new worlds within them, waiting to be explored. What's exciting, really interesting? What will I learn? What will others want to know about it in the ongoing professional dialogue? Will there be surprises, preferably happy ones? If all of the questions can't be answered and the projects don't pan out, what subordinate questions and issues can be salvaged from the detritus? That "nothing can be made out of nothing" (*King Lear* 1.4) is an implied premise of graduate education; you have to start somewhere.

Even before I had learned enough to understand these disciplinary considerations, two book projects emerged serendipitously from the mountains of notes that arose while studying for Michigan's comprehensive preliminary exams—Beowulf to Virginia Woolf (one of six women on the twelve-page list—one line of which read "Shakespeare, Complete Works [including poetry]"). Martin suggested to me and Arthur Kinney, my study buddy, "You have so many notes you should turn them into a book." From the long list of possibilities, the most innovative was an edited collection of essays on Faulkner's *The Bear*, which we submitted to Scribner's. Soon the word came back: Francis L. Utley, professor at Ohio State, had made a comparable proposal. Would we TAs be willing to collaborate with this scholar whose publication record was longer than both our arms? You bet we would. As serendipity would have it, during a year's exile from Michigan[5] three years earlier, I had aced Professor Utley's linguistics course, which proved to be the kismet kiss of collaboration. Random House (which wouldn't sell the Faulkner rights to Scribner's) published the first edition of *Bear, Man, and God* in 1964, the year after I earned my PhD.

A freshman composition textbook also emerged from our notes, *Symposium*. Like all novice textbook authors, Arthur and I intended to revolutionize the field through readings from (mostly Western) Great Books on love, religion, justice, nature, science, and the arts—literature on which it was presumptuous of us to pontificate, but we did so anyway, and Houghton Mifflin published the book in 1969, with a section—*Symposium on Love*—as a separate casebook a year later.

WRITING DOCTOR SPOCK, BIOGRAPHY OF A CONSERVATIVE RADICAL, RESEARCH SERENDIPITY

To write the biography of American's best-known living author when I was right out of graduate school required top-flight preparation, the imagination to transcend received knowledge and conventional research paradigms, good luck, and the risk-taking self-confidence of a babe in the woods. Energy and ingenuity trumped naïveté. Despite New Criticism's premise that a work of literature should stand alone, silent upon a peak in Darien, abstracted from its author, time, and place, as an aspiring author myself, I wanted to understand the creative process.

How did one become not merely a writer but a great author? Could literary biographies explain this? In my doctoral dissertation, "How Literary Biographers Use Their Subjects' Works: A Study of Biographical Method 1865–1962," I concluded that whether an author wrote poetry (George Herbert), prose (Jonathan Swift), fiction (Charles Dickens), or drama (George Bernard Shaw), biographers read all their subject's creative writing as autobiography. They documented the documentable—date, place, circumstances of a work's composition—but not the ineffable—how the author thought and worked.[6] An illustration depicting Herbert inspired by an angel in a garden was the closest anyone came. I surprised myself by concluding that all these autobiographers, including esteemed scholars whom I'd been taught to revere, were wrong.

To gain the textual understanding and authority I needed to justify that claim, I myself needed to write a biography to find out whether it was possible for me to explain what others couldn't, a position Robert Scholes would later advocate in *Textual Power*. To do truly original research, I decided I'd have to write the first biography of a major author, mostly from primary sources accessible in Cleveland,[7] where we were living when our sons were babies. Benjamin Spock, world-renowned author of *Baby and Child Care*, was the logical—perhaps the only—choice. He held a distinguished professorship at Case Western Reserve, where I was splicing adjunct teaching into days filled with childrearing and carpools. We lived two miles and several social strata apart. Nevertheless, innocent of celebrity protocol, I simply called him up and got right to the point. "I'd like to write your biography." "Well," he hesitated for a few seconds, "I'd thought about doing it myself, but I probably won't get around to it. I'm retiring so I can spend more time on the anti-war movement. Why don't you come to my office so we can talk?"

I was there in a shot—clad, I confess, in the miniskirt and fancy stockings of the period. During that fateful first meeting, Dr. Spock granted me access to unlimited interviews with him and his family, friends, colleagues, enemies; to a lifetime accumulation of professional and personal papers; and to his secretary, who could translate his handwriting and spell the obscure references in the interviews I was taping. He would let me follow him around the hospital, clinic, skating rink (he was taking ice dancing lessons), peace marches, anywhere.[8] Whether Spock ever balanced my utter inexperience against the flattering fact that I was the first person eager to write his biography, I never knew. That I would also be happily willing to spend limitless hours and energy working on this project for seven exciting years could not have been anticipated at the outset; nor could the drama that increased over time as Spock's anti–Vietnam War activities accelerated.

There was no manual to consult on how to write a biography, particularly about a living person whose life was continually in flux—anathema to my department head, who told me that to write about Spock rather than safely dead men would be "to cut my throat professionally." Nor did graduate school teach me how to do the improvisatory guerrilla research necessary to follow Spock's antiwar protests. A question would arise and I'd look for the answers; a problem would emerge and I'd figure out how to solve it; part of the excitement of the research was that everything was new and different and therefore never boring. As both the war and Spock's own life erupted in unforeseen directions, I, like my subject, acquired an FBI record. For associating with Dr. Spock, I was under FBI surveillance throughout most of my research. Mysterious clicks on our phone meant that spies were listening in on conversations with students, neighbors, babysitters, but never with Dr. Spock, whom I saw only in person, usually in his office, which presumably was bugged. Because his life was in jeopardy, so was mine, though I was scarcely aware of the danger until Benjamin Spock and Martin Luther King Jr. led a parade of 50,000 antiwar protestors down Fifth Avenue. My participatory research—right up front with my subject—meant that I too could have been hit by an assassin's stray bullet. I would not have known how to behave had I been beaten or jailed. Although harassment and risk might be considered the downside of serendipity, I was too preoccupied with research and childrearing for the dangers to register. As *Mad* magazine's Alfred E. Neuman said in the day, "What, me worry?"

Indeed, the entire research process was exhilarating, not terrifying. Dr. Spock taught me how to live. It was inspiring to write about a man willing to act on principle and to plunge happily into controversy that would provoke vice-presidential scorn ("Nattering nabobs of negativism," ghost-wrote William Safire), death threats, and a federal indictment for conspiracy to incite resistance to the draft. Convicted in 1968, he was acquitted on appeal a year later. His down-to-earth good will and relaxed good humor were perpetual illustrations of the maxim, "Don't sweat the small stuff"—easier said than done by a tense young mother. Best of all, he taught me how to write. He not only explained his own writing process, he acted it out, pacing up and down in reminiscence as he had done when dictating the first edition of *Baby and Child Care* to Jane, his wife and amanuensis. The pacing, I realized, was a way to capture the sentence syntax and rhythm; the oral delivery enabled him to re-create the sound of human speech—the small stuff of writing that is actually huge. But his biggest concerns were step-by-step precision, and lucidity: "If you don't write clearly, someone could die." With clarity as my mantra, I resolved always to write for a real-world audience and have evermore avoided academic jargon even when the hermeneutic demands of the text mandated its promulgation.

Finding a publisher was another stroke of serendipity. Dr. Spock had moved to Manhattan after retirement to be closer to the antiwar action. I occasionally visited him there to catch up with his kaleidoscopic activities and read his latest mail, flying from Indianapolis, where we had moved in 1968 for Martin's new professorship at Indiana University. Spock had given me a copy of his latest book, *A Teenager's Guide to Life and Love*, which I was reading on the return flight. The man next to me was also immersed in my book, his face grazing the pages. "I'm sorry," he apologized, "I've broken my glasses or I wouldn't be so close." As I explained why, at my age, I was perusing advice such as, "It's sensible for a teenager not to go beyond kissing and embracing the person he loves until there is some kind of commitment to marriage" (L. Bloom, *Spock* 219), my seatmate grew more and more excited. "Why are you writing this?" he asked. "How do you know Dr. Spock?" His exacting questions never stopped; was he an FBI agent? Finally he explained, "I'm a vice president of Bobbs-Merrill. I'd like to see your manuscript." The verdict was swift, "I love every word of it."

FORBIDDEN DIARY, EDITING THE MOTHER LODE

When a diminutive, politically radical Bostonian, Natalie Crouter, after hearing my lecture on Spock's antiwar activities when I was writing his biography, approached me with a five-thousand-page typescript diary of her World War II internment in a Japanese civilian prison camp—"If you're good enough for Doctor Spock, you're good enough for me"—I said I'd take a look. Although I'd always avoided editing other people's books, black holes for time, both topic and author were compelling. As an experienced editor (and what English teacher isn't?) I knew that a single sentence, any sentence, would reveal whether it was publishable. The opening was enthralling, December 8, 1941:[9] "Almost over the house . . . came seventeen big bombers in formation. . . . As they passed . . . we heard a long ripping sound like the tearing of a giant sheet and saw an enormous burst of smoke and earth near officers' quarters at Camp John Hay—the first bombing of the Philippines before our eyes. Huge billows of smoke and dust covered the Post" (3).

Yes, I said, yes, after I finish *Spock*, I'll edit this, which Natalie and I agreed meant cutting it down to readable size—omitting ninety percent of its bulk to accentuate the story's good bones, and annotating military and cultural information unfamiliar to American readers. In transforming a chronicle into a narrative, I would emphasize the spirited replication of Western family life and culture in a community of five hundred Americans and British confined to a captured U.S. military base in Baguio, summer capital of the Philippines throughout World War II. My editing of *Forbidden Diary: A Record of Wartime Internment 1941–45* would have to weave the themes of American ingenuity, multiculturalism, international politics, and military strategy into an aesthetically satisfying whole for a readership forty years and seven thousand miles distant.

Natalie did not regard the pervasive shortage of food, clothing, amenities of life, and family living space (Natalie shared a single bunk bed with her teenage daughter throughout the war) as insurmountable privations, but as reminders of class privilege and an opportunity to learn and grow stronger. Most importantly, in captivity, paradoxically, she found liberation—from socially assigned roles, from class constraints—and freedom to live, existentially, on the cutting edge of the history whose significance she was recording in her inspiring, idealistic diary. On the verge of starvation, as the Marines firestormed the prison gates, Natalie had never been more fully alive: "We had the best time of our lives in here—sorry to leave"—surely a unique accolade from a newly released prisoner of war (February 5, 1945, 475). *Forbidden Diary* would transcend time and confinement, published first by Burt Franklin in 1980 and then reissued in 2001 by Alexander Street Press as one of two hundred distinguished North American Women's Diaries and Letters. At my suggestion, the Crouter family donated the entire manuscript to Radcliffe's Schlesinger Library on the History of Women in America.

Editing this work required an understanding of autobiographical portraiture as a rhetorical construct with historical, psychological, social, intellectual, cultural, economic, religious, and artistic dimensions. As Adam Gopnik has observed, "Histories are narratives we make up as much as chronicles we discern" (36). Everyone has a life to invent, interpret, define, defend, reconfigure, or regret, and every editor alters these dimensions. Carving a graceful narrative from a mountain of redundancy (Natalie identified camotes and beans or rice for at least 2,500 of the 3,785 meals) became especially powerful as the central character's personality and numerous roles emerged, of which upper-middle-class American expat wife, mother, captive, feminist, social activist are but a few. Soon her role as self-appointed scribe and therefore interpreter of her confined universe became paramount.

What appeared at the outset to be a self-effacing choice—to subordinate my professional reputation to that of an unknown, unpublished author on a huge project on a subject I didn't know anything about that would take unknown years (six, actually) to complete—turned out to be full of serendipitous opportunities for professional growth. Editing and publishing *Forbidden Diary* enabled me to gain expertise in brave new worlds of American and South Pacific literature and the culture of World War II. I learned how to do feminist scholarship from the ground up; remember, I began this in 1974. As a scholar and writer, I am ever aware of Henry James's advice, "Try to be one . . . on whom nothing is lost." Once I've done a major research project, its essence is burned into my subliminal consciousness, providing a mother lode of new material to add to mine whenever I choose to do so. *Forbidden Diary*'s new perspectives on issues of race, class, families, culture, and human rights, along with friendships formed with Natalie and other internees, have led to forty years of publications and conference presentations. These have arisen not according to a logical or systematic plan—I don't work that way—but through a series of aha! mostly feminist discoveries on topics as varied as *human relations*—between mothers and daughters, husbands and wives, captors and captives, religious dissidents; *genre*—single experience autobiography, diary as popular history, public vs. private writing, editing another Philippine internment diary of an adulterous love story, Margaret Sams's *Forbidden Family*; *pedagogy*—teaching about trauma; *editorial practices*—collaboration with authors, shaping manuscripts; and *human rights*—nutrition and health, food insufficiency, witnessing.

THE SERENDIPITY OF A FIRST JOB

Although I had finished most of the work on *Spock* in 1969, it hadn't been published when I began looking for a job that would begin in 1970–71, the first year our sons would be in school full-time. As fate would have it, a rare tenure-track position in English at Butler University—just down the street from our house—was being advertised. Whether or not a single textbook could transform any field, in defiance of the academic maxim, "Textbooks don't count," *Symposium* was my entré to that job. Werner Beyer, head of Butler University's English Department, found the book "ideal for honors courses," as he wrote Houghton Mifflin when adopting it in 1969. And then, dear reader, he adopted me, hiring me for my first full-time position ever.[10]

I loved that job, despite the fact that if I wanted to do any writing, I (a night person) had to get up at 5:30 a.m. for a half-hour of furious concentration before the paper-grading kicked in. "We are not, thank God, a publish-or-perish university," the dean had asserted during my interview, oblivious to the fact that if writers don't write they will indeed perish. However, as utility infielder I scarcely had time to write, for I taught four different courses every semester from Freshman Composition to Great Books to a Master's-level Non-Dramatic Literature of the Renaissance, and advanced writing courses whose enrollment grew and grew, and then grew some more. The students, especially the corps de ballet from Butler's ballet program, were highly motivated and fun to teach. The university's small-college culture, which functioned as an extended family, embraced us all. Even though I was thirty-six, with children of my own (and a cat named Paradox and a border collie named, no kidding, Serendipity—a signal of our family's pleasure in unexpected findings), in the English department I was assigned the role of kid sister. Dr. Beyer served as a benevolent paterfamilias; my office mate, a senior Twain specialist, filled in as a kindly big brother. If there were serpents in this Garden of Eden, I was oblivious to them.

So why, four years later, after I'd earned early promotion and tenure, did I leave that happy place to leap into the unknown, with no job or the prospect of any in St. Louis? We were moving there for my husband's new super job at Washington University, but what was I thinking? (I was thinking I needed more writing time and research funding, that's what I was thinking. Oh yes, and a better salary. In short, I had the usual reasons for making academic moves.)

THE SERENDIPITY OF QUITTING—AND OF A NEW BEGINNING

To make this move was the biggest professional risk I have ever taken in my life, truly a leap of faith. And why not? Buttressed by my Michigan PhD (and arrogance to match), I believed I could light out for any new territory and get the best job in town. After all, this had been so easy in Indianapolis. Wrong! I couldn't get *any* full-time job in St. Louis in the lean year of 1974. Furthermore *Doctor Spock: Biography of a Conservative Radical*, had just been named a Book-of-the-Month Club selection. Surely I was on my way to best-seller stardom. Wrong, oh so wrong, again!

No jobs had arisen during preliminary inquiries, despite Dr. Beyer's jokey claim, "I've perjured myself to the hilt," in my reference letter. During the long hot summer of our arrival, the adjunct teaching I had landed at three universities (Washington U, U of Missouri-St. Louis, Webster U) neither paid well nor paid off. By then I was at work on two other books that proved to be my credentials into women's studies scholarship and feminist politics—*Forbidden Diary*, and *The New Assertive Woman* (1975), coauthored with two St. Louis women's counselors. With its promise of "how to know what you feel, say what you mean and get what you want" (cover), this self-help guide to assertive training proved to be useful in my subsequent administrative work. I would not have worked on either if we hadn't moved, nor would I have responded to the invitation—out of the brilliant blue—from the University of New Mexico to apply for an associate professorship a thousand miles away. Firm in the belief of the time—any time—that adolescent children deserved a mother-in-residence, "I can't do that," I told Martin. "Oh yes, you can," he said. "If you get the job, I'll be home when the children," then in junior high, "come home from school." So I did. And so he was, for the three-to-four nights a week that I was perched in Albuquerque.

That exhilarating job was a Rocky Mountain high, literally and figuratively. New Mexico's one hundred percent raise over my Butler salary paid the airfare and the rent—cheap tuition for all that I learned during the dazzling days and starry nights in the Land of Enchantment. As Writing Director (my dream job, undertaken, as was common at the time, with no prior experience, anyone could do it), my professional perspective ballooned immediately from local to national. Early composition studies faculty everywhere were acrobats, high-wire performers and jugglers, working under a huge tent whose shape shifted continually. It took imagination, teetering up there on the high wire, to anticipate problems and troubleshoot issues raised by deans, athletic directors, TAs, adjuncts, the SAT, the ACT, litigious parents, and their lawyers. It took grace and goodwill, reinforced by the most supportive department head ever,[11] to make tough solutions look easy.

The biggest, most pervasive, and most enduring question of all, and the most complicated to unpack and try to answer, was how to teach a wide range of students to write with ease and accuracy in standard English, the lingua franca of the flagship university in a multicultural, bilingual state[12] where even in the '70s Anglos were a minority. Other big questions addressed reading and writing among first-generation college students, what Mina Shaughnessy called "basic writers," how to help them find the time, space, and supports for success. UNM's full-service writing program provided a naturalistic milieu for large-scale composition studies research. What happened in Albuquerque did not stay in Albuquerque, but was occurring across the nation. I learned, often the hard way, about high- and low-stakes testing of writing, program assessment, academic politics, for good and for ill. I learned the white-knuckle thrill of lighting out for unknown territory, how hard it was to get a good research design adapted to the students' diverse languages and cultures, funding, and answers that would hold up (many didn't).

In New Mexico, I also learned to teach women's studies courses, beginning with Women in Literature. "Are there any questions?" I chirped at the end of my first lecture, on *The Doll's House*. A man's voice boomed from the back of the auditorium, "I want to know how you get along with your husband." I blushed, "We get along fine, but what does that have to do with this course?" "Every reading on the syllabus," he shot back, "has a negative view of marriage, and of men." Even though I retorted with Tolstoy's "happy families are all alike" to justify angst in literature, the student was right. Positive writing needed a fair shot, and we would find it in nonfiction, such as nature writing (Annie Dillard, Gretel Ehrlich), essays, diaries, and autobiography (Mary McCarthy, Maya Angelou)—genres now striding into the literary canon and academic inquiry. So on the spot, I added sections of Elinore Pruitt Stewart's *Letters of a Woman Homesteader* and Crouter's *Forbidden Diary* as positive examples of grit and gumption, feminist survival.

I taught a much wider range of students—in income and age, as well as ethnicity—than I'd ever taught before: veterans and parents, ranchers and bikers, political activists and artists from the rez, skiers and hikers and rodeo riders. And they taught me: the complications—familial, cultural, logistical—of being a first generation college student; what it was like to balance full course loads and full time jobs; how to survive in extreme mountain climates ("always drive with water, blankets, sand, and a shovel, even in summer"); how to eat fry bread and blue corn tortillas and (essential for this effete Easterner) to avoid any chilis hotter than anchos; and how to flat out have fun in fiesta, but duck the rifle shots on Cinco de Mayo. Best of all, they taught me to listen to the lilting lingua franca of flutes, guitars, and the throbbing drums carried high on the Western wind that never stopped, heartbeats of the mesa.

What I learned would have been utterly impossible had I never left home and settled for the alternative—part-time, dead-end adjunct work in St. Louis. I had learned, too, that it was possible to take huge risks with my family and my career (what if I'd fallen flat?), because the foundation was in place, so when Martin and I were interviewed about our "alternative lifestyle," we—nerds to the core—maintained that it wasn't alternative, it just occurred in two different places. Although we lived apart, what I learned during those three pivotal, high-altitude years where hot air balloons grazed my office's walk-out balcony that faced the ever-changing Sandias, ultimately brought us together. New Mexico's serendipitous job offer set the administrative and disciplinary trajectory of the rest of my career; my experience at UNM enabled other choices of jobs where I could rejoin my family, and provided the intellectual basis for research support from NEH, Fulbright, even the Department of Agriculture. The flow of the second half of my career culminated a decade later at the University of Connecticut in an Endowed Chair in Writing[13] and a Distinguished Professorship. This could not have occurred without the prolific serendipity of the first half, the unexpected buoyancy of currents, and the uncharted directions—the exhilaration of the flight. I like always to be in motion, like the tumble of acrobats in my favorite painting, *Aerial Troupe*, swooping up and down, back and forth, never at rest, always searching for serendipity, forever in mid-. . . .

NOTES

1. Letter "To Horace Mann," January 28, 1754.
2. Bear in mind that because failures don't "count," all academic vitas read like unbroken strings of success.
3. Even as a mature adult, I feel as if to say this in print is to court disaster. Yet as the daughter of two, at times, clinically depressed parents, I have an intimate understanding of the blessings bestowed by good cheer.
4. A corollary of this is travel, which has taken me and my husband, sometimes with children and now with grandchildren, many places in the world. Although I have circled Everest via a Buddha Air twelve-seater, I am not brave or bold enough to tackle this provocative peak on foot. Other less masochistic prospects for exploration abound.
5. Michigan's English graduate advisor said my undergraduate 3.97 GPA, for which I'd received a best-in-the-honors-program award, wasn't good enough for admission to the doctoral program. "But the catalog says applicants need a 3.5," I ventured, and he replied, "What it means is that women need a 4-point. Men can get in with a 3-point." So I accepted a proffered doctoral fellowship from Ohio State, reapplied to Michigan the next year post-MA, and returned to Michigan with my new husband to begin doctoral work all over again.
6. I realize as I'm writing this that I'm attempting to explain my own creative process, not only in writing the Spock biography but also in general. Because we don't articulate much of the way we think and work, let alone analyze it, it's tough to reconstruct, either in process or in retrospect. As in breathing, we don't pay attention to the inspiration and exhalation unless the process is painful or stops altogether. Indeed, self-consciousness itself could be fatal, as X. J. Kennedy observes in "Ars Poetica": "The goose that laid the golden egg / Died looking up its crotch / To find out how its sphincter worked. / Would you lay well? / Don't watch."

7. The speed and ease with which the Internet has transformed document-based research from local to worldwide within the past fifteen years is astonishing, yet so ingrained in our current thinking that it's hard now to imagine working in far more time-consuming ways that required personal access to all the sources. Yet that's what we did, just as we wrote on typewriters, using carbon paper, manual erasers, and Wite-Out.
8. Susan Cheever, while writing a biography of E. E. Cummings, identifies three "official" types of research that are "the foundation of writing biography": primary sources (original papers, and in my case, contact with the subject himself); secondary sources (other writers' work—there wasn't much except newspaper articles and repetitive interviews with Spock); "interviews with experts, people whose memories are useful"—among whom I would include the parents of present and former patients; parents who used *Baby and Child Care*; Spock's students and employees—secretary, maid. Cheever's fourth kind of research is "just going to the places where the story happened" (47), what anthropologists would call field research. Living and working in the same milieus meant I knew the territory; I could overhear casual conversation in the supermarket, visit Spock's classes, don a white coat to sprint after him in the hospital corridors. Our family's summer interviewing trips were the most fun. Arriving with small children in tow proved disarming. With my sons on the scene, people would tell me anything; all I had to do was smile. And to know how to swim; treading water, I interviewed one of Dr. Spock's sisters in her swimming pool. I also figured out how to read upside down in order to interpret documents on people's desks and the importance of supporting any fact with two, preferably three corroborating sources.
9. The international dateline determines whether December 7 or 8 is the date "which will live in infamy." In the Philippines, it was December 8.
10. There were doubtless many factors that influenced this appointment. In my more cynical moods, I think I was hired because as a local, I had no bargaining power and was thereby a cheap date. Indiana University–Purdue University Indianapolis, far better funded, and Butler had an informal agreement not to raid each other's faculty; my starting full-time salary, $8,600 was a third less than the going rate at IUPUI. Moreover, by being on the scene, however serendipitous, my selection spared Butler's home team the time and expense of attending MLA.
11. This essay is dedicated to the memory of Dr. Joseph Zavadil, department head whose grace under pressure sustained my own.
12. Not counting the variety of languages spoken by Native Americans and numerous overseas immigrants.
13. Lore says this was the first endowed chair in composition studies in the U.S.

WORKS CITED

Bloom, Lynn Z. *Doctor Spock: Biography of a Conservative Radical*. Indianapolis: Bobbs Merrill, 1972. Print.

———. "How Literary Biographers Use Their Subjects' Works: A Study of Biographical Method 1865–1962." Diss. U of Michigan, 1963. Typescript.

Bloom, Lynn Z., Karen Coburn, and Joan Pearlman. *The New Assertive Woman*. New York: Delacorte/Dell, 1975. Print.

Cheever, Susan. "'Why Didn't Rebecca Stop at the Railroad Crossing?'" *New York Times Magazine* June 28, 2014: 46–47. Print.

Crouter, Natalie. *Forbidden Diary: A Record of Wartime Internment, 1941–45.* Ed. Lynn Z. Bloom. New York: Burt Franklin, 1980, Print [also North American Women's Diaries and Letters. Alexandria, VA: Alexander St. P, 2001. CD format].

Gopnik, Adam. "Word Magic." *The New Yorker* May 26, 2014: 36–39. Print.

James, William. *The Varieties of Religious Experience: A Study in Human Nature.* Charlottesville, VA: Electronic Text Center, U of Virginia Library, 1902. Web. July 1, 2014.

Kennedy, X. J. "Ars Poetica." *Nude Descending Staircase.* New York: Doubleday, 1961. Print.

Kinney, Arthur F., Kenneth W. Kuiper, and Lynn Z. Bloom, eds. *Symposium.* Boston: Houghton Mifflin, 1969. Print.

Merton, Robert K., and Elinor Barber. *The Travels and Adventures of Serendipity: A Study in Sociological Semantics and the Sociology of Science.* Princeton: Princeton UP, 2004. Print.

Murray, Donald. *A Writer Teaches Writing.* Boston: Houghton Mifflin, 1968. Print.

Scholes, Robert. *Textual Power: Literary Theory and the Teaching of English.* New Haven, CT: Yale UP, 1985. Print.

Smith, Sidonie, and Julia Watson. *Reading Autobiography: A Guide for Interpreting Life Narratives.* 2nd ed. Minneapolis: U of Minnesota P, 2010. Print.

Spock, Benjamin. *Baby and Child Care.* New York: Meredith P, 1946.

———. *A Teenager's Guide to Life and Love.* New York: Simon and Schuster, 1970. Print.

Utley, Francis Lee, Lynn Z. Bloom, and Arthur F. Kinney, eds. *Bear, Man, and God: Seven Approaches to William Faulkner's* The Bear. New York: Random House, 1964. Print.

Walpole, Horace. "To Horace Mann," January 28, 1754. *Horace Walpole's Correspondence.* Ed. Lewis Walpole. Yale Edition. Lewis Walpole Library. New Haven, CT: Yale UP, 1937–38. Web. February 17, 2016.

CHAPTER 5

Composing a Poetic Life

LIBBY FALK JONES

> Tell me, what is it you plan to do / with your one wild and precious life?
> —Mary Oliver, "The Summer Day"

> Ask me whether / what I have done is my life.
> —William Stafford, "Ask Me"

As I reflect on the seven decades (to date) of my wild, precious life, I wonder, like the speaker in William Stafford's poem, in what ways that life is defined by what I have done. It's a life that's been rich—indeed, serendipitous—with opportunities for meaningful self-discovery and contribution, work and art, relationships with family and community. A life composed, to use a metaphor suggested by Mary Catherine Bateson, as music: theme and variations, through silence and sound (66–67). A life in which I am both composer and composed; where what I have done flows from and into who I am. My single note needs to be heard not in isolation but reverberating among people, places, times, and circumstances into shades of consonance and dissonance. The theme is constant: I've spent my adult life working with word and image and, for all but a single year, as an educator. But it's the variations that are the heart of the story. As Bateson notes, we can compose multiple versions of a life, all true, and there are advantages in understanding the control we have in choosing how we see our lives (67–68).

Within my professional life, I've experienced various serendipitous interruptions and opportunities, as I moved through graduate school and part-time administration and teaching in Chicago and Tennessee before landing in 1988 at Berea College. Initially the Director of the Center for Effective Communication and Associate Professor of English, I'm now Chester D. Tripp Chair in Humanities and Professor of English. Variation, as well, has marked my time at

Berea: thirteen years ago, my career turned dramatically, as I moved from my primarily administrative appointment directing what had become, under my leadership, a nationally known teaching/learning/writing center to a full-time faculty position teaching primarily creative writing as well as professional writing, literature, and photography. When I began my academic career in 1967 as a graduate student at Stony Brook University on Long Island, I would never have predicted that fifty years later, I'd define myself as poet and photographer. Looking back, however, I can see this surprising evolution as natural—though not to say inevitable. In this essay, I want to explore several different truthful versions of my story and reflect on the insights each version yields into the roles of preparation, opportunities, and challenges—in a word, the resilience—that mark women's career paths in English studies.

Bateson argues that Americans privilege life stories that are continuous, where the end is contained in the beginning (71). Indeed, I can tell such a story about my movement to a lifework centered on creative work, particularly poetry. Here's how it might go:

BECOMING A POET, TAKE ONE: A CONTINUOUS STORY

1946: Sent to my room in tears for sassing my mother, I copy "Rome Beauty Apples" from a shipping crate-turned toy box onto my chalkboard. Mother, herself an accomplished writer and reader, waxes rhapsodic. I am two years old.

1948: My parents, godparents, and grandparents give me *Mother Goose* and *A Child's Garden of Verses* and *When We Were Very Young*. Mother reads them aloud to me, many times. She also reads me poems she loves, like Alfred Noyes's "The Highwayman" and Walter de la Mare's "The Listeners."

1954: I get gold stars for my stories made from the week's twenty spelling words; I make a collection of poems on construction paper, laced with a piece of yarn. Mother waxes rhapsodic.

1959: With Jeanne, my best friend and partner-in-crime, I draft the first chapter of a novel which we (modestly) title "Teachers Who Have Known Us."

1960–62: In high school and community dramatics, I deliver heartfelt performances as Mrs. Stevenson in *Sorry, Wrong Number* and Cornelia Otis Skinner in *Our Hearts Were Young and Gay*. My creative writing wins praise from my beloved high school English teacher, Blanche Sandefer.

1962–66: Studying fiction writing at Duke University with Reynolds Price and William Blackburn, I learn about voice and style, place and perspective, structure and narrative arc. I frame my postcard from Reynolds Price awarding me an A, with the comment, "With real thanks for your careful, beautiful story." Two years later, that story, "The Morning Light," is published in *The Archive*, Duke's venerable campus literary magazine.

1967–72: Earning my PhD in English from Stony Brook University, I sit for field exams on English and American poetry and prose from the Renaissance through the twentieth century.

1973–76: Working at Columbia College Chicago, I take evening classes in the Story Workshop approach to creative writing and in black-and-white photography.

1983: At the University of Tennessee as an adjunct English instructor, I study poetry writing with Marilyn Kallet and publish poems and photographs in the university's literary magazine.

1984: Gloria Steinem visits campus, urging outrageous acts and everyday rebellions. Sitting on our living room sofa while my husband and two sons prepare the supper I refuse to produce, I write sonnets.

1990s: At Berea College, I teach a winter-term, one-month poetry writing course called "Wordplay," and, when our resident poet is on sabbatical, a semester-long poetry writing course. I publish two poems on teaching writing in *Writing on the Edge*.

1997: By my dying father's bedside, I read him poems from my informal collection, which I've titled "On Cats, Children, Words, and Other Living Things." After his death, I write many more poems.

1998: Unpacking boxes from my parents' attic, I discover a small collection of poetry by my maternal grandmother, who'd died in 1965.

2003–04: On my first-ever sabbatical, I write poems, give my first poetry reading, study poetry writing with Thylias Moss at the University of Michigan, and produce a chapbook of poems, photographs, and brush paintings titled "From the Darkroom."

2004: I begin teaching a variety of creative writing classes, including creative nonfiction and introductory and advanced poetry writing.

2010: My chapbook of poems, *Above the Eastern Treetops, Blue*—a collection I develop while teaching my first contemplative writing class—is published by Finishing Line Press. I enter the MFA Creative Writing program at Eastern Kentucky University.

2011-12: During my second sabbatical, with a ten-page sample of poetry and a CV recast to emphasize creative work in poetry, creative nonfiction, and photography, I am granted writing residencies at Hambidge Center for the Creative Arts and Sciences and Virginia Center for the Creative Arts.

Today: I teach a wide range of creative writing courses, give readings, publish poems, lead poetry workshops, integrate poems and poetry writing into all my professional work, write about writing and teaching poetry, study poetry through local and international workshops, and have served as President of the Kentucky State Poetry Society. Poetry is a center of my life.

Telling this continuous story yields a satisfying coherence, helps me to see myself as whole—to realize the creative thread running through my professional life. Telling a continuous story also makes clear that this seemingly-inevitable progression was indeed marked by serendipitous turns—as, for example, when two talented poets generously welcomed me unofficially into their classes. But a continuous story has its limitations, Bateson notes; such a story is often retrospective, rather than reflecting lived experience (73). It may also suggest a model of control impossible for others to enact. In contrast, a discontinuous story reflects the role of interruptions, fits and starts, and surprises. Discontinuous stories stress the possibility within change and help the teller as well as younger listeners realize that different turns are indeed possible (73). These turns, too, can be seen to arise from underlying threads of continuity.

Here's how I might construct a discontinuous version of my movement toward poetry/creative work:

BECOMING A POET, TAKE TWO: A DISCONTINUOUS STORY

1954: Neighborhood organizer non-pareil, I regularly lead a dozen kids in outdoor games. I play touch football with the three boys next door. A budding entrepreneur, I set up a lemonade stand at the street and a used comic book store on our front porch. On the ornament I make for my fifth-grade class's Christmas tree, I list my career goals as ballet dancer, astronomer, and taster in a candy factory.

1956: With my mother masterminding my campaign, I'm elected president of my elementary school's Student Council, beating three boys named John.

1960: Following in my mother's and aunt's journalistic footsteps, I found and edit the Robert E. Lee High student newspaper, *The Traveller* (named for Lee's horse). Mother waxes rhapsodic.

1962: Through giving a presentation to 600 attendees at the Sales and Marketing Executives National Conference, I'm named National Junior Achievement Sales Champion and awarded $1000. I tell an interviewer that I plan to use the money to study psychology at Duke University.

1964: At Duke, after I understand that psychologists study rats before they study people, I major in history, host a weekly show on the university's radio station, and am elected editor-in-chief of the university's newspaper, *The Chronicle* (third woman editor in the paper's then-sixty-year history).

1966: Graduating with a portfolio of news stories, features, and editorials, I get a job writing advertising and mental health fact sheets for a pharmaceutical company in Philadelphia.

1967–72: In grad school in English and American literature, I write analyses, annotated bibliographies, and arguments and teach Freshman Composition.

1973–76: I become Assistant Dean at Columbia College Chicago and teach British literature survey courses part-time at a local community college.

1977: At the University of Tennessee as an adjunct instructor, I teach composition and, occasionally, sophomore British and American literature surveys. I'll go on to teach Women's Studies, Interdisciplinary Studies, and Honors as well as English. I'll also edit an anthology of good first-year writing, used for several years in the first-year program. I'll win the English Department's Instructor Award for Teaching Excellence.

1985: I serve as interim director of Tennessee's Interdisciplinary Studies Program and as Master Learner in a year-long University Learning Community on the theme of Technology, Society, and the Common Good. I begin publishing and presenting at CCCC, MLA, and elsewhere in the fields of rhetoric/composition, pedagogy, higher education, and feminist utopias.

1988: With the support of my husband, who's willing to resign his tenured position to follow me, I move to Berea College as Director of the Center for Effective Communication and Associate Professor of English. I found and lead a writing center that includes work with oral communication as well as faculty-staff development programs in communication and learning.

1990: My coedited essay collection, *Feminism, Utopia, and Narrative,* is published by the University of Tennessee Press.

1994: Meeting Reynolds Price at a conference, I apologize to him for not having pursued creative writing.

1998: Based on a dossier including teaching and scholarship in rhetoric/composition, writing centers, writing across the curriculum, and faculty development, I'm promoted to Professor of English.

2002: My administrative position having been reconfigured, I apply for and am awarded tenure. Under my leadership, Berea's Center for Learning, Teaching, Communication, and Research opens in expanded facilities.

2003–04: On sabbatical, I pursue an interview project on women as teachers/scholars/administrators, write and publish essays on teaching, and serve as a Visiting Scholar at the University of Michigan's Center for Research on Learning and Teaching.

2006: I develop new courses, including technical communication and an English capstone seminar in literacy studies, as well as a general education capstone seminar in vocation. I inaugurate and direct an embedded tutoring program to support Berea's first-year writing seminars.

Today: I teach first-year writing and advanced rhetoric-composition and regularly lead writing assessment projects. I speak and write frequently on faculty development and composition and contemplative pedagogies. Teaching and learning—particularly the teaching and learning of writing—are centers of my life.

This version of my story shows that continuity on one level can reflect discontinuity on another. Here, the logical progression of my work in composition studies, faculty development, and administration flows continuously.

What's masked is the undercurrent of creative work my first story version makes visible.

But both these versions, despite their truth, are in fact incomplete. Each contains gaps, silences. There is yet a third version of my story, a radically discontinuous one that names those gaps, that highlights failure rather than success—a story of what Quakers call "way closing." In *Let Your Life Speak: Listening for the Voice of Vocation*, writer and educator Parker Palmer argues for the value of the guidance that comes from the things that don't happen in our lives (39). Bateson notes that a truly discontinuous story is difficult to claim (69). I can testify to the fact that this third version of my story is indeed painful to voice. Yet if I am to "live / All of myself," as urged by the speaker in May Sarton's poem, "Now I Become Myself," I need to tell it.

BECOMING A POET, TAKE THREE: A RADICALLY DISCONTINUOUS STORY OF WAY CLOSING

1967: With a fine undergraduate degree but with a major in history rather than English and with mediocre scores on the GRE English exam, I enter SUNY Stony Brook's MA in English program. All the other graduate students have read everything ever written. On the second day of class, when my Boswell-Johnson seminar professor asks me to name the thesis of one of Johnson's *Rambler* essays, I have to ask him what "thesis" means.

1970: Despite being given extra time to write my first doctoral field exam, in eighteenth-century British literature, I barely squeak through.

1972: Having passed my major orals (with flying colors!) and my second language exam through the generosity of my Latin professor, I submit a one-page proposal for a dissertation on education plots in five Victorian novels and move the next day to Chicago, where my husband enters a doctoral program in history and philosophy of science.

1973: Becoming our chief breadwinner, I take two part-time administration/teaching jobs. One day a week, I walk to the university's library to work on my dissertation, which I've narrowed to two novels. I typically spend the first half of the day trying to figure out where I was the previous week. I need help from my always responsive dissertation director, but I never seem to be able to write a clear enough question. Long distance phone calls are expensive and e-mail doesn't exist. My second reader takes six months to return chapter drafts with elaborate pencil scrawls in which he demolishes my argument.

1976: Six weeks after I move with my husband to Knoxville, Tennessee, for him to begin a tenure-track job in philosophy of science at the University of Tennessee, our first child is born. When our son is six months old, I begin taking the bus two afternoons a week to the university's graduate library to continue work on my dissertation.

1978–79: In the semester after which I will no longer be able to be granted a dissertation extension without having to retake all my exams, I defend my dissertation successfully and then, while my parents watch our two-year-old, spend two frenzied weeks on revisions.

1980–81: After our second child is born, I use all my adjunct instructor salary to pay an in-home nanny so I can keep breastfeeding.

1982–85: My husband earns tenure in Tennessee's philosophy department; I apply for two different tenure-track jobs in English at Tennessee but am not even interviewed.

1985–86: When Tennessee's Interdisciplinary Studies program director leaves unexpectedly, I'm the only person qualified and available to step in. In nine months of 80-hour work weeks, I lead the program through an external review that results in a doubled budget and institutionalization of the program in the Provost's office. But the permanent director position is limited to tenured associate or full professors, so I'm not eligible to apply.

1992: In my third year at Berea, my collaborative learning philosophy and practices are openly criticized, especially by my colleagues in English. A friend tells me in confidence that some say I should be asked to leave.

2003: Two months into my first-ever sabbatical, in a routine check-in conversation with the (new) Provost, he tells me he's decided to dissolve the administrative position I've held successfully for fourteen years. He's asked the chair of English to find enough courses for me to teach full-time the next year.

Today: A full-time professor of English and holder of the Chester D. Tripp Chair in Humanities, I teach writing, literature, and general studies as well as write and publish poetry, creative nonfiction, and photography.

As I write this radically discontinuous story—replete with failures, near-failures, and downward turns—my body clenches yet again with the very real emotions of fear, despair, frustration, grief, anger, and loss I experienced at various points. Yet despite these difficulties, this version of my story validates Palmer's argument: way closing is in fact way opening. "Each time a door closes," Palmer writes, "the rest of the world opens up" (54). Consider, for example, three crucial chapters from my story:

> **Chapter 1: The Long Road to the Doctorate (1972–79)**
> Moving away from my supportive grad school environment, taking two jobs, moving again, and having a baby, I despair of finishing my dissertation. Yet these moves also open key creative, professional, and life experiences and result in a stronger dissertation to boot.
>
> **Chapter 2: Finding a Cross-Disciplinary Academic Home (1980–88)**
> Denied traditional English positions, I discover interests and develop abilities that eventually qualify me for a more interesting and satisfying position than those I originally thought I'd wanted.
>
> **Chapter 3: Claiming Myself as a Poet (2003–04)**
> My first sabbatical, at age 59, allows me to discover that I truly love writing poems; the elimination of my administrative position frees me to pursue creative writing and teaching.

WAY OPENING: THE ROLE OF FEMINIST RHETORICAL RESILIENCE

> . . . what I heard was my whole self / saying and singing what it knew: *I can.*
> —Denise Levertov, "Variation on a Theme by Rilke"

What are the mechanisms, then, through which way closing leads to way opening? Each of these times of challenge has called forth from me what Elizabeth A. Flynn, Patricia Sotirin, and Ann Brady describe as "rhetorical resilience," a creative, improvisational, relational response to a challenging situation. As storytelling reveals the power of creatively viewing a life (Bateson 68), so the concept of feminist rhetorical resilience helps us understand how a life can be transformed through an "ongoing responsiveness" involving "determination, perseverance, hope, and imagination" (Flynn, Sotirin, and Brady 7).

Flynn, Sotirin, and Brady argue that feminist rhetorical resilience involves three particular elements: agency, *métis*, and relationality. Agency is a matter of "recognizing and seizing opportunities," of understanding the power of change that is "small, local, fluid, provisional, and ongoing" (8). Being able to reinvent the self—to refashion identity in a proactive way—is central to feminist rhetorical resilience (8). Such refashioning also draws on the concept of *métis*, or shape-shifting, in which one confronts power "with flexible, subtle, active responsiveness" to both limitations and possibilities (9). *Métis* "combines forethought, resourcefulness, opportunism" so that hope functions "as practical agency" (9, 11). Through relationality, the third component of feminist rhetorical resilience, inward adaptation moves outward, seeking support and creating "an ethic of connection" along with "mutual empathy and empowerment" (11). These elements have marked my experiences. Three moves, especially, have been crucial: changing my thinking about myself and my situation; enacting a new identity; and building networks of support for new roles. I'll give a key example of each of these moves.

Changing My Thinking

In spring 1986, the Interdisciplinary Studies program holds a faculty retreat. As acting director, soon to be succeeded by a tenured associate professor who was eligible to apply for the continuing position, I organize the daylong meeting and concluding banquet. There, to the applause of some seventy-five colleagues, the Provost thanks me for my leadership and smilingly presents me with an inscribed glossy coffee-table book of regional photographs. I smile back, outwardly expressing the gratitude I'd regularly displayed when given an opportunity to over-extend myself for a limited reward. Holding the book in my hands, I continue to smile as my colleague, the incoming director, rises to speak to the group about the program's continuing work. Suddenly the book seems both very heavy and very light.

After the retreat, I tell friends that the Provost's gift is like the prize awarded to the young black narrator in the first chapter of Ralph Ellison's *Invisible Man*—the scholarship to the prestigious Negro college that he comes to understand is a means of continued oppression rather than genuine opportunity. I never open the book but begin preparing my dossier for a national job search. Two years later, during my first year at Berea College, I will write "Moving Toward the Center," an essay which tells the full story of the changed thinking that was necessary for me to go forward in my career. I'll present that essay at MLA and publish it in *Women's Studies Quarterly*.

Enacting a New Identity

In November 2003, the day before my meeting with Berea's Provost where I will learn that, by the way, he's decided to dissolve my administrative position, I draft this poem:

The Absent Director

I wander the hall, a ghost
in jeans. Strange students smile,
overlook my sweatshirt. The blinds
on my office door are down.
I never turn off
the out-of-office e-mail reply.

People rush to meetings,
I don't know where. Behind
closed doors they talk about
what used to be my stuff.
I meet some friends in the gym,
they're going to a dance
I didn't know was now.
They miss me, though.

I read Roethke on the dolor
of paper clips, never need
to empty my garbage can.
Where do I matter,
who am I? My life's
re-centered on the margins
of my old world.
Nice place to visit.

At the time, I felt that this poem expressed loss and uncertainty. In retrospect, however, I see that the poem speaks to the new identity I was already in the process of creating. I'd spent the first two months of my sabbatical less on my official project, a study of women's academic lives, and more on writing poems. This poem shows my growing understanding that change was happening, had already happened, that I was no longer who I had been. Deep within me, all of myself wanted to be born—wanted, as May Sarton describes it in "Now I Become Myself," to become a self that was then hovering on the margin, waiting to be brought from shadow into light. When the English department chair asked me, two days later, if I wanted to fight the Provost's decision or instead teach a roster of writing classes—creative nonfiction, essay-writing, journalism—I did not hesitate in accepting the teaching schedule he offered. Like Parker Palmer, I found I was "already standing on the ground of my new life" (55). The part of me that wanted justice—wanted to protest the Provost's unwarranted, politically motivated, decision—was silenced by my sudden realization that, though my old professional life had been richly rewarding, this new life was where I already was, where I now needed to be.

As my poem reflects, of course, even without the trauma of injustice, reinventing an identity means embracing loss and uncertainty as well as possibility. In responding to loss we must, as Reynolds Price advocates in his memoir, *A Whole New Life*, give ourselves time to grieve, but then we must move on. The new marginal world that I described in my poem turned out to be where I wanted not just to visit but to live.

Building Networks of Mutual Support

I could write here with truth and passion about the women colleagues who've supported and counseled me through my professional development. They've helped me prepare a persuasive CV and dossier, they've encouraged me to deepen and expand my thinking, they've taught me skills and helped me cope with failure. But I want to give a different example of the relationality component of my resiliency: the support—the championship—of my husband. His response, in 1986, when I brought up the possibility of my seeking a job elsewhere and his resigning a tenured position to follow me? "I've had the first ten years" since his doctorate, he told me. "You can have the next ten." It's been twenty-nine, a testimony to his continuing generosity and his own ability to reinvent himself as a writer. In addition to having become primary parent to our then 8- and 12-year-old sons, Roger still backs me up daily in my professional and creative work. As I do him. Beginning in graduate school, we have woven an ethic of mutual support that has undergirded our careers and our relationship.

If my two moves to follow Roger in his career (1972 and 1976) brought initial challenges followed by serendipitous advantages, a third move of Roger's was serendipitous from the start. Though embarked on a new career himself as an essayist and science fiction writer, he agreed to be a visiting professor in the philosophy department at the University of Michigan for the winter 2004 term. Thanks to my husband, I was able to spend the second half of my sabbatical in the richly creative environment of Ann Arbor. In particular, I was able to step through the opening door of poetry writing into a new world of kinetic poetry with Thylias Moss, where I was introduced to poems as fractals, where I found ways to weave my visual creativity (photography and brush painting) into my work with words, where I discovered a new voice.

CONCLUSION: UNDERLYING CONTINUITIES AND COMMUNITIES

Living a life does not by itself lead to insight; discernment is necessary, as both Bateson and Palmer argue (Bateson 70, Palmer 42). Through telling multiple versions of my life story, I've realized the underlying coherence as well as the complexity and versatility that have marked my path. Articulating the third version of way closing has been a freeing experience and has helped me to understand that, despite the pain that accompanied many of the turns, I've indeed found openings to worlds that are richer than I ever imagined. A key part of this discernment has come through probing the mechanism of change, through naming and examining the elements of resiliency that have enabled me to reinvent myself to meet challenges and opportunities.

Reviewing my stories, I've also become aware of the role played by institutional contexts and the field of writing studies itself. The yearning for community and interdisciplinarity that arose through my 1986 interdisciplinary studies/learning community experience at the University of Tennessee led me to seek a position at a liberal arts college. Such colleges typically encourage—even demand—continued reinvention, as core programs, cross-disciplinary courses, and scholarship opportunities evolve. Teaching full-time in English at Berea College since 2004, I've received institutional support to develop new courses such as contemplative writing, imagined landscapes, nature writing and photography, artists books, and experimental writing. We in writing studies can also be grateful that our field is so rich in opportunities for change and connection. The creative writing arena where I now concentrate is indeed a part of our field, and our national conferences and publications are testimony to the myriad interests of our colleagues.

Reviewing my stories also confirms that all experience, all study, fuels creative work; I see that there is nothing from my work, study, or life that is not potentially of use to me as a writer and poet. I may find material for a poem in talking with a writing student, reading a text on globalization for a capstone seminar, or bicycling with my husband. In exploring the form for that poem, I may draw on my knowledge of literary models like sonnets or villanelles, reach for the genre of an advertisement or table of contents, or create a map, mixing words and images. And always, my stories show me, I can find and create communities of knowledge and passion—communities where I can advance my abilities and help others grow as well, through courses I develop and teach, through participating in workshops led by other poets and writers, through dialogue with community writers.

As I begin the eighth decade of my journey, I'm confident that ways will continue to open and that resiliency can persist. The following poem, triggered by a photograph of myself at eight months old and published a month before I turned 70, names a cornerstone of my "one wild and precious life":

About

It's about amazement,
and sound and smell,
coffee dark and thick,
words I didn't know,
bubbling up the clear column,
and the photo Daddy took,
my eyes huge
under wisps of golden hair,
my mouth a dark circle
of wonder, it's about Mama's
rich voice, telling me
the percolator story,
telling me again,
it's about the way
she gave me
myself, invented me,
that great gift
of her life.
    It's about
the way her words,
my face, that amazement
still move in me
and on this page.

WORKS CITED

Bateson, Mary Catherine. "Composing a Life Story." *Willing To Learn: Passages of Personal Discovery*. Hanover, NH: Steerforth, 2004. 66–76. Print.

Flynn, Elizabeth A., Patricia Sotirin, and Ann Brady, eds. *Feminist Rhetorical Resilience*. Logan: Utah State UP, 2012. Print.

Jones, Libby Falk. "About" (poem). *Still: The Journal* 15 (Summer 2014). Web. May 31, 2017. <www.stilljournal.net>.

———. "Moving Toward the Center." *Women's Studies Quarterly* 18.3–4 (Fall/Winter 1990): 128–35. Print.

Palmer, Parker J. *Let Your Life Speak: Listening for the Voice of Vocation*. San Francisco: Jossey-Bass, 2000. Print.

Price, Reynolds. *A Whole New Life*. New York: Scribner, 2003. Print.

CHAPTER 6

Choreography

Running Away, Moving Toward, Living In

SUELLYNN DUFFEY

Years ago, as my hiking friend and I approached a low gate we would soon step over, I asked him whether we would turn right or left after we passed it. "Ah," he said. "You want to pace your steps so the leg you lift over the gate lands you in the direction we're headed." "Yep," I thought. I didn't want to pivot clumsily toward the next step or waste motion. I wanted my steps leading up to the gate choreographed, the choreographed movement purposeful, and my leisure walk on a summer day physically smooth. I love kinesthetic elegance.

As an image for the life paths I write about here, my walk that day and the motives that guided me are both supremely apt and completely misleading. Since I've studied dance for most of my life, it's not surprising that smooth choreography, purposeful movement, and kinesthetic elegance appeal to me— in physical realms of course but probably in most if not all others, a sort of bodily experience in the mind, if you will. As feminist research on rhetoric and feminism (Ede, Glenn, and Lunsford), on affect (Liljeström and Paasonen), and on rhetoric's sensorium (Hawhee) show us, that which is other than rational—affect, the body's materiality—is functionally important in driving our lives and is not separable from epistemologies, goal-setting practices, decision-making, and many if not all other parts of our lives. Thus, my claim that I like kinesthetic elegance in many realms is not simply a metaphorical abstraction; it is an embodied reality of my life as well. Much as it is real, forces beyond my control have sometimes structured my steps, and the paths I took were often jagged instead of smooth, patched together out of missteps rather than elegantly choreographed, evolved from a combination of opportunity, improvisation, desperation, and resilience rather than consciously designed, but nonetheless deliberate and agentive.

The concepts of *métis* and rhetorical resilience as Elizabeth A. Flynn, Patricia Sotirin, and Ann Brady explain them in *Feminist Rhetorical Resilience* come close to describing the inarticulate force that I think has guided me. Invoking Debra Hawhee, they write: "Hawhee's case for *métis* as embodied intelligence [of which kinesthetic elegance may be one example] points the way to rhetorical strategies that do not depend on positivistic reasoning but on an overlooked alternative: the ability to understand shifting contexts and the opportune moments for change or subversion that emerge through them" (10), an intelligence needed in situations where one's path is jagged. Further, this *métis* consciousness enables what Flynn, Satirin, and Brady call rhetorical resilience, which "offers an alternative when rational thought and action may be ineffective. . . . [It emphasizes] situational intelligence and innovative resourcefulness rather than rational planning" (9). Rhetorical resilience, then, is party to a perplexing and paradoxical dilemma that is part of this book's project, it seems to me: how we guide our lives often without fully knowing why and how. We attempt to describe the trajectories our lives have followed and explain them rationally; we attempt to attribute causation pushing us along this or another path; we try to understand intersections among kairos, resilience, and serendipity. We create stories that seem much more coherent than the lived experiences they narrate, and from that coherence we create advice for others to follow.

Advice, however, about how to succeed often rests on the rational alone. While advice given in such books as *Women's Ways of Making It in Rhetoric and Composition* can be wonderfully helpful, it assumes rational planning as well as contexts, paths, and results absent from many nonetheless successful, productive, satisfying academic lives.[1] As a woman in rhetoric and composition, I have had a successful career without following much if any of the received wisdom about how to succeed. If I fully believed in professional advice such as that outlined, I would judge myself (as I have done) as *less-than* those who've "made it" by following the hard-work, strategized existence of the tenure-track (research university) academician. Alternately, I could assume an oppositional stance—in spite of not following the best ways to "make it," I've done just fine. "Look at me," I could crow. But neither is the stance I want to take and neither frames my stories well.

My professional life story is in some respects not unlike those others could tell. Lives that have walked rocky paths, that have pushed us away from where we thought we were headed and left us apparently shipwrecked. Others of us, even without jagged stories of professional life, have traveled paths we would have been advised not to. We haven't planned our careers strategically by establishing goals and timelines and following them scrupulously. We haven't chosen dissertation topics that would get us through graduate school expeditiously (Aisenberg and Harrington). We have trailed spouses in their careers or stayed in place because of family(ies) nearby. While we may work in regional universities or small colleges, often we work in research universities, as I have. We may work off the tenure line, but some, maybe many of us work *on* the tenure line and are tenured. By many measures, certainly by the *rational* model of how to "make it," we are misfits, but we are many and varied.

And so I tell stories. It is feminist relationality that has invited my stories into this collection. Mine—and the stories others tell here—invite readers into feminist resilience.²

MY FAMILY'S INFLUENCE

I grew up the daughter of rural, southwestern Ohio parents who, like many others, had moved to an urban area for factory work during World War II, so the family backgrounds that influenced my upbringing were country and blue collar. When we grew gardens, it wasn't out of an ecological consciousness; it was because that's what generations of my country families had done. It's one of the ways they and we lived frugally. But because of our country ways, I sometimes ate high on the hog (a term we often used); meats that are now considered exotic by carnivores—quail, pheasant, rabbit—came to our table because my father hunted. Some of the vegetables we grew were so unusual for most of my life that they are only now making it to mainstream markets, kohlrabi, for example. My dialect was nonstandard until sometime in upper elementary school when, because my ear was good enough to hear the differences between my and my teachers' speech, I matched mine to theirs. I was also good at memorizing Walsh and Warriner handbook usage rules and following the linguistic etiquette they promulgated. I suspect, too, that I intuitively learned the lessons about language and power implicitly embedded in school teachings. My language is pretty much standard now. I don't think I ever slip back into the pronunciation of my home state's name the way I said it then: "Ahia" instead of "Ohio." I sometimes wish I did.

My father was a machine repairman in a huge factory, and his was, as I understand it now, a position of some privilege because of the skill it required. His work was important to the factory's smooth operation because when machines broke down, assembly lines didn't run, production stopped, and profit was jeopardized. What I knew then about my father's work is that it sent him home with dirty clothes and once a metal shard in his eye. But I didn't see him arrive home in those clothes because, for most of my growing-up life, he wasn't home from his second shift job until long after I was asleep. I remember, though, the feel of a blanket wafting over me as I slept, my father covering me when he came home from work. I roused slightly from the blanket's breath and felt my father's care.

It was he, I somewhat surprisingly say now, who guided me to college. Yet he provided no model for the importance of school learning, having not been a particularly good student himself—a poor speller and a nonreader. It was my mother who had done well scholastically in high school, had earned state honors for French, and had earned (but declined) a scholarship to the Conservatory of Music in Cincinnati. It was in my mother's family where reading materials were present and where school learning had a modest place. It was in my mother's family where I felt an occasional air of *gentility,* though only in brief moments, as when one of my aunts, a librarian, gave me a book on ballet for Christmas or when my grandfather arose as we were seated at the dining room table and made a speech honoring my grandmother, a speech that included a poem, or when for my grandparents' fiftieth wedding anniversary, my aunt from the cosmopolitan (to me) city of Detroit directed us in making hors d'oeuvres for the celebration. We didn't call them that, but I knew that the tiny, delicate, artful sandwiches with such surprising and delicious ingredients belonged to a world different from my everyday one. I struggle with using the word "gentility" here. It does not *necessarily* have a connection to higher learning, but it captures much of what myths about literacy and learning suggest: With more learning, one becomes refined; one enters a different class of people. A whole constellation of attributes follows, ones that we often use language as a marker of. A refined and genteel class I was not part of then and caught only glimpses of.

So when I say that my father guided me toward college, I mean "guidance" in a very narrow but nonetheless powerful way. It had nothing to do with what many of us now consider essential—and rational—advice for the college-bound. It included nothing about choosing a school, seeking scholarships and financial aid, studying well, choosing a major, or shaping a career. Never did he advise me about the intellectual benefits of a college education. His guidance looks like barely a nudge, and it happened in just a single moment. It rested on a kind of logic, but logic is not what produced its effect on me. In the car on the way to somewhere, my dad's mother asked me, the young teenager who by then had demonstrated a school career of high grades, if I were going to college. Unsure how to answer because I had no plans, I was silent for a moment. In the silence and at a time when a college degree was not the expected credential it has become, my dad said "Yes, she will. She and her brother will go to college so they won't have to work as hard as I do," his logic very working class.

In that serendipitous moment, my post–high school future was settled. That moment's choreography was smooth, the unlikely choreographer, my father, whose impact was joined by all the other forces that gave me the abilities to "do school" well, that nurtured them, and shepherded me along. The life resulting from that choreography, improvised.

RUNNING AWAY

Eager though I was, I entered college as a first-generation student, and the promise of excitement was undercut by my socioeconomic class, which gave me no knowledge of college and the middle- and upper-middle-class lives that dominated the small liberal arts school I attended. In my first semester, I got the lowest grade I had ever received, a C in world history after I failed the first exam. I know now that having never taken a high school class in the subject, I was totally unprepared for learning in one semester all I had to know about Europe across several centuries. Like many working-class families, mine never talked about worlds outside our local ones, so my store of common knowledge lacked much that would have made my life easier and more successful academically. I had no family-acquired historical, political, economic, or Renaissance art world knowledge to help me with school and that history class. I had no conceptual framework or geographical knowledge or vocabulary of names and places through which to ground what my professor wanted me to learn about the plethora of German and Italian principalities, the Holy Roman Empire, or unification movements in Europe.

I also had no learning strategies to fall back on when school became hard because it had always been easy; I had no resources to help me even though I did meet with the history professor who was awkward and ill-equipped to handle my tears and embarrassment. With insights from having studied socioeconomic class and higher education (Dews and Law; Peckham, Linkon, and Lanier-Nabors; Shepard, McMillan, and Tate; Welsch), I look back now and see the missing resources that would have made my young adult life easier. While parts of that undergraduate life had been smoothly choreographed (by scholarship aid, for example), its paths also covered rocky terrain familiar to many first-generation college students. I transferred to another college, eloped when I was twenty, and dropped out of school to follow my husband to Germany, where the Air Force had stationed him. After two lonely years there and a few more in the States, we divorced and I headed back to college.

In all these early moves, I suspect I was guided by promises that the new held in my imagination. In other words, I was guided by the desire to *move away from* what I knew but did not know what I was moving toward. That each new location in these years had rarely lived up to its imagined promise is not a surprise. I was young, ill-informed about what I headed into with each change in life circumstances, and ill-prepared by any of my previous experiences to anticipate accurately how real the promise might be. In these, my early vagabond years through my mid-twenties, I was often unhappy, and as I tell the stories now, I traveled rocky paths that I seem to have chosen without very much deliberation. I believe, however, that even though I didn't have articulable career goals and I made decisions in ways that were not necessarily goal-oriented, my decisions were grounded in an unspoken, inchoate, powerful place in my being, just like the kinesthetic sense that led me on my walk. I also believe that the paths they led me on, professionally and personally, were good ones for me to follow even if they were not rationally planned. Something guided me well.

MOVING TOWARD

At twenty-four, I returned to college, and by spring of my first year, universities across the country were afire with student protests about the Vietnam War. National Guard were on my and other Ohio campuses, and on one day in May 1970 when my university closed, eighty some other campuses across the nation did also (Tebben). Before school closed, we had lived through a two- or three-week period of campus turbulence, and during that time, one event set the stage for a significant part of the pedagogical beliefs that have guided my career. As student protest groups were milling around various places on Ohio State's expansive campus and voicing discontent about both national and campus events, one of my professors taught me my first lesson about integrating personal and professional lives, a lesson with great impact particularly since my personal life to that date had been so very far removed from the "professional" life of school. Julian Markels, a Melville scholar who taught my small honors seminar, came to class in his usual blue blazer, shirt and tie, and dark trousers. But at the outset of class, he stood, dramatically removed his blazer, hung it carefully on a hook, and rolled up his sleeves all the while explaining that he *could not* remain in his more formal, detached professorial role when campus was in turmoil. The esteemed professor in front of me had broken out of a role, crossed a boundary, and his actions and words invited us to speak about what we were living instead of Melville.

The classroom discussions I initiate now that integrate personal and academic subjects surely had their beginning then.

LIVING IN

As an undergrad, I majored in English because I was good at "doing" it, but I had no career goals. My attempt to major in English education, which would have offered a career path, had left me unsatisfied. Like many of the students I now teach, I was relatively ignorant about higher education's institutions, cultures, and professional pathways. Not surprisingly, I had only a dim notion that schooling after college existed, but as I was finishing my bachelor's degree, the Honors College dean suggested, during another brief discussion like my father's and grandmother's about college, that I'd be much happier once I was in graduate classes. His words surprised me, but I believe that just like my father's, they propelled me onward in higher education, into graduate school, the next path I would travel and a good place for me to land given the kinds of learning and thinking I do. Another nudge, a simple choreography, a dance I entered without much training but one I eventually learned the steps of. I thus became, like many of the students I now teach, a first-generation *graduate* student.[3]

Shortly after I began graduate study, OSU's English department hired Susan P. Miller as Writing Program Administrator (WPA), and her influence on me affirms what Lisa Ede says in this volume: "To say that Susan Miller brought energy and intellectual excitement to the writing program is an understatement" (18). Susan gathered up graduate students and taught us, in informal reading and study groups and in many other ways, how broad and deep the study of rhetoric could be. From these and other informal sources, rarely if ever from classes I took, I learned of and then read unbelievably exciting work by contemporary compositionists and language theorists that shaped my beliefs about pedagogy and the nature of English studies. Extracurricular learning opportunities, new classroom pedagogies, and participation in departmental affairs added to this make-shift rhetoric and composition study and allowed me, through a rich synergy, to move into and thus learn professional roles on which I would build later philosophies and scholarship.

Julian Markels's class during the 1970 campus turmoil had shown me a new model of classroom interaction. Susan Miller and our Milton scholar, Joan Webber, who moved out of her specialization and taught contemporary women poets, added to and sanctioned my sense of new ways to teach and learn—informally, interactively, nontraditionally, blending the personal with the professional. The department culture and the character of the times invited me into professional roles I'd never imagined. For example, early in my graduate career, the department invited me to its retreat. That was my first inside view of how the department was a community with its own driving forces and conflicts, a community that was a political entity instead of a collection of the individual faculty members I saw in classrooms. I was completely immersed in the work of that retreat and felt like something of an insider. Except for Susan Miller, those who involved me in the department's workings were literature faculty. But the writing program gave me many sustained, participatory ways in which to learn how programs are developed and managed. An important one is a graduate student committee concerned with First Year Composition (FYC) matters. Such committees are familiar and common now, but they were not then. In it, I was party to many long discussions in which we evaluated strategies for handling meetings, discussed writing issues and pedagogies, planned the direction for FYC, and kept abreast of department politics. In doing so we developed our intellectual and professional composition worlds. I found the work, both in committee and informally outside it, stimulating and productive. I was, I realize now, undertaking an apprenticeship in writing program administration, an apprenticeship that prepared me for administrative positions I would hold from 1985 onward.

What OSU offered me in informal and extracurricular learning situations profoundly complemented what I learned from courses, a curriculum I created that was itself surprising for the time. Via paths with unpredictable twists, I was able to take a considerable number of rhetoric and related courses as I worked on my doctoral degree, not because Ohio State was the rhetoric/composition center it has become. With the exception of one rhet/comp course taught by Ed Corbett and a two-quarter-long linguistics course, the English department offerings were all in literature or literary theory. Because I wanted to take more rhet/comp courses, I left the English department and for a time became a doctoral student in OSU's Department of Communication where I took courses in rhetorical criticism, history and theory, speech act theory, statistics, and more. After a year, though, I returned to the English department, preferring the humanities to social science. The fact that OSU had a strong rhetoric and communications department available to me and that I could follow its study for a year and then return to English allowed me to create a foundational knowledge base, opportunities not available to others elsewhere, circumstances for me that were kairotic and serendipitous and that allowed me opportunities to exercise resilience and agency as interactive processes.

Further, I made choices during this time by following my interests and taking advantage of what was available, not by exclusively rational planning. Serendipity, kairos, agency, chance, and a *mētistic* intelligence all played roles in my improvised graduate education at OSU.

My further life at Ohio State, as I will show, violates several requisites of how to "make it" professionally. For example, I earned all three degrees there. Unadvisable, they say, to have all three degrees from the same institution. Maybe two degrees, but not three. I see wisdom in this advice: It seeks to avoid the potential narrowness of learning what only one institution and its faculty can offer, and yet I earned all my degrees at OSU. Why? I'll explain more below, but one of the main reasons I stayed is that I was *in love* with the riches OSU offered in composition and rhetoric, or I might say in clichéd terms, I followed my heart, a claim that is also accurate. In the 1970s and early 1980s, OSU offered an exciting intellectual and professional milieu that substituted for the not-yet-developed world of published scholarship in rhet/comp. OSU's culture also worked against narrowness in many ways, not the least of which is through the scholars who visited: Mina Shaughnessy, Ed White, Joe Comprone, Barry Kroll, Rich Enos, Mike Rose, David Bartholomae, Richard Lanham, Susan Jarratt, Linda Brodkey, and many more. OSU was in the midst of rich scholarly networks in rhetoric and composition, a result of faculty vision while I was there as well as certain kairotic moments such as the founding of a basic writing program, which I'll say more about below.

What I have written above about my graduate work makes clear why I stayed at OSU for my doctoral work, and what I write below about my full-time professional positions there will add to my reasons for doing so. In addition to the rich milieu at OSU, I stayed also for personal reasons. I had remarried and had a son, and staying in Ohio allowed me to be near many members of both families and my son to be near all of his grandparents as he was growing up, something my own familial and perhaps class backgrounds caused me to value. Getting all three degrees from one institution is not my only seemingly *ill-advised* step. Before I finished my dissertation, I took on full-time work, another arrangement most of us would advise against. But that work shaped my professional life thereafter in very good ways. My experiences, however, in no way deny the problems of women in the academy. For example, I participated in what Ballif, Davis, and Mountford call the "'leaky pipeline for women PhDs in which women enter and complete doctoral programs but disproportionately drop out of the running for tenure-track positions" (3). It was not until my fourth full-time position that I entered the tenure line.

At OSU I also willingly participated in writing program directorships without faculty rank and without the job security of tenure, requisites often seen as necessary for such administrative work. It is thus accurate to say that I violated my profession's standards. Yet, books such as *Untenured Faculty as Writing Program Administrators: Institutional Practices and Politics* (Dew and Horning, eds.) trouble blanket proscriptions about the requisites for administrative work, as does my contribution to that collection, "Defining *Junior*," an essay that grew out of my lived experience and that challenges orthodoxy, a recurring theme in this essay. Ill-advised as one may describe my time at Ohio State, staying there laid the groundwork for a very satisfying career, one that has allowed me to develop and—productively and satisfyingly—use the talents I have, experience the excitement that classrooms can give our lives, design writing programs creatively and with wonderful collaborators, work often with colleagues who were doing cutting-edge work, and, in later years, discover the satisfaction research can bring. What I learned and was able to do at Ohio State was both broad and deep.

I began full-time work in the mid-1980s when the director of OSU's basic writing program resigned midyear, and the department decided to replace her with a nonfaculty appointment. The program's beginning in 1977 was a kairotic moment in Ohio State's rhetoric and composition identity and, in some ways, for the whole field.[4] I had taught in the basic writing program since its inception, and so my experience and perhaps other qualities led the department administrators to solicit my interest in the directorship when the position was suddenly vacant. I applied for the job and was hired in 1985— my first time professional job with a *real* salary. I was thrilled. In terms that would seem to matter, I was in a terrible position—I was ABD, without faculty rank, with a year-to-year contract, and isolated in satellite offices miles away from the main campus. But in fact, that position was in many ways the best gig I've had in my professional life in terms of opportunities, support, and the degree of control I had over my work life. When I was hired to direct this writing program, my mandate from the English department was little more than "keep the lid on." There had been conflict in the program shortly before that, and calm was foremost in the department administrators' minds. What that minimal directive allowed, what physical distance from the department allowed, what a strong staff allowed, I realize now, was a significant degree of freedom. Guided primarily by an inchoate sense of how I wanted the program to develop, I took advantage of the freedoms I had.

For example, when my assistant and I decided to team-teach a version of the curriculum David Bartholomae and Anthony Petrosky laid out in *Facts, Artifacts, and Counterfacts* (FAC), the program took a significant experimental step. From a program that had begun less than a decade earlier and at its outset asked students to write nothing longer than paragraphs, it was a huge change to move into the difficult *FAC* reading and writing curriculum. In fact, my assistant, Mindy Wright, and I had both attempted the curriculum previously and given up midquarter because it was too hard—for both the students and us. When one of Mindy's sections and one of mine at the same hour were both under-enrolled, I suggested we combine them into one and teach it together, something I'd probably have had a hard time getting *permission* to do because team-teaching is expensive when each instructor gets full work-load credit. But Mindy and I were able to do just that because I managed the program's budget, scheduling, and staffing and was in the position to facilitate our team-teaching.

We jumped in and then continued team-teaching for several quarters. Along the way, we expanded and changed the model to include in-class tutors who were other instructors in the program. As they tutored, they simultaneously learned how to teach the curriculum itself, and it expanded eventually into all the other sections in the grassroots, bottom-up way I had wanted it to. Notable about the program is that none of us held a degree beyond a master's.[5] Many of us were place-bound, and most of us had little or no training in composition; in other words, we were typical of many invisible instructors around the country. Yet, we were drawing on respected scholarship and pedagogy and following what were then and still are seen by many as best practices in composition pedagogy. The results of the team-teaching project were widespread in this fertile ground, both for the program and for me professionally.

Although I didn't know it at the time, the decision to teach a *FAC* curriculum would lay the groundwork for my first sustained forays into wider professional arenas, both regional and national ones. It gave me conference presentations, a few consulting jobs, and leadership positions in the Council on Basic Writing (CBW). These leadership roles (executive board member and then president) began serendipitously, as my father had nudged me toward college and the Honors College dean toward graduate school. A friend beside me in a conference hall nudged me to volunteer for a CBW position. Soon, I was president, working on the executive board with colleagues from across the country, designing national conferences, judging proposals for their merit, and holding Special Interest Group (SIG)-sponsored functions at CCCC.

Significant is the 1992 Conference on Basic Writing that I planned with Peter Adams and Carolyn Kirkpatrick. At this conference, David Bartholomae's keynote address, "The Tidy House: Basic Writing in the American Curriculum,"[6] was in the center of a major shift. As Jeanne Gunner explains:

> Whereas [basic writing] once clearly operated as its own community of practitioners and theorists, . . . [it] seems to be shifting from a term for a specialized teaching and research in the field of rhetoric-composition to a pedagogical and sociopolitical concern dispersed across the spectrum of composing issues, writing curricula, and socio-educational theory, with the continuing argument over mainstreaming serving as a central site of this transformation. (25)

This 1992 conference was at the heart of scholarly discussions in basic writing and beyond, and my coplanners and I were at the center of it, a serendipitous occurrence perhaps. Or kairotic. Or agentive. Or all three.

Happily, I continued directing the basic writing program after 1985, doing programmatic research, redesigning curricula, applying for and getting grants, and bridging the distance between our offices and the English department both by finding my way onto departmental committees and enticing graduate students, with their new knowledge, to teach in our program. During that time, we paired honors and basic writing students, which undergirded one of my early publications, an invited comment on mainstreaming in *CCC* ("Mapping"). By the early 90s, we had invented basic writing courses with an attached Writing Center component, an arrangement sometimes called a *studio* design. To support the undergraduate tutors, we invented a course in writing and learning, which I taught. My teaching further expanded to the graduate course in teaching basic writing. This variety in my work life excited me. I had opportunities to invent and implement programs and projects, and I had support for whatever I did. By this time, I was doing much the same work as regular faculty even though I wasn't on a faculty line, a comment that seems merely to record factual information but that is a window into many of our profession's conflicts as well as moments of significant tension and dismay in my individual professional life. When, much later, a textbook based very much on a program I had developed was published under other authors' names, the university lawyer told me that if I were a faculty member, I would have a right to own intellectual property, but as staff I did not.[7]

By the early '90s, cultural, political, and economic forces combined to threaten the existence of basic writing programs in four-year institutions, and so when, again, our department sought a non-tenure-track professional to direct a writing program, I put myself forward and left the basic writing program. This time, I became interim director of all OSU's writing programs and moved to the main campus into an apparently more prestigious position, one that I had reason to believe would become permanent. Interestingly, I had less office support and far less budgetary and staffing control than before. Charged with upgrading the TA training, I designed peer mentoring and teaching circles. Charged with enhancing the first-year writing curriculum, I chose a staff of advanced TAs who worked collaboratively with me to create it and then lead peer teaching groups. Included in this staff were both composition and literature students, such as Carrie Leverenz, Jane Greer, Jennifer Phegley, and Paul Hanstedt. With them, I reiterated and expanded the kind of graduate school extracurriculum I had had.[8] Later, a coauthored publication grew out of these projects, "Conflict and Collaboration in Peer Teaching Groups."

My career in these two years, though, was tenuous. Although I saw only glimpses of foment among regular faculty, a major storm was brewing about my directorship, part of it philosophical (nonfaculty should not direct programs) although I have only the barest sense of what really happened. Before I knew it, someone else in the department had been assigned my job and I was to be demoted. Serendipitously, another job appeared on the horizon, serendipitous especially because we were well into spring at the end of the hiring cycle. I applied for this position I could commute to,[9] was hired, and by midsummer, had left Ohio State to become Ohio University's director of writing across the curriculum. Thus began my (second) vagabond life. I had been at Ohio State for twenty-six years (first as an undergraduate then a graduate student and then a professional), but within the next eleven years, I would hold jobs at four different institutions in different parts of the country.

While my work life after I left OSU was far from dismal, in the vagabond years afterwards, I did have long, unhappy professional stretches. At Ohio University, I worked primarily alone, outside of a department, directly under a dean. It was lonelier work than I was accustomed to, with inadequate infrastructure, and internal resistance to what I undertook. I left there after three years and took my first-ever faculty position, assistant professor and director of writing at the University of Wisconsin-Eau Claire. In this job, I began to learn how different institutional cultures can be from one another, and my interest in *place* began to form and has resulted in publications.[10] Another pressure on my professional life was my mother's health. She had become terminally ill as I was leaving Ohio, and I disrupted both of our lives when I moved her to Wisconsin with me. While her health had some negative effect on my professional life, having her with me for the last year of her life, during which she was often fully functioning, was a great gift to me personally. Unexpectedly, her death rekindled my incidental interest in family stories, an interest that grew and eventually led to a book chapter, "Come Sit at the Table," that locates my mother's family and some of its stories in southern Ohio's racialized climate, including its Underground Rail Road history. As should be clear by now, my scholarly life is very much intertwined with my personal one.

After a problematic third-year review at UWEC, I once again benefited from a serendipitously late-advertised position at Georgia Southern. Quickly, I applied to direct its writing program and was hired as its (untenured) WPA. With my membership in a relatively new department of Writing and Linguistics, however, I thought I had landed exactly where I was meant to be, finally. I had a bevy of congenial colleagues in my field, something I'd missed since I'd left Ohio State. We were developing a major in writing and linguistics, which was new and wonderfully exciting work, as exciting as the first programmatic work I had done at OSU. When I, the Midwesterner, lived in Georgia, my interest in institutional locations took a geographical turn, out of which grew the article, "Student Silences in the Deep South: Hearing Unfamiliar Dialects." I earned tenure at GSU and thought I would never again want to work in a department of literature because the writing department offered me so much more than it seemed a literature department ever could.

I was wrong. I ultimately *did* leave Georgia Southern to take the position I now hold in the University of Missouri-St. Louis's English department, one that satisfies me professionally, personally, and geographically. I did not feel compelled to leave Georgia Southern, as I had felt compelled in the three previous moves, but by this time, I had learned to evaluate what *promise* the new offered, something I had been unable to do as a young adult, and St. Louis promised me a return to the Midwest, to a climate I liked better and landscapes that were not foreign, and (relative) proximity to my son. It also gave me a significant salary increase and a lower teaching load. I found, too, a department of literature that was amenable to rhetoric and composition, having had a specialist or two for decades. In my current department, I have as much freedom to design courses as I did at Ohio State, the opportunity to design a wider *range* of courses, and considerable freedom to choose what I teach. These opportunities keep my teaching life stimulating, and since I have designed courses related to my research interests, they have nourished my scholarly endeavors as well.

Collegially, I am fortunate. Here, more than at any place except OSU, I meet with colleagues socially as well as professionally, which adds a satisfying dimension to my life. Here, also, I have developed extensive collaborative networks, with colleagues and, as importantly, with graduate students and alumnae networks I learned the importance of at OSU. An important and shaping component of OSU's environment, I realize now, is how the academic world was embodied in the people and places and activities. Collaboration wasn't merely a scholarly topic to investigate. It was embedded, materially, all around me—in the informal study groups I've mentioned, in programmatic decision-making; in grant-writing projects; in curriculum design; in team-teaching;

and, especially important for me, in frequent social events often centered on a visiting scholar. My family background had given me no models for nor instruction in the kind of social interactions that happen among professionals, but I had learned a certain variety of them at OSU. Just as important as social niceties and networking were the many ways in which the line between the personal and professional was blurred. Witnessing that blurring, in many ways and many times, gave me experiential knowledge of the feminist assertion that the personal is political and thus enriched my academic learning. My instruction and learning there were *embodied* and thus materially grounded as I continually aim for them to be in all my professional work.

One recent collaboration is a writing and study group that evolved from my well-developed sense of and affinity for the extracurricular at OSU, a kind of group I'd not been able to form at any other institutions since I left Columbus, a group that lasted for several years and satisfied many of my interests. We began initially as four who were finishing a course in Women, Literacy, and Multicultural America in which we had read, for example, Beth Daniell's *A Communion of Friendship: Literacy, Spiritual Practice, and Women in Recovery*, Katherine Corbett's book about St. Louis women (*In Her Place: A Guide to St. Louis Women*), articles about rural women, and some of Deborah Brandt's work. When the group first met, all four of us were attending a local conference at which Shirley Brice Heath spoke. Energized by Heath's research, we paused before we left the conference to explore what we'd just heard and begin to shape plans for continued study. I wanted the group to form because I thought we'd not gone as far as we could in our explorations of women and literacy, particularly via the personal inflection the students' lives had contributed to our academic study. I wanted to learn more about and from them.

Our study group began originally as a research group in which the students reflected on their reasons for beginning graduate school, how those reasons and/or the perceptions of them had changed, what literacies the students had brought with them, and how those had changed as a result of graduate study. Because the students had all written literacy histories in a class they took together, we investigated the effect of that project on their lives and on classroom dynamics. Before the group formed, I had already developed scholarly projects growing out of my interest in the particular paradigm for graduate study that our location invites. For example, I have developed the concept of *local* disciplinarity that appears in two articles.[11] With the group's help, my interest in the locale of my institution and its students has blended with my earlier interest in *place*, and I envision these insights as part of a book about Midwestern literacies.

In its second year, the group expanded to include three more members, one an alumna of our program, one a teaching professor, and one a tenure-line faculty member. Sometimes we functioned as a writing group and vetted conference proposals, poetry, articles-in-progress, and grant-proposal ideas.[12] Sometimes we were a teaching group, all of us being literacy teachers. Sometimes we found our explorations reaching into religion and spiritual practices; sometimes we investigated motherhood from our various roles as daughters and (some of us) mothers and grandmothers. The group blended the professional with the personal, met in domestic spaces, and always included food with its meetings—just my kind of group, the prototype for which arose long ago at OSU and which enriches my intellectual, personal, and professional lives. The group's origins are in some ways as serendipitous as my being able to study rhet/comp at OSU but also a product of agency and collective desire.

My life between Dayton, Ohio, and St. Louis, Missouri, has been troubled and rich, complexly choreographed as I see it in retrospect. By cyclically leaving, returning, staying put, moving away from, and revisiting, I have developed, as I've mentioned, a wide-ranging interest in *place*—in geophysical and human-created locations, as well as culturally created locations and the people in them. My earliest interests were motivated by intellectual and emotional drives to understand wherever I'd landed, to move beyond what I had known, and to adapt. In the long years while I was at Ohio State, I lived in new personal and professional spaces and flourished, sometimes, through what they offered. As I moved into my second vagabond years, I studied *place* for something like professional and emotional survival, and then I began to write about what I was learning. Publications followed the initial ones about WPA locations and institutional cultures. At Georgia Southern, the location called me to learn about both geographical location and cultures. Now, at yet a different kind of institution with different students, I study the literacies of place-bound graduate students in an urban, master's-only program. Along the way, I've explored my family places, geophysical locations, their shaping influences on me (or humans in general), and humans' shaping influences on lands and landscape.

Like what drew me to OSU, I have been guided to my current institution and find my satisfactions here by a complex combination of kairos, serendipity, and agency. Collaboration at Ohio State laid the groundwork for a relational resilience; my sometimes desperate job situations have shown me how much I need a satisfying professional life. The many crossings that my family and working class backgrounds required and in some ways taught me how to perform have contributed to *mêtistic* moments in my professional life. The diversity of backgrounds, credentials, professional goals, and opportunities I've seen in my vagabond years show me that there is a much wider world of professional life in rhetoric and composition than our how-to-make it rational advice uses as models. We, as women in rhetoric and composition, move with different choreography through dances that show diverse ways in which one can "make it." I tell stories now to limn the complex choreographies we dance by.

NOTES

1. To be fair, I need to point out that the authors of *Women's Ways of Making It* acknowledge explicitly that they aim their book's advice to women seeking tenure-line positions at research universities. Baliff, Davis, and Mountford write, "Our focus on women in tenure-track and tenured positions is in no way meant to ignore the number of women in non-tenure-track or non-tenured positions or part-time positions across the country, who represent approximately 80 percent of those teaching writing" (3). Other models of professional life—even ones on the tenure-track at research universities like mine and others this volume includes, offer much-needed alternatives. In addition, the positions open at research universities are only a small percentage of the jobs available and are not the ones all doctoral candidates seek.
2. I use the terms "feminist relationality" and "feminist resilience" as do Flynn, Sotirin, and Brady.
3. As I write this essay, I realize the many and powerful ways in which the 1970s at Ohio State shaped my beliefs and values about the nature of learning, pedagogy, disciplinarity, and professional/personal life, but the environment at OSU in the 1970s and later also stands out as especially pertinent for rhetoric and composition. Ohio State's English Department, from the mid-70s until I left in the '90s, was an extraordinary place for someone interested in rhet/comp, and so my entry tale into graduate school and the profession is, perhaps, more than merely my story alone. It sketches part of our discipline's history.
4. Mina Shaughnessy's *Errors and Expectations* was published in 1977, and *1977: A Cultural Moment in Composition*, Henze, Selzer, Sharer, et al. explores the Penn State writing program at that cultural moment; still there is more for historians to explore.
5. For accuracy's sake, I should add that after two years directing the program, I completed my doctoral work.
6. This keynote address was later published in the *Journal of Basic Writing*.
7. I have written about this juncture in my professional life in the article "Whose Work?"
8. After securing a faculty position at Roanoke College, Paul told me, more than once, that he attributed his success on the job market and early in his position to the professionalizing work I sponsored, a comment about rhetoric and composition as much as about me.
9. Commuting was important. I had no time to plan a major move because of the timing of the hire.
10. "Place, Culture, Memory," "Skeletons in the Closet," "Defining *Junior*," and "English Departments."
11. "English Departments" and "Sites."
12. One member has just published a haiku.

WORKS CITED

Aisenberg, Nadya, and Mona Harrington. *Women of Academe: Outsiders in the Sacred Grove.* Amherst: U of Mass P, 1988. Print.

Ballif, Michelle, Diane Davis, and Roxanne Mountford. *Women's Ways of Making It in Rhetoric and Composition.* New York: Routledge, 2008. Print.

Bartholomae, David. "The Tidy House: Basic Writing in the American Curriculum." *Journal of Basic Writing* 12.1 (1993): n. pag. Web. February 17, 2015.

Bartholomae, David, and Anthony Petrosky. *Facts, Artifacts, and Counterfacts: Theory and Method for a Reading and Writing Course.* Portsmouth, NH: Heinemann, 1986. Print.

Corbett, Katherine T., ed. *In Her Place: A Guide to St. Louis Women's History.* St. Louis: Missouri Historical Society, 1999. Print.

Daniell, Beth. *A Communion of Friendship: Literacy, Spiritual Practice, and Women in Recovery.* Carbondale: Southern Illinois UP, 2003. Print.

Dew, Debra Frank, and Alice Horning, eds. *Untenured Faculty as Writing Program Administrators: Institutional Practices and Politics.* West Lafayette, IN: Parlor, 2007. Print.

Dews, C. L. Barney, and Carolyn Leste Law, eds. *This Fine Place So Far from Home: Voices of Academics from the Working Class.* Philadelphia: Temple UP, 1995. Print.

Duffey, Suellynn. "'Come Sit at the Table with Us': Traces of Racial History and Women's Agency in Place." *Feminist Challenges or Feminist Rhetorics? Locations, Scholarship, Discourse.* Ed. Kirsti Cole. Newcastle upon Tyne: Cambridge Scholars, 2014. 24–38. Print.

———. "Defining *Junior*." *Untenured Faculty as Writing Program Administrators: Institutional Practices and Politics.* Eds. Debra Frank Dew and Alice Horning. West Lafayette, IN: Parlor, 2007. 58–71. Print.

———. "English Departments' Relationships to Community: An Experiment at the Heart of Disciplinary Identity." *Journal of Public Scholarship in Higher Education* 1 (2011): 47–65. Print.

———. "Mapping the Terrain of Tracks and Streams." *College Composition and Communication* 47.1 (1996): 103–7. Print.

———. "Place, Culture, Memory." *The Writing Program Interrupted: Making Space for Critical Discourse.* Eds. Jeanne Gunner and Donna Strickland. Portsmouth, NH: Boynton/Cook, 2009. 186–93. Print.

———. "Skeletons in the Closet, Ghosts, and Other Invisible Creatures." *The Promise and Perils of Writing Program Administration.* Eds. Theresa Enos and Shane Borrowman. West Lafayette, IN: Parlor, 2008. 139–46. Print.

———. "Student Silences in the Deep South: Hearing Unfamiliar Dialects." *Silence and Listening as Rhetorical Arts.* Eds. Cheryl Glenn and Krista Ratcliffe. Carbondale: Southern Illinois UP, 2011. 293–303. Print.

———. "Teaching and Literacy in Basic Writing Courses." *Practice in Context: Situating the Work of Writing Teachers.* Eds. Cindy Moore and Peggy O'Neill. Urbana, IL: NCTE, 2002. 3–11. Print.

———. "Whose Work?" *Writing Program Administration: Journal of the Council of Writing Program Administrators* 20.3 (1997): 19–20. Print.

Duffey, Suellynn, Ben Feigert, Vic Mortimer, Jennifer Phegley, and Melinda Turnley. "Conflict, Collaboration, and Authority: Graduate Students and Writing Program Administration." *Rhetoric Review* 21.1 (2002): 79–87. Print.

Ede, Lisa, Cheryl Glenn, and Andrea Lunsford. "Border Crossings: Intersections of Rhetoric and Feminism." *Rhetorica: A Journal of the History of Rhetoric* 13.4 (1995): 401–41. Print.

Flynn, Elizabeth A., Patricia Sotirin, and Ann Brady, eds. *Feminist Rhetorical Resilience.* Boulder: UP of Colorado, 2012. Print.

Gunner, Jeanne. "Iconic Discourse: The Troubling Legacy of Mina Shaughnessy." *Journal of Basic Writing* 17.2 (1998): 25–42. Web. February 14, 2015.

Hawhee, Debra. "Rhetoric's Sensorium." *Quarterly Journal of Speech* 101.2 (2015): 2–17. Print.

Henze, Brent, et al. *1977: A Cultural Moment in Composition.* West Lafayette, IN: Parlor, 2007. Print.

Liljeström, Marianne, and Susanna Paasonen, eds. *Working with Affect in Feminist Readings: Disturbing Differences.* New York: Routledge, 2010. Print.

Peckham, Irvin, Sherry Lee Linkon, and Benjamin G. Lanier-Nabors, eds. *Special Issue: Social Class and English Studies. College English* 67.2 (2004). Print.

Shaughnessy, Mina. *Errors and Expectations: A Guide for the Teacher of Basic Writing.* New York: Oxford UP, 1977. Print.

Shepard, Alan, John McMillan, and Gary Tate, eds. *Coming to Class: Pedagogy and the Social Class of Teachers.* Portsmouth, NH: Boynton/Cook Heinemann. 1998. Print.

Tebben, Gerald. "Columbus Mileposts: May 6, 1970: Riots Force Closure of Ohio State's Campus." *Columbus Dispatch* [Columbus, OH] May 6, 2012. Web. January 11, 2015.

Welsch, Kathleen A., ed. *Those Winter Sundays: Female Academics and Their Working-Class Parents.* Lanham, MD: UP of America, 2005. Print.

CHAPTER 7

Embracing Scrappiness

Troublesome Knowledge and Serendipity

LINDA ADLER-KASSNER

In the graduate pedagogy class I taught most fall quarters from 2000–2014 (at two different institutions), I asked students to write "Classroom Observation Reflections" or CORs. Usually, these were observations of their own teaching of the lower division general education writing course in which they were TAs and, once a term, of someone else's teaching. In the fall of 2014, though, I added a new COR that asked TAs—who come primarily from other disciplines in the Division of Humanities and Fine Arts (e.g., history, English, religious studies, film studies, etc.), where the Writing Program is housed—to spend time reflecting on and describing their experiences with threshold concepts in their home disciplines.

Here, a brief explanation is necessary. "Threshold concepts," identified originally by learning researchers Jan Meyer and Ray Land, are concepts critical for epistemological participation—seeing through and seeing with. Meyer and Land's work located threshold concepts in academic disciplines. With a number of colleagues (e.g., Adler-Kassner; Adler-Kassner and Majewski; Adler-Kassner and Wardle), I have suggested that they also can be viewed more broadly as concepts critical for epistemological participation in communities of practice (including, but not limited to, disciplines). Beginning in 2013, I used threshold concepts of writing studies in the TA pedagogy course as a way to ground TAs' thinking about teaching in aspects of the field's knowledge about writing, writers, and writing development as this knowledge applies to their teaching of writing as well as teaching in their home disciplines.

The threshold concept COR asked students to

> identify the [threshold] concept [in your discipline] and explain it for an audience outside of the discipline. Please then explain an instance when this TC has come into play for you (in your own work or your teaching in the discipline.) Then, spend the bulk of the COR reflecting on: 1) How you identified this TC—an experience? Something in a class? 2) How/whether the process of identifying/using this TC helps you think about the work that you're doing in Writing 2; and 3) Anything else related to identifying TCs.

By asking the TAs to think about a moment of learning associated with the threshold concept, I hoped that they would spend some time reflecting on the wrestling that inevitably comes as learners encounter threshold concepts and come to see through and see with them. This wrestling was important both for the assignments that they were working on with their own first-year students in Writing 2 (assignments that asked students to engage with the threshold concept "Writing is an activity and a subject of study" [Wardle and Adler-Kassner 15] in different ways), and for their work with students in their home disciplines.

The responses to these questions were incredibly rich and thoughtful. TAs described a threshold concept in their disciplines, explaining that concept clearly and considering its relevance for their teaching of Writing 2. At the same time, some had a hard time accessing what happened as they learned the threshold concepts they named. In class, we talked about the implications of what it meant for us as teachers (of whatever discipline) to not only be able to define these concepts that were so important for our success as learners, but also to remember the affective experience of learning those concepts and the messiness that surrounded that learning.

I'm very familiar with the literature on novice-expert practices; I work with faculty regularly to articulate the constituent elements of their own expertise. But I hadn't ever asked expert learners to recall their processes of learning in quite the same ways that I did in this COR. I was a bit surprised at how little some of the responses focused on what it was like to develop that expertise and, perhaps, how hard it could be. I quickly realized, though, that this was a projection. For me, this kind of messy, visceral struggle sits at the core of my experience as a teacher, researcher, program administrator, and human being. Another term from the threshold concepts literature is relevant to these moments: "troublesome knowledge." Meyer and Land, as well as David Perkins (who has also used this as a lens to consider learning processes), describe this as knowledge that interferes with learners' movement toward participation in threshold concepts as those concepts butt up against knowledge that is inert, alien, or that otherwise interferes with or runs counter to the concept. But drawing on literature from learning and development, Julie Timmermans argues for a reconsideration of the idea of troublesome knowledge. "If we accept that some degree of dissonance is necessary to stimulate development," she contends, "then the troublesome . . . nature of threshold concepts may be the very quality that reveals their developmental potential. . . . Their power may be that they trigger dissonance not only at the cognitive and affective levels, but also dissonance at the epistemological level, calling upon learners to 'change their minds' not by supplanting *what* they know, but by transforming *how* they know" (11).

What I most appreciate about Timmermans's reconsideration (along with the literature she draws on for it) are the connections she makes between the epistemological and affective qualities of troublesomeness. Both qualities are central for growth and contribute to a sort of resilience through which that growth can occur. As Timmermans describes them, these connections reflect an orientation to troublesome knowledge that also constitutes a central part of my identity. Defining that identity now, I'd say that I am a very determined scrapper, that I try to find my ways into opportunities, cracks, moments of possible entrance. Though I've never thought about it in this way (until the opportunity provided by this collection), it's clear that this identity has been shaped by serendipitous encounters that have contributed to a sense of resilience and even agency as defined by Flynn, Sotirin, and Brady—an ability to analyze a moment or a context, build alliances with others, and adapt in a principled way.

This journey started with struggle and affective experiences with both troublesomeness and just plain trouble. I was a not-at-all-accomplished junior high and high school student with what felt like a litany of unsuccessful experiences to my credit. I applied to and was rejected from many opportunities for "gifted" students through junior high and high school. Looking back, I see myself feeling like I couldn't crack any number of codes that were being placed before me. Once I was in high school, I reveled in history and English classes, which were taught through an integrated curriculum and included immersive reading and writing. But my performance in math and science classes ranged from awful to abysmal. Meanwhile, my home situation, while economically stable, was less so emotionally. My junior year, I heard about a way out of all of it when a visiting college admissions officer mentioned the concept of "early admission," whereby students could go to college after that third year of high school. I understood it as a very real possibility for escape. The beginning of my serendipitous journey, then, was what I still consider my miraculous acceptance to Macalester College. The dean of admissions saw something in my application, so he took a chance. Flashing forward four years, I graduated from Macalester with a major in history, a "core" in political science, and serious emphases in extracurricular activities (e.g., spending a lot of time protesting and writing vocally strident articles for the campus's many publications) and socializing. I had no desire to do homework after graduating from college. But I *did* want to be a teacher. I applied for a few positions teaching history in private high schools (since I didn't have a teaching credential); while I came close to them, I wasn't hired.

Looking back, this might have been the moment where my experience with troublesome knowledge and scrappiness began to intersect. I spent a couple of years working at a local bookstore in St. Paul. While there, I started to put together my own teaching job. I created The Personal History Project, a nonprofit through which I taught neighborhood history in elementary schools around the city. I divided my time: writing grants to fund myself, doing primary historical research (since the curriculum was neighborhood- and school-specific) at archives from the Minnesota Historical Society to the Minnesota Department of Transportation, teaching, arranging locations for exhibitions that the kids from each school made, finding new schools and new money . . . in other words, working a lot.

Looking back, this experience was full of troublesome knowledge. While I wanted to *be* a teacher, I'd never really taught (since I didn't minor in education in college, nor try to get a teaching certificate). I have a distinct memory during the time I was developing the elementary school curriculum of reading *Democracy and Education,* trying to figure out what it meant to take Dewey's ideas and actually turn them into the real work of teaching. Then there was the culture of the public schools. I met with administrators, principals, and teachers to try to get them to agree to have me come into their classrooms. And the culture of archival, primary research—I'd been a history major, but my primary interest was in popular culture. I'd spent a lot of time watching old movies and reading and writing about hard-boiled detective novels in order to examine postwar culture. I had no experience reading plat maps, looking at letters from African American citizens displaced from their neighborhoods by the construction of I-94 (the freeway that bisects the Twin Cities and was placed straight through St. Paul's long-established black neighborhood), or gathering and analyzing architectural artifacts. Then, of course, there were the students, all between nine and twelve years old. I was in some of St. Paul's most diverse schools, working with kids from a wide variety of income levels, backgrounds, and racial and ethnic groups. And then there was the fundraising. I knew what grants were, but I'd never written a grant. Still, I made it work. I taught in schools around the city, working in classrooms several hours a week. At the end of each of my month or six weeks' worth of work with each class, we'd create a special project—a photographic collage of the neighborhood annotated with what we knew about the history of the places in the picture; a map comprised of each student's own student-eye view of their block and its history; or other artifacts that connected "then" and "now."

The PHP (as I called it) was successful. After the project's first year, schools started to call me, and a local business invited me to apply for a significant grant that would have meant much less hustling for funds. Despite these signs pointing to greater stability, though, I realized after eighteen months that I needed a life and a stable salary, so I took a position at a local arts agency. This was back to just plain trouble: the job was so profoundly boring that there were many days that I nearly exploded watching the clock move from 9 to 5. I turned to the contacts I knew in the nonprofit world to ask them what would help me to get a better job; they said a master's degree. A friend had told me I could earn an MA at the University of Minnesota's School of Journalism and Mass Communication (SJMC) in a year. That was perfect: one and done.[1] And I did love history and journalism, so I thought it would be a nice break. I applied to begin the fall quarter of 1989; when I was accepted, I quit my job.

In their introduction to this collection, Elizabeth A. Flynn and Tiffany Bourelle write that individuals sometimes find themselves at "the intersection of agency and fortuitous choice: if the circumstances are right, we begin to learn from the past and trust our intuitions." These moments, they say, are not "solely coincidence or luck but the willingness to act on hunches or trust one's own intuition—to learn from one's experience" (5). My arrival in the SJMC heralded the beginning of many such moments, all of which contributed to what I am suggesting was a shift from "trouble" to an appreciation of "troublesomeness" that, ultimately, led me to move toward the scrappy persona I have described earlier.

When I arrived at the SJMC that fall quarter, I enrolled in the then-required Theories of Communication Studies course. The course was taught by Theodore (Ted) Glasser, a faculty member whose research focused broadly on critical communication studies, then including public journalism and law. Glasser would be at Minnesota for the first ten weeks of the five years I spent in graduate school because he moved to Stanford; however, to my great fortune, his departure wasn't until winter quarter. The first book we read in Ted's class, James Carey's *Communication and Culture*, introduced what I would now call a threshold concept that was as troublesome and powerful as a tsunami for me. Carey writes:

> Reality is brought into existence, is produced, by communication—by, in short, the construction, apprehension, and utilization of symbolic forms. Reality, while not a mere function of symbolic forms, is produced by terministic systems—or by humans who produce such systems—that focus its existence in specific terms. . . . To study communication [therefore] is to examine the actual social process wherein significant symbolic forms are created, apprehended, and used. . . . Models of communication are, then, not merely representations of communication but representations *for* communication: templates that guide, unavailing or not, processes of human interaction, mass and interpersonal. Therefore, to study communication involves examining the construction, apprehension, and use of models of communication themselves—their construction in common sense, art, and science, their historically specific creation and use. (25, 30, 32)

These ideas were electrically energizing for my returning-to-school self. It led me to rethink every assumption I'd made about what language was and what it did. There were, to be sure, elements of this in Dewey's work—in fact, Carey drew enormously on Dewey and aligned himself with the same tradition of American pragmatism with which Dewey was affiliated. (There are also references to Burke in Carey's work, but at the time I didn't know who Burke was so I wouldn't have recognized these. Still, serendipity . . .) There were other books, too, most notably Daniel Czitron's *Media and the American Mind*, that also integrally connected communication with ontologies, ideologies, and orientations. My engagement with these texts contributed to a realization, per Flynn and Bourelle's, that I might be facing an intersection between "agency and fortuitous choice." The ideas I was taking from the texts (as well as discussions with Ted Glasser) were challenging my thinking and leading me to consider the ways in which communication helped to constitute senses of reality encompassing time and space in all sorts of new ways. I quickly realized I actually *liked* thinking about these ideas, and maybe graduate school would be more interesting and useful than I had originally thought it would be, and I should stick around.

My commitment to graduate school via serendipity and the intersection between agency and choice was also fueled by my employment situation. The MA program at the SJMC was a bit of a cash cow—all students were required to have an MA before pursuing PhD study, but my application probably made it clear that I wasn't focused on an academic career. As a result, I'd been accepted without funding. During the first year of my MA program, I worked full-time in the Office of Student Financial Aid administering a program that provided federal financial aid for students to participate in community service learning positions—but I really wanted to teach. For my second year, then, I applied for two TA positions: one in the composition program (which was housed in the English Department) and one in General College (GC), a stand-alone college for students labeled "underprepared" for admission to degree-granting units. I wasn't offered a position in composition, but I was in GC.

Being hired in GC represented probably the most serendipitous moment of my academic career. The seven years I spent there were foundational for my identity as a teacher and a researcher, for my orientation toward what it meant to be a compositionist and a writing program administrator, and for my sense of why advocacy is so important. In the language of this collection, then, I could say that GC was where I began to develop conscious agency; it certainly is where I realized the value of scrappiness. I learned these lessons from Terry Collins, who was the WPA when I was hired but quickly moved to a position as academic administrator for the college. For my first two years in GC, I worked with Terry as a TA. In the third year, my position was converted to a lecturer line, a job I kept through graduate school and for two years following. Through this stretch of the mid-1990s, the University of Minnesota was attempting to raise its standings in the national rankings and the then-president, Nils Hasselmo, made it clear that he didn't think GC (with its mission of working with students labeled "underprepared") would contribute to that effort. Terry, however, was a fierce advocate for the college and for our students—and so I also learned from an incredibly talented mentor about how to work with students and community allies to create a relevant identity for an institution populated by students the university might have preferred to not admit.

My identity was also shaped by the ways in which I learned to teach the so-called "basic writing" courses that GC offered. Terry laid out the guidelines for the first (of two) required classes when I was hired: it should focus on literacy, and it should use a full-length book about a person with a challenging educational experience. Terry provided some sample assignments and syllabi and let the TAs run with our own ideas. After one term, I found Mike Rose's *Lives on the Boundary* (*LOB*), recently published. There, I read this:

> Through all my experiences with people struggling to learn, the one thing that strikes me most is the ease with which we misperceive failed performance and the degree to which this misperception both reflects and reinforces the social order. Class and culture erect boundaries that hinder our

vision . . . and encourage the designation of otherness, difference, deficiency. . . . Some of our basic orientations toward the teaching and testing of literacy contribute to our inability to see. To truly educate in America, then, to reach the full sweep of our citizenry, we need to question received perception, shift continually from the standard lens. [We need to] sit close by as people use language and consider, as we listen, the orientations that limit our field of vision. (205)

Mike Rose's voice in *LOB* (and through every other piece of his writing and research) continues to serve as a model for the ways in which I approach every aspect of my work. There's the amazing reach of Mike's intellect, the careful and rigorous attention to method, all of those things that we value as scholars. All of that can be learned. But the orientation that is reflected in the paragraph I've quoted above—the kindness, patience, and generosity—that's not something that can be learned in graduate courses. Serendipitous moment #2, then: good teaching is also about orienting one's self as a whole person.

I started to learn this by reading *Lives*. But it became even clearer to me when Mike became a real presence, if only over the phone, in my classes from about 1991–93. As it happened, *LOB* resonated with a lot of my students who, remember, had themselves been labeled "underprepared." They also had a lot of questions—about why Mike did one thing or another, about what happened to him, and so on. I had no answers for them, knowing nothing about Mike beyond what was printed on the page. So I decided to call this guy, Mike Rose, to see if he would be willing to answer some of my students' questions by corresponding (in letters, since this was mostly pre-email) with them. Mike wasn't in when I called, but the voice on his machine at UCLA sounded pretty nice, so I decided to leave a message explaining who I was—a graduate instructor at a university 1200 miles away, a person teaching two classes a term to students who hoped to transfer to another college at the university where they could then actually *get* a degree. And hey! Would Mike be interested in answering letters from these folks?

It didn't take long for Mike to call back and explain that while writing letters to more than fifty students wasn't possible, he'd be happy to do a conference call. Terry Collins thought this was a fine idea, too, and went through the then-complicated process of actually getting a telephone (and a speaker box) into a classroom. That term and the following—for two or three years, three times a year—we arranged these calls. Mike listened to my students thoughtfully, carefully, taking them seriously, responding to them in ways that made clear he was honoring their ideas. And he did the same to me, a second- or third-year graduate student who had taught writing for a year or two. As a researcher, the ideas in *LOB* also exponentially expanded the connections I was starting to make between my work as a composition TA in General College and the ideas about communication and reality that I was encountering in the SJMC. The boundaries that were erected by "class and culture" were created in and through communication, and that communication led to designations—like "basic writer," or "illiterate," or "unsuccessful"—that had been applied to GC students. I also empathized with these labels, having spent my own share of time experiencing at least a taste of what it was like being labeled as a screw-up in junior high and high school, and knowing what it was like to be able to escape those labels, too. All of these, I realized through my research and teaching, were situated in ideologies, values, currencies (cultural and financial), times, and spaces. This, it seemed to me, was critically important as we thought about the "standard lens" mentioned in the excerpt from *LOB* that I've included above. From my perspective now, I realize this is a long-established fact in the field, but at the time it felt momentous.

By the middle of my second year at the SJMC, I was deeply invested in thinking about communication as it was manifested in ideas about "good literacy" and, even more specifically, "good writing" and loving my job at General College. I was about to finish my thesis on the perceived threat of comic books to children in the 1950s.[2] I needed to stay for a PhD to keep my job in General College, and I wanted to stay for a PhD because I was becoming ever-more invested in research. And again, resilience, serendipity, and scrappiness came together. By this point, I'd started enrolling in graduate composition courses in the English Department, where Chris Anson was then a faculty member. My graduate advisor, Hazel Dicken-Garcia, was enormously supportive of the uncharted territory I was exploring as I tried to bring together communication studies, historiography, literacy studies, and composition. When I talked to her about staying on for a PhD, I also said that I really wanted to focus on education as a form of communication. I also let her know I wanted to focus on composition, rather than journalism and mass communication—and how could I do that? I put the same question to Chris and, with his help and Hazel's support, carved a path that would help me bring communication, composition, historiography, and American Studies (my other two areas of focus in graduate school), together. For my dissertation, I would look at the historical formation of ideas about "good literacy" in American schooling. This shift, from mid-twentieth-century popular culture to nineteenth and twentieth century American intellectual culture, was profoundly affected by three books: Warren Susman's *Culture as History*, David W. Noble's *The End of American History*, and Benedict Anderson's *Imagined Communities*.

From Susman:

> One of the more striking observed results of the structural changes in the social order [in the 1920s] was that a larger proportion of it was increasingly engaged in professionals seeking to understand it, with a special calling to "know" the world as writers, artists, intellectuals, journalists, scientists, social scientists, philosophers, teachers.... The great fear that runs through much of the writing of the 1920s and 1930s is whether any great industrial and democratic mass society can maintain a significant level of civilization, and whether mass education and mass communication will allow any civilization to survive. (107)

From Noble:

> Implicit in our common usage of the term, America, is a profound commitment to isolating our national culture.... American historians from the Puritans in the 1630s through the writings of Charles Beard in the 1930s have not used a concept that combines political independence with cultural interdependence to define our national identity. They have thought and written as if the United States was absolutely independent, standing apart in its uniqueness from the rest of human experience.... The rhetorical ritual of the American jeremiad as described by [Sacvan] Bercovitch provided the structure for the narratives of [Frederick Jackson] Turner and Beard, as it had for the most influential historians of the nineteenth century. (7, 10)

And from Anderson:

> [A nation] is an imagined political community—and imagined as both inherently limited and sovereign. It is *imagined* because the members of even the smallest nation will never know most of their fellow-members, meet them, or even hear of them, yet in the minds of each lives the image of their communion.... Communities are to be distinguished, not by their falsity/genuineness, but by the style in which they are imagined. (6)

Through these texts and the intellectual (and moral) support of Hazel and Chris, I started to articulate a big picture. From them, I took the idea that historical narratives contributed to a sense of national identity (through their portrayal of the past) formed in the midst of their creators' understandings of the nation, and especially of threats to that idea of the nation as these were reflected in the American jeremiad that Bercovitch described and the African American jeremiad as described by David Howard-Pitney (who finished his PhD at Minnesota a few years before I arrived). And while none of these authors directly addressed conceptualizations of literacy as a critical part of that historical narrative, it certainly seemed important—after all, ideas about what "good literacy" was formed the foundation and backbone of American schooling, the institution through which students would become enculturated into those narratives about American identity.

Over the next three years, I finished my coursework, blending communication studies theory and methods, composition, and American Studies/historiography, and wrote that dissertation on historical constructions of public literacy.[3] With this research, I had to balance on many lines. I was among the first few students in the history of the SJMC, a school founded and deeply invested in industry-driven research, to complete a dissertation based in cultural studies and cultural theory. As with any dissertation, I also had to demonstrate mastery of the field's methods, other theories, and approaches. I knew I wanted to go on the market in composition, not communication, so I had to make connections between my research and the interests of compositionists. The weekend before I defended I remember sitting on a bench in my kitchen, my two-year-old daughter running around the house, grading the sixty student papers I had just gotten in because I was determined to *not* have grading waiting for me after my defense. At this point, my relationship to struggle and troublesome knowledge felt fundamentally reoriented. While I had swum upstream against some dominant thinking in my home department (i.e., I was pushing on ideas of "mass communication" with my focus on education and literacy; I was teaching writing in another college), I encountered incredibly supportive faculty members. I was working like crazy, but this work was deeply satisfying, if all-consuming, and I was surrounded by supportive and provocative teaching mentors and colleagues in Terry Collins and Geoff Sirc. And I had the freedom and intellectual resources to approach troublesomeness, challenge, and difficulty in ways I never could have imagined as, for instance, I departed high school for college fifteen years before. The results of these experiences—defending my dissertation, moving a year later to a tenure-track position—reflected the "convergences of choice, change, and serendipity" that Flynn and Bourelle describe in their introduction to this collection (118). My arrival in graduate school was one kind of risk (for me, for the SJMC); my progress through it was enabled by others like Hazel Dicken-Garcia, Terry Collins, Chris Anson, Geoff Sirc, and others with whom I worked in my home department, the composition program, and GC. It was also fostered by what I took to be composition's fundamental commitments to students (initially, students like me; later, students like the ones I was working with) and their abilities.

•

As I reflect back on the experiences I've written about here, I can see both how my "scrappiness" and the ability and to make something *of* those scraps has come from them. I think of graduate school as a time where I was given an incredible gift by my advisor and mentors: the intellectual freedom to piece together pieces into a whole that isn't quite like anyone else's. What I've taken from this gift can, I think, can be seen in the work I've done as a teacher and a writing program director, a role I've occupied in one form or another for over twenty years. I left General College in 1997; after three years in a tenure-line job that wasn't the right fit for me (nor I for it), I was hired as the director of first-year writing at Eastern Michigan University. Some of the students there had experiences similar to those of the students I taught at GC—they had been labeled "underprepared" or "underperforming." But they had made it to this comprehensive regional university in the outer-outer ring of the Detroit area, ready to do something. And many of the faculty who taught them in our first-year classes—a group consisting largely of adjuncts who were paid $3500 a class—were ready to jump in and create a writing program that provided space and support for these students to develop and demonstrate their amazing intelligence.

I was privileged to spend ten years at EMU, and even more privileged to spend the first five of those working with Heidi Estrem, who was hired as assistant director of first-year writing at the same time I was as director. To chronicle the moments where Heidi and I (along with our colleagues) were provided the opportunity to exercise the collective scrappiness that comes from working with an amazing and creative group at an underfunded institution in a one-industry state in economic decline would require an entire book. I'll point to just one, though, that illustrates "the intersection between agency and fortuitous choice" that comes together in serendipitous moments. During our first semester at EMU, Heidi and I were in a meeting, talking with other first-year writing instructors about the tremendous work that their students were doing in our second-semester research writing course. Since EMU was deeply invested in community connections (and we were deeply committed to situating writing in real contexts), students in that course grounded their research in a community site, gathering preliminary observations in order to develop research questions that they then pursued through ethnographic-style and/or multigenre research efforts—an approach that one of our colleagues, Clarinda Flannery, had initiated just before we arrived. The student projects that faculty were describing sounded simply spectacular. One of our colleagues asked, "How can other people see these? They can't just go into a drawer."

From this question, the Celebration of Student Writing—an event started at EMU and now replicated at hundreds of campuses around the country—was born. Why not, we thought, have students create a project based on their research work, then display these in the ballroom of EMU's student union so that the entire university could see them? Why not invite the provost and ask him to deliver opening remarks, then bring in every other administrator and faculty member we could lay our hands on for the event? Why not? Because we'd never done it. Because we had no idea what students would actually create, because we had no idea who would attend, if anyone, or what would happen. Because at the time, we were both untenured, and this seemed like a high-exposure project, *but* our department head, Russ Larson, was enormously supportive, and the acting provost at the time gave us $300 for chips, salsa, and lemonade (the cheapest items available from catering, and ones that became the traditional fare of the CSW), so full speed ahead. Because of my own aversion to labels, prizes, or anything else that declared one person's work better or smarter than another's, there would be no awards at the CSW; if an instructor decided their class was going to participate, *everyone* in the class participated. And for the first few years, every participant received a certificate (until everyone agreed that signing that many hundreds of certificates was, perhaps, too much work).[4]

Though it's been fifteen years since the first Celebration at EMU, I still remember standing in that ballroom with Heidi, wondering whether this whole thing would amount to a giant and very public disaster as we waited for the first class to bring whatever it was that they created for that first event. And as they did, taping whatever it was they had created to the walls, we realized that it would be *great*. Whatever those things were—and that, I don't remember—we realized that they truly were engaging representations of what students *could* write, what they *had* learned (not what they hadn't)—regardless of whatever labels had been affixed to them in their previous schooling or would be attached to them subsequently. We (through their instructors) had asked them to take a risk, just as all of us in the first-year writing program had taken a risk in creating the CSW to begin with—and through the collective and determined scrappiness of all of us, scrappiness that involved working strategically and tactically from what we knew was a really strong curriculum being implemented by a really creative group of underpaid teachers, it paid off. The CSW became a signature program for EMU; by now, it's been replicated and/or adapted by many (hundreds?) of campuses around the country.

While I left EMU in 2010, the lessons that I took from there about the importance of scrappiness, inserting programmatic toes into institutional cracks, and collaboration became integral to my work as a writing program director. At UC Santa Barbara, where the director is also the department chair, it helped me learn to work with another spectacular group of faculty members—this time, happily, everyone employed full-time, with salary, benefits, and opportunities for advancement—to contribute to a writing program that was outstanding when I arrived and extended its reach in all sorts of ways in the five years I served as director. They're also lessons I've taken with me as I've moved from that position as director of UCSB's writing program to a position as associate dean of undergraduate education, where part of my responsibilities involves adapting the strategies that come with scrappiness and toe-inserting to working with teaching, learning, and assessment across campus. In the job, I've found that my experiences have led me to an orientation that seeks out and remains open to serendipity. Encounters and collaborations with allies, mentors, and friends seem to lead to unimagined results.

•

Both personally and intellectually, I feel a pull to deconstruct the narrative I've just laid out. The intellectual trajectory it describes does, in retrospect, constitute some of the most important thresholds and threshold concepts in my intellectual development as a composition researcher and teacher. At the same time, it's pretty tidy. There were bumps, moments of troublesomeness that probably contribute to other pieces of my identity and my approach to teaching, research, and working with people in and through writing programs and undergraduate studies more broadly. At the same time, it does highlight some of the moments of what I still consider an exceptionally serendipitous journey. Through this journey, I've continued to engage with what I describe in the introduction to this chapter as "troublesome knowledge"; however, my orientation to that knowledge has shifted considerably. Initially, it was simply "troublesome"—things didn't work out as I wanted them to. But through the moments I've described here—moments that were facilitated by mentors who saw something and gave me the intellectual, moral, and sometimes emotional support I needed to figure out if those somethings really *were* something—I've been able to develop a deep appreciation for troublesomeness and troublesome knowledge that has led me to the scrappy orientation I mention earlier. Those moments, too, are integral to my own identity—I'm not sure it's even possible for them to leave me, because they are part of who I am.

I'll end with another story, this one a moment from a 2009 symposium convened in honor of Hazel Dicken-Garcia's retirement from the SJMC. I was invited to speak, along with a handful of Hazel's other former advisees. They all held terrific positions in journalism and mass communication; not only was I the only person there who was in writing studies, but I'm also the *only* graduate student in the more than sixty-year history of the SJMC to focus on education, much less composition. At a dinner following the event, I was seated next to a faculty member who had been the director of the SJMC during my time there, a man who taught the required quantitative research methods seminar—a class in which I did not do very well. He said to me, "Linda, I had no idea what you were doing while you were here, but you seemed to have had fun and I guess it worked out for you." Indeed, I think that faculty member had it about right. At the beginning of the period I describe here, I didn't really know what I was doing. I'm clearly a believer in troublesome knowledge and the power of intellectual struggle and am not sure it's healthy or productive for any entering graduate student to *really* know what she wants to do upon arrival (just as research by Sommers and Saltz as well as Reiff and Bawarshi suggests that undergraduate students need to question their way into postsecondary learning); at the same time, I certainly wouldn't want to present my own story as a model for others, because I truly believe we all find the ways that are best for and open to us. For myself, I can say that thanks to the serendipitous moments and people I describe here (along with others), I know the experience of moving from trouble to troublesome knowledge in its best sense. I appreciate the ways in which these moments of serendipity helped me to muck through troublesome moments and thinking and have provided me with a deep appreciation of troublesome knowledge that remains at the core of my identities as a researcher, teacher, and program director.

NOTES

1. This was incorrect. Two years, master's thesis . . .
2. . . . a reader-response study of letters from fans to the publisher of E. C. Comics (*The Vault of Horror, The Crypt of Terror, A Haunt of Fears*) situated in the context of comic book censorship in the mid-1950s. After E. C. Comics was singled out during Congressional hearings on comic books in 1954, the publisher decided to shift his attention to a new venture. That's when William M. Gaines started *Mad* magazine, which I had devoured through childhood and which remains an important contributing factor to my outlook on life. I interviewed Gaines as part of the research for my MA thesis, probably the funniest, most fun, and most engaging interview I've ever conducted. Of course, I was interviewing a rock star, so my perceptions may have been skewed.

3. Specifically, I examined constructions of public literacy in two chapters in each of eight history textbooks published during the Progressive Era: one chapter in each of the eight books focusing on the Civil War, one on the Spanish-American War. Writing my dissertation countered the experience of my MA project: a long slog through a fascinating subject, but examined in sometimes painful detail.

4. I am familiar with the argument that not everyone should get a trophy, not everyone gets to win, etc. I also realize that in academe, we work in a system that is inherently hierarchical, where some are more privileged than others. I don't like this, and I don't buy the argument. Sometimes, everybody *does* get to be recognized.

WORKS CITED

Adler-Kassner, Linda. *The Activist WPA*. Logan: Utah State UP, 2008. Print.

Adler-Kassner, Linda, and John Majewski. "Extending the Invitation: Threshold Concepts, Professional Development, and Outreach." Adler-Kassner and Wardle 186–202.

Adler-Kassner, Linda, and Elizabeth Wardle. *Naming What We Know: Threshold Concepts of Writing Studies*. Logan: Utah State UP, 2015. Print.

Anderson, Benedict. *Imagined Communities*. London: Verso, 1991. Print.

Carey, James. *Communication and Culture*. Boston: Unwin and Hyman, 1989. Print.

Czitrom, Daniel. *Media and the American Mind*. Chapel Hill: U of North Carolina P, 1982.

Dewey, John. *Democracy and Education*. New York: Macmillan, 1916. Print.

Howard-Pitney, David. *The Afro-American Jeremiad*. Philadelphia: Temple UP, 1983. Print.

Meyer, Jan, and Ray Land. *Overcoming Barriers to Student Understanding: Threshold Concepts and Troublesome Knowledge*. New York: Routledge, 2006. Print.

———. "Threshold Concepts and Troublesome Knowledge: An Introduction." Meyer and Land 3–18.

Noble, David W. *The End of American History: Democracy, Capitalism, and the Metaphor of Two Worlds in Anglo-American Historical Writing, 1880–1980*. Minneapolis: U of Minnesota P, 1985. Print.

Perkins, David. "Constructivism and Troublesome Knowledge." Meyer and Land 19–32.

Reiff, Mary Jo, and Anis Bawarski. "Tracing Discursive Resources: How Students Use Print Knowledge to Negotiate New Contexts in First Year Composition." *Written Communication* 28.3 (July 2011): 312–27.

Rose, Mike. *Lives on the Boundary*. New York: Penguin, 1989. Print.

Sommers, Nancy, and Laura Saltz. "The Novice as Expert: Writing the Freshman Year." *College Composition and Communication* 56.1 (September 2004): 124–49.

Susman, Warren. *Culture as History: The Transformation of American Society in the Twentieth Century*. New York: Pantheon, 1984. Print.

Timmermans, Julie. "Changing Our Minds: The Developmental Potential of Threshold Concepts." Ed. Jan Meyer, Ray Land, and Carolyn Baillie. *Threshold Concepts and Transformational Learning*. Rotterdam: Sense Publishers, 2010. 3–19. Print.

CHAPTER 8

Word by Word, Bead by Bead
Making a Scholarly Life

MALEA POWELL

> SLOW WORK / WE DO THIS / WORD BY WORD / EACH WORD A STORY / EVERY STORY BEADED / WITH WORDS
> —Kim Shuck, "DHLA:NUWA"

This is a story.

This story is a making, a tracing of relations, a beadwork of choices, of words, stitched around and through an accumulation of stories, anchored with poetry,[1] shot through with chance. If you could see what I am making in beads instead of words, you'd see a peyote-stitched[2] making—a three-dimensional tree rising against a landscape of rivers, fields, wildflowers, and sky. In North American indigenous communities, peyote stitch is a practice of making commonly used to bead around objects—fan handles, hair sticks, lighters, shakers—or to create stand-alone sculptures like this one. To begin, you create a row of beads loose enough so the thread is tight but there's about half-a-bead's worth of space between each bead on the string. For this making, I'm holding the thread of that first row taught between the fingers of my left hand. The second row is created by adding a new bead to the thread and then running the needle through one of the beads in that first row. If I were beading around something, that would be the second bead in that first row; because I'm going stand-alone, I'll grab the next to last bead on the thread, now holding the last bead in that row between my fingers. Then I'll add a new bead and go through the fourth bead in that first row, and will continue in this fashion until I get to the end of the first row when I'll move down again to bead back across—right to left, left to right, adding a new bead and going back through a bead from the previous row. Eventually I'll go back to that first row and bead in the other direction—the "first" row always becomes the middle of the finished piece. In this way, the entire piece of beadwork is composed by weaving relationships between the previous row and the new one—a practice that creates a web of relations that leaves both the first and the last row open to an infinite possibility of future makings. I offer these words here, then, as beads in a new making constellated through place, space, story, relatives, and chance—accumulations that have led me to particular moments of choice in my (scholarly) life.

When I began preparing the thread for this making,[3] I searched through boxes of old photographs looking for a specific picture of me I hold in my memory: age four, my small girl's face dominated by big brown eyes, I am dressed in overalls, a T-shirt, a red bandana on my head, standing in my great-grampa's soybean field. In the photo, the beans are as tall as I am, which is why my great-grampa wanted to take the picture. It was a good year for beans, and he wanted to mark it the way he would mark many other things—with a photo taken on his prized 35 mm camera.[4] But I'm getting a little ahead of myself here, starting a pattern in greens and blue before I've laid down the field of earth upon which this larger story is balanced.

This is how it goes. I grew up at 975 West 400 South, Grant County, Sims Township, Indiana. Located in the middle of the eastern edge of what had once been the Big Miami Reserve.[5] The land there continuously proved up evidence of its centuries-old occupation by Miamis in the form of arrowheads and potsherds and grinding stones. I lived on a small farm in the middle of a cornfield in a house built around the turn of the century for Elsie, the local "old maid" schoolteacher, by her father who finally resigned himself to the fact that Elsie would never marry. It's pretty clear from the stories I've heard about Elsie that she didn't really have much use for men, if you know what I mean, and that she was a fine neighbor to my great-grandparents, Russell and Dorothy Baker,[6] who lived just across the road.

Most of my memories of childhood are outdoors, growing up on the land in close relationship to seasons and weather and crops and stock and chores. I went to school with kids from town—"walkers," we called them because they walked home from school—and envied many components of what I imagined to be their lives. But I also went to school with a lot of kids who seemed to be just like me. Farm kids who learned early how to weed gardens and pick vegetables and put them up in ball jars or in the deep freeze, who learned about killing and butchering pigs and chickens and cows kept on the farm expressly for such purposes, who learned to work in the kitchen even before they were old enough for school, who learned to hunt and fish and forage as well. Kids who generally understood the natural world as a place of sustenance, work, adventure, danger, and joy.

Late in the 1960s, the racial violence in towns all around us in north-central Indiana had my mother and step-father worried. In 1967, a fight broke out between one hundred black and white students at Southside High School in Muncie. In August of '68, the lumber yard in Marion[7] was said to have been burned down by the Black Panthers, the one in Swayzee[8] rumored to have been burned by the Klan[9] because the owner was known to sell to blacks. After that, I overheard some of the old folks in the community talking about the lynching in Marion back in 1930, remembering just who showed up in that infamous photo.[10] Their stories wove genealogies of white-black racial violence into my imagined landscape of the other histories in that place.

So I should tell you—I'm not very good at peyote stitch. It's one of those beadwork practices that eluded me for many years, and I still feel a little awkward doing it. I'm not good enough to just go along and bead in the patterns without drawing them out on paper first, then carefully accounting for each bead. In beginning to craft the pattern above, I'm making the same mistakes with words that I usually make with beads. So, I'm gonna tear out some beads and go back to Elsie's, since that's the way I want the pattern to work. At least for the moment, that's the choice I'll make.

So, I grew up in Elsie's house across the road from my paternal great-grandparents. Their farm—established in 1921 and named, hand-lettered in white on the big red barn, "The Little Ideal Farm"—had cows, pigs, chickens, a two-acre truck patch, and a house garden in addition to the "regular" acreage of corn and soybeans from which they made their living. And a big golden dog of decidedly mixed ancestry named "Cookie." The chickens, though, are the point in this part of the story. Because there are a *lot* of chicken stories in my past—stories about hatchets and cleavers and scrub buckets full of Tide—I probably need to tell you now that when I think about an account of my scholarly life focused on resilience, agency, relationships, and chance, I'm just as likely to think about chickens as beadwork or poems or graduate school. They're all related in my mind and in the things I've chosen to make as an intellectual.

My great-grampa Russell wrote in a diary every day as he sat in his chair after supper. Their house had a real bookcase—a fancy one with glass doors—full of books by folks like Homer and Shakespeare, Faulkner and Harper Lee. My great-great-grampa Lemuel Shull had been a schoolteacher, had taught in little one-roomed schoolhouses in Indiana and Oklahoma, and his books were in Latin and Greek and French and German as well as English, and were kept in a box in the cedar closet—exciting fodder for a young, curious girl. But I'll spare you the strange articulations of farmer/Native/intellectual that were fostered in their house and stay focused, instead, on the farm in the spring, because spring is when the baby chicks would arrive in the mail.

My great-gramma Dorothy sold eggs for her bread-and-butter money, and every year we'd butcher a bunch of retired "layers" to stock our freezers. So she ordered chicks early in the spring each year, and they'd arrive via the U.S. postal service. In the weeks before they came, we had to mow the south lot (where the baby chicks lived until they were big enough to be moved in with the hens), clean out the brooder house, move in the brooder stove, and make sure it still worked (this inevitably required several trips to the barn, the tool shed, and town, and was the beginnings of my own extensive education in cussing "a blue streak"). After what seemed like a million preparations, the heralded day arrived, and we'd drive to the post office to pick up the chicks—not our own tiny post office in the nearby 200-souls-and-no-stoplights town of Sims but the "big" post office in Swayzee, the town with the stop light and the school, just three miles away.

Now, baby chicks are, well, baby chicks. They're fluffy and soft and seem pretty sweet even if they do make a lot of noise. They're vulnerable. They need a brooder stove—ours looked like a big canvas tent on a wide metal base—to keep warm. And they need to be protected from the plentitude of foxes and the occasional coyote who lived in Russell's woods—a patch of hardwoods at the corner of their forty acres where Russell frequently hunted. So for the first couple of weeks after the chicks arrived, someone had to sleep in the brooder house to make sure the stove stayed lit and to chase away the critters. I don't know what the setup was when my great-grampa slept out there, but I know how it worked when my great-gramma did because she frequently invited me to join her.

On those nights, I'd wander across the road at dusk in my nightgown. We'd shift the straw bales around to form a barrier between us and the chicks, then she'd lay down an old wool blanket and a hand-pieced quilt for us to lie on. I'd bring my pillow and "our" book, *Raggedy Ann Stories*, and she'd bring crackers (graham or saltines), a flashlight, and a shotgun. She'd read to me until I fell asleep. Sometimes I'd wake to her yelling "get out of here now" at some critter bent on a baby-chick dinner as she stood just outside, shotgun held loosely in her hands. Sometimes it was her own form of cussing—"jumping Jehoshaphat's" being about the worst of it—as she tinkered with the stove. And sometimes I'd simply wake in the deep, cool dark of the night and want to go home. She'd stand outside the little wooden shack with that shotgun in the crook of her arm and watch me walk all the way to my front door. I'd wink the light at her once I got inside. We had a pretty similar going-home ritual for the next thirty-plus years—I'd head for wherever I called home, and she'd wait for me to signal my safe arrival (through a phone call) before she relaxed her vigilance. She lived to be ninety-four, and when she died, three years after my mother's death, I mourned the absence of that vigilance.

There are a couple of choices to make here in terms of how the pattern plays out. I could construct a beadwork story-sculpture for how I became the kind of scholar I am, one that starts with my telling of this "brooder house story" back when I was a grad student, enrolled in a summer seminar on feminism and rhetoric. I only vaguely remember the paper where I used this story to make a point, I suppose, about feminism or strong women or learning from elders. What I remember more clearly are the suspicions the story raised among my classmates. Some of them flat-out didn't believe anything like that could have happened to someone my age because "no one lived like that" within my lifetime. Others were more troubled by what they perceived as competing identity claims. Was I, they queried, a Native scholar now laying claim to a settler-colonial class narrative as well? Was I suddenly "writing as" a rural woman? Even in the midst of their mid-90s postmodern embrace of the multiplicity of subjectivities, my "outing" of a piece of my past that pointed to what they saw as a "non-Native" experience was troubling, perplexing even. They encouraged revisions of the story that emphasized the "Native-ness" of this experience with my decidedly Euro-American great-grandparents. Maybe, they suggested, I should mention that these were the folks who had taken in my mixed-blood grandmother after she had run away from boarding school—White's Institute[11]—and eventually adopted her. That would make it clear how I was "maintaining" a Native subject position within this story.

That was one of my first introductions to the prison house of "writing as," and to some of the well-intentioned ways in which we categorize one another and use writing as an ending, not as a beginning. It was also one of the all-too-frequent reminders of the ways that even highly educated "liberal" folks thought of "Native" as a single, stable identity that couldn't at all overlap with any kind of dominant culture experiences in order to be "real." I wish that I could say that this kind of categorizing doesn't happen anymore—that it was a symptom of a kind of anxiety around authenticity and postmodernity—but it still happens all-too-frequently to me. So before I'm sidetracked into a genuine rant about settler-colonial attachments to authenticity, I want to go back, turn left instead of right after flipping that porch light switch and make a different choice.

The story-row of beads here also recalls a difficult choice, one that could become a different kind of tangled mess. The words themselves are old ones written for an assignment in my very first college writing class at Indiana University at Kokomo, taken with Dave Gaskill in 1989. I was a twenty-seven-year-old single mother. The room we met in overlooked Wildcat Creek[12] as it wound its way along the edge of campus. The assignment: to write about a moment when we made an important decision in our lives and to include enough detail that readers would feel like they were there.

Richardson, TX, 1981, an anonymous 2-bedroom apartment on Belt Line Road just a 15 minute walk from my job as a quality control clerk at Blue Cross/Blue Shield.

I'm standing in the only bathroom in our apartment getting ready for work. I live with 6 other people but I'm the only one who works a full-time day job. My husband (Ed) works as a cook at Red Lobster at night, and one of our roommates (Rod) periodically works construction. The rest of them are construction day-laborers who wait on street corners and parking lots each morning for work. Some days it feels like I'm the only one working to get ahead, to make something of myself, to be somebody. They all work to use. They're junkies—heroin, crystal meth, speed. They're always high. Always.

I'm looking in the mirror, straightening by bleach-blonde hair, checking for roots. I finish and start to put on makeup. I lean in close to the mirror and concentrate on my eyeliner. I'm startled by pounding on the door. "Get the fuck out of there now. I'm gonna fucking puke." I open the door and slide past Rod who rushes in and does, in fact, throw up. Not in the toilet where he could flush it away but in the tub. He doesn't clean it up. He staggers back to his bedroom instead mumbling, "too much fuckin booze & 'ludes last night . . . sorry."

I walk back into the bathroom, start the shower to clear the tub, shut and lock the door, get out my eye-shadow and lean back into the mirror. I finish my makeup, turn off the shower, and do one last check into the mirror. I'm staring at myself in a fairly objective way. Attractive but tired looking. I'm always tired. Everyone else in the apartment parties until 3 or 4 in the morning while I try to go to bed by midnight at the latest. Well, we don't actually have a bed, but we do have a pallet of blankets on the floor that I head for every night. I usually lock the door. I'd rather take the off-chance that Ed will make it to our bedroom and pound on the door to be let in than what can happen if I leave the door unlocked. I'm thinking about locked doors, how I'm always locking myself into rooms in this apartment, when it comes to me.

"I can't do this anymore." I actually say it out loud. I repeat it. "I fucking can't do this anymore." I keep saying it as I leave the apartment, walk down the street. I start to get angrier as I get closer to work. I stop saying it out loud once I'm in the parking lot and other people I work with might hear me. But I'm thinking it so vehemently that the guard at the door where we swipe our security badges asks me if I'm ok. I say, "Yes," but he doesn't look like he believes it. I'm usually so cheerful, I know. I usually flirt a little. Today, I just can't.

There are all sorts of things I could say in this paper right now. All sorts of explanations and reasons. But what I did was on the way home from work, I went to the bank and took all the money out of our account and moved it to a new account in my name only. Then I went to an apartment complex closer to my work and put a deposit down on an apartment, just in my name, with a lease starting in two weeks—the first of the month. My salary would barely cover it. I didn't care. I didn't tell anyone that I was moving. I just moved one Saturday when they were all up at the lake getting high. One of my friends from work helped me. I left a note. A lot of things happened after that. Some of them good, some of them bad. But when I think about important life decisions and why I made them, I always think of that moment in the bathroom mirror, the steam from the shower not really clearing the smell of Rod's vomit in the tub. I always think of what could have happened if I hadn't left. Who I'd be. (Powell)

A lot of things happened in the eight years between that moment in the mirror and the moment when I decided to quit my very good job working as a project engineer at Westinghouse in San Antonio in order to come home to go to college. Other men, other women, the birth of my daughter. Good decisions. Bad decisions. Chance conversations with my grandfather before he walked on that started to unravel the puzzle of who we were as mixed, Native people. Choices. Coming home for the birth of my daughter—a decision that certainly rivaled the mirror moment for drama and danger. Risks. An attempt to reconcile with my biological father. But in the moment in that class when I decided to tell the "mirror" story, I took a chance that was also a beginning, a row of beads central to what I'm making here. I want to emphasize, though, that neither the moment in the bathroom in Texas, nor the moment in that classroom at IUK were "bootstraps" moments. The first came out of sheer exhaustion and revulsion, the second out of simply not being savvy enough as a student to be coy about my past in a class assignment. These weren't great shining turning points after which I triumphed. These were moments of chance that have become teachings in how easily the smallest decisions can accumulate, teachings to be mindful of the positive *and* negative effects of my own actions. Teachings I'm still taking[13] about the ways in which my actions are always related to other humans and other consequences for those humans. But in that classroom on the banks of the Wildcat, I also learned that I had stories to tell, that my classmates also had stories to tell, and that all of those stories mattered.

Next row. This one starts to twist itself out into separate branches—some reaching toward the future, others drooping down toward the roots of the past. One of the things I love about beadwork is that, if you're lucky, you're frequently making things in the company of other makers. Sitting at a table, gathered on couches in a living room, under a shelter at a powwow, you work for a while and talk for a while and talk while you work and work while you talk. Stories come out of the beads and want to be told, so you tell them. My time in those circles has also taught me that stories come out of places too, and those stories need to be told, heard, beaded, held. There are too many stories like that from my time at Miami University in Oxford, Ohio. The place itself has some powerful stories to tell—most of which won't fit into this making. Stories about the formation of the University itself. Stories about the relationship between the University and the two Miami tribes—the Miami Tribe of Oklahoma and the Miami Nation of Indians of Indiana, Inc.[14] Stories about the mascot controversy at the University.[15] Stories about driving home to visit my family on roads and highways that traced the path of Mad Anthony Wayne's march to Ft. Recovery, to the site of the Battle of Fallen Timbers, and to Kekionga (Ft. Wayne) during the Indian Wars of the late eighteenth century. Too many stories. And the tree here has too many branches of family, history, ancestors, colonialism. If I try to outline all of the branches, the beaded structure will collapse under the weight of them

The choice I want to make here, then, is to offer a story I didn't know until years after I left Oxford. One that happened in a place about 192 miles east and north of Oxford in a place called Coshocton, Ohio.[16] A place where two story strands come together, weave themselves around each other and form a branch. In 1816, Henrietta Howells (born 1783 in Breconshire, Wales) and her husband Thomas J. Powell (born 1787 in Lower Staffordshire, England) gave birth to Joseph Powell in London. The family immigrated to Coshocton, Ohio, where Joseph married Margaret Leighninger (born 1819 in White Eyes township, Ohio).[17] Margaret's parents were George Leighninger (born 1793 in York,

Pennsylvania) and Anna Mary P. Wolfe (born 1791 in Cumberland, Pennsylvania). Joseph and Margaret's son, Lewis Powell, was born in 1850 in Converse, Indiana.[18] Lewis married Mary Etta Bealle (born 1857 in Amboy, Indiana) and their son Joseph A. Powell was born in 1889 (in Converse). Joseph—"Big Joe," as he would be called by the time I came along—married Maude Larrison. By the time of her death in 1916, three children—including my paternal grandfather Floyd G. Powell—had been born. Big Joe married Florence Yoars in 1918. I can remember attending their fiftieth wedding anniversary party when I was about six years old. At any rate, Floyd married Audrey Speece Baker—the adopted daughter of Russell and Dorothy Baker who'd spent almost her entire childhood (age two to sixteen) in orphanages and boarding schools. They had three children—the middle one was my father.

So far this feels like just the standard genealogy chart, arranged to connect me directly back to ancestors in England and Wales. But the beads here aren't lettered; instead, they're arranged to indicate ancestral roots following that old familiar settle-colonial pathway from east to west, movement marked by settlement in particular places in that geographical space historians call the Old Northwest Territories or "the middle ground."[19] These roots open this beaded landscape to yet another set of stories. In 1778, as part of a treaty provision promising them their own state, Lenape peoples[20] who had been living around Fort Pitt in Western Pennsylvania agreed to serve as guides for Americans moving through the Ohio Country in order to undermine British and Native forces gathered around Detroit. The Lenape leader *Koquethagechton*, White Eyes (sometimes also called Capt. Grey Eyes), was the main guide and negotiator for that trip.[21] By 1777, many of the Lenapes not involved in the militia trip had moved to the Muskingum River Valley in what is now eastern Ohio. The Muskingum River is a meeting place for the Tuscarawas and Walhonding Rivers, the lands there once home to Moundbuilders. Lenapes built a village there—*Goschachgunk*[22]—where sixty to eighty families lived until the village was destroyed by Colonel Daniel Broadhead in 1781. In 1800, white settlers began to arrive in large enough numbers to form a town near where the village had been. First called Tuscarawas, then Coshocton (1811), it lies in White Eyes township, established 1823.

See how this story is getting out of hand? How the beads trail down from the branches in disarray? Let's pull them back up and anchor them down more firmly. My great-great-great-great grandmother, Anna Wolfe Leighninger, is the thread that binds this all together. Johan P. Wolfe, Anna Waggoner Wolfe, and little two-year-old Anna Wolfe were among the early settlers who moved to Ohio in 1799. Little Anna grew up watching the Ohio Country in the Northwest Territories become the settler-colonial state of Ohio instead of the promised Lenape state.[23] She watched everything change. She took a husband there (1817), and she died there (1889), and in between she sometimes lived in Oxford, where she was rumored to have relatives, a place whose indigenous inhabitants were still sizably present during her time there (1830–40). At this point, it seems, I've beaded this tree limb down into the ground—the needle sunk deep beneath the buckskin backing and into my own flesh. This, too, is a choice—a deliberate attempt to mark the implications of my colonial and indigenous ancestors. A moment of deliberate agency amidst the long story of the colonization of the Americas.

So there I was in Oxford in 1996, desperately trying to make peace with an institution built on lands from which Miamis had been removed 150 years earlier, only fourteen miles north of Fort Hamilton—one of the primary gathering points for that removal. I was at the beginning of the third year of my doctoral work, studying for my comprehensive exams and working as assistant composition program director when my mother died.[24]

Growing up, my mother was presented to me through other people's eyes in a myriad of ways. The nice girl from the city who married the wealthy farmer's bad-boy son. The uppity city girl who then divorced that same bad boy. In 1967. When no-fault divorce didn't exist, when *no one* decent got divorced. Ever. Moved out? Sure. Divorced? Never. Divorce was for those who had no morals. Who weren't good Christians. In my mother's mind, divorce was the only answer to a husband who'd "stepped out" with a sixteen-year-old girl, even though she had a small child at home and another on the way. In my mind, this is one of my mother's most important qualities—she followed her own sense of right and justice. Over the years, she gathered a highly diverse, highly talented group of friends—folks of color, LBGTQ folks, artists, makers, writers, risk-takers. Many of whom attended her funeral and gave their own tributes to her impact on their lives. They marked her as "odd" in our small, rural community. But she'd marked them as well, as her relations.

When she died I had to (eventually) face one of the central truths of my story as a scholar—that I'd been doing much of it for her. To lend credence to the way she had lived her life, to her father's decision to pass for much of his life. To lend respectability to our family stories. To do what hadn't been available to her—go to college, get a degree, get another degree, get another degree, be a poet, a writer, an artist, an intellectual. So she died, we mourned. I mourned. I started reading for my comps. If I could suspend a beaded sky above this making, it would be gray beads, somber and matte, with just the barest glimpse of the blue sky and the rainbow bridge that opened during her wake.

So, it's January 1997. I'm sitting in a coffeehouse on High Street, reading and taking notes. Drinking too much coffee. Going outside to smoke. Nodding and smiling and scowling and generally trying to look like what I think an edgy intellectual might look like. Faded 501s with black thermal underwear showing through the rips in the knees and at the pockets, scuffed Harley-Davidson screamin' eagle harness boots, black leather classic Harley riding jacket, plain black T-shirt and thrift-store flannel underneath. Beaded earrings, tobacco tie in my pocket, Joy Harjo's *In Mad Love and War* visible on the table inside. I am a living, breathing stereotype of a diasporic mixed-blood intellectual, but I don't know it.

I'm puzzling over a question one of my committee members has asked me during our latest meeting: what would it mean to construct a theoretical frame from the work of Native women writers and activists? Remember, this is 1997 and there's little, if any, Native scholarship that's broadly acknowledged as theoretical. There's a ton of Native poetry and fiction that seems pretty theoretical to me, but I had yet to acquire the language for making that argument. Instead, I was using Warrior, Vizenor, Allen, and Green with a little (as little as I could get away with) Krupat thrown in for respectability.[25] I was trying to weave what I could gather from these scholars against European and Euro-American scholars in order to argue for Harjo's poetry as theory; thus Vicki's question. My committee will eventually choose this question for the "seven days to write an essay" portion of my exam in April. I will choose to answer it. It will become a question that defines much of my intellectual life. But there, in that coffeehouse, I was still puzzling through the implications of being able to answer it *as a theorist* of Native rhetorics. I desperately wanted to feel like I had permission to make this kind of theory. But I knew the positionality of "theorist" was light-years away from the traditional rhetoric historian identity that my chair had mapped out for me. I was deeply torn between my desire to theorize, my fear of failure, and my exhaustion with rhetoric traditions. And in that moment, in the full-out stupidly-self-destructive phase of mourning for my mother, I was suddenly filled with sparkling red cut-beads of rage.[26] Rage at "a fucking University built on Miami land that's completely arranged for the comfort of the most privileged students I've ever met" (Powell private journal). Rage at my mother for dying and turning the only safe place I'd ever known—the farm—into a space of deep despair. Rage at myself for not having the confidence, the knowledge, to be the theorist who I wanted to be.

A few days later, while talking with an aunty, I realized that there was something about trying to play that part—the edgy intellectual in the coffeehouse—that almost always filled me with this kind of cascading rage. Her advice was to find my relatives there, the ones who live in the natural world.

So I went to water in the form of Acton Lake at Hueston Woods State Park. In February and March it was often too cold to sit at a picnic table, so I'd just park in the picnic area and work in my car. Once it got warm, I started carrying a blanket and a lawn chair in the trunk of my car. I transitioned to writing, reading, and studying at the picnic areas or sitting on the beach. Sometimes I took my journal up the trails and hiked and wrote. I went while my daughter was in school on days I didn't have to be on campus. I eventually took a couple of trusted friends up to the Woods to show them where/how I worked, but mostly I was alone.

Like that moment back along the Wildcat when I learned that I had stories to tell, the lake had teachings for me as well, teachings that weren't about how "special" I was; instead, it showed me the opposite—my very small role in the much larger story, the much more enduring continuum of existence. This was where I was taught to hear the brush of ancestors, the voices of all my relations, learned to understand my small bit of agency in this network of relations as one of accountability. The land and the ancestors there taught me how to take those teachings as a maker and a listener; in that way, I learned how to prepare for the many teachings that have come since. Those teachings are merged in my memory with the still-painful process of mourning my mother. As beads, they are sharp in my memory—those bright red cut-beads against a lake of blues. A transitional field—a multiplicity of greens—comes next.

This was the year I learned how deeply connected my work was to my mother, to my grandparents and great-grandparents, to my ancestors and all of my relations. Even as I work the copper beads of those connections onto threads, I want you to know it's taken more than a decade of stepping back to see the larger pattern emerging and to move outside my own head and heart toward that larger spiraling story of all of us, together, struggling through. But it was there in Ohio after my mother's death that those bits of copper started to appear. Copper as I've learned and relearned the collective power forged in the stories of our survival. Copper as those stories push me through choice, through chance, through place into space and other patterns beaded in the weave of this making that will simply take too long to tell. But they're here. And the rage? It's still here too.[27]

So, where does that leave us? The only cure for the deadly poison of rage that I've ever found has been to let the push and pull of my relatives, of ancestors, of land guide me. What does it mean to locate myself as a scholar in this way? It means spending weeks in Nevada and Oregon using Sarah Winnemucca Hopkins's *Life among the Piutes* as a map in order to walk with those ancestors in that place, to travel that set of histories, instead of just reading about them. It means driving through northeastern Nebraska in order to stand in front of the hospital that Susan LaFlesche Picotte built in Macy, staring north into the wind blowing down the long road that was her route across the plains to her patients on the Omaha-Winnebago agency. It means standing alongside the river outside Flandreau, South Dakota, using the directions in Charles Eastman's *From the Deep Woods to Civilization* to find the approximate location of his father's cabin, then walking from there to the Flandreau Indian School where he was a student. It means rushing up Main Street in Harbor Springs, Michigan, in order to stand on the porch of the tiny house where Andrew Blackbird wrote *Complete Both Early and Late History of the Ottawa and Chippewa Indians of Michigan, a Grammar of Their Language, Personal and Family History of the Author* (1897, a revised version of his 1887 *History of the Ottawa and Chippewa Indians of Michigan*) and "The Indian Problem, From the Indian's Standpoint" (a slim monograph published in 1900) then trekking the shore of *Iniwewi-gichigami* (Lake Michigan)[28] in order to move through the ancestors and relatives still present in *Wawgawnawkezee*.[29]

But more than that, in each of those places, among those specific relations, it means learning to feel that subtle push of blood pounding, the feel of houses and farms encroaching, crowding in, the pain and outrage of loss, the push of stories, the accumulations of history here, to open this place into a space by listening to those stories, learning to weave them into patterns whose shape is just slightly out of reach. Sometimes this means allowing a swathe of matte white to nearly overwhelm the balance of an entire making, only to be pulled back by this truth—the land itself never forgets; it holds our stories, our ancestors, and quietly reasserts itself in copper, green, chocolate brown, the blue of sky and water. As human beings, we are all intimately connected to the land. We depend on it to such a degree that sometimes it disappears from our immediate vision. Our lives happen on the land, in places practiced into spaces of discursivity, of rhetoricity. If there's a "meaning" to this story I've been making, it's this. You live in a geography, a particular space written on a place, a body of land. You work, study, teach, write there. Who else lives there? Who lived there before? What other practices of composing exist there? What other spaces are practiced there? As scholars and humans, we have choices to make, questions to ask, stories to listen to, things to make. Don't be afraid of what happens between asking and listening. Don't be afraid to take a chance, to listen, to practice, to tell.

I know I haven't made any claims about how all of this has turned out so far. It's a work in progress, and future generations will judge what I've done better than I am able. What I do know is that I keep beading, keep telling stories, keep listening to stories because I want Native folks to understand, learn and use the power of the academic institutions that have their roots sunk deep on our lands. Because they are on Native lands, these are, at least in part, our institutions (despite all rumors to the contrary). At least ours to reinhabit and remake in our own ways. That means I have to do my part to make the academy more livable for Native people, and to make the knowledge created in the academy more accurate about and accountable to Native ways of being. I'm happy to be one of the many working to make this happen. And most days that's enough, that's my part of it. And I'm at the part of this piece where I need to stop, need to anchor the thread up, through, under the beads that are just starting to become something. Time to put the beads, and the words, away. For now.

> OFFER UP THESE STORIES LIKE / SKINNED CORN / MADE READY FOR SOUP AND / I AM HOME.
>
> —Kim Shuck, "TALECRUMBS I LEFT MYSELF FOR NAVIGATION"

NOTES

I want to thank Daisy Levy for her persistent ability to make my writing better and for the generous, loving spirit with which she offered comments on several drafts of this essay. I also want to thank Karla Kitalong and Bernice Olivas for their productive and enriching commentary on the early draft of this essay. Finally, I want to thank Elizabeth A. Flynn and Tiffany Bourelle for their patience and persistence in getting this important collection published.

1. This story begins and ends with lines from Kim Shuck's wonderful poems from *Clouds Running In*. Read these lines as openings out to other makings, other makers. Kim Shuck is one of those Native poets who's known especially well by other Native poets—one of those beadworkers known especially well by other beadworkers. Her work pushes out the edges of what we're all trying hard to do, creating new practices rooted in older ways. Her stories (like those of Joy Harjo, Qwo-Li Driskill, and Deborah Miranda) always weave themselves into me like an old relative. *Kim: neewe and wado for your stories, words, beads, generosity, and strength.*
2. For a demonstration of peyote-stitch beadwork, see Renee Bedard's tutorial *Peyote Stitch Tutorial* on YouTube.
3. To prepare a length of thread for beading, I cut off a piece of Nymo the length of my outstretched arm then wax it well, using a piece of beeswax gifted to me by my teacher, Evelyn Bellmeyer. Already dark with the excreted nectar of wildflowers when she gave it to me fifteen years ago, it is a tiny piece of mahogany now. I run the thread across the wax a few times, then lick my index finger and thumb and run them down the length of the thread. Holding up the tiny #13 needle, I look for the light in its eye, push the thread through, and fold about a third of it down. I don't tie a knot. I won't need one. I'll weave the thread around and through, anchoring it in the weave of the beads.

4. I wish I could remember the specific brand. It was a black-and-silver camera in a brown leather case that you wore around your neck. The cover of the camera dropped down, but stayed attached when you opened it to take pictures.
5. The Big Miami Reserve was 760,000 acres set aside during the 1818 Treaty of St. Mary's, the same treaty that stripped Miamis of their claims to some lands south of the Wabash River. The Reserve ran along the Wabash River from the mouth of the Salamonie River to the mouth of the Eel River North. It contained all of what is now Howard County in Indiana and portions of seven surrounding counties—Wabash, Miami, Cass, Clinton, Tipton, Madison, and Grant. At the time of the survey of the Reserve itself (1819–20), there were no white settlements between Terre Haute and Fort Wayne along the Wabash River.
6. Our family stories emphasize that the Bakers weren't blood relations—they adopted my paternal grandmother Audrey when she was sixteen. No one ever had any explanations, though, for the strong physical resemblance between photos of Dorothy at eighteen and those of myself and my daughter at the same age.
7. Marion is about eleven miles from the farm.
8. Swayzee is about three miles from the farm.
9. The Grand Dragon of the KKK lived in Tipton, about thirty-five miles from the farm.
10. In 1930, in Marion, two young black men were lynched on suspicion of murdering a white man. Their hanging was captured in a gruesome photo that became an iconic depiction of American lynching, and that served as inspiration for the song "Strange Fruit." A third teen, James Cameron, was spared, served time in prison, and later wrote a book about the experience, *A Time of Terror*. He was eventually pardoned by the Indiana Gov. Evan Bayh in 1993 and opened America's Black Holocaust Museum (Milwaukee, WI), dedicated to the thousands of blacks killed by white lynch mobs. On and off growing up, I would hear grown-ups talk about local businessman, elected officials, or law enforcement officers who either showed up in that picture or were there but not pictured. This was always communicated in shorthand, "Well, you know he's in that picture," or "Well, he wasn't in the picture but he was there."
11. White's Institute was opened in 1850 by Quaker railroad entrepreneur John White. It still operates today, having served as an orphanage, an Indian boarding school, a reform school, and now a family services facility. White's was made famous as an Indian boarding school in Zitkala-Sa's (also known as Gertrude Bonnin) *American Indian Stories*. There is much debate among Miamis in Indiana about whether Miami children were sent to White's—some families have stories about relatives who went there while the official tribal history says none did. White's wasn't the first institution where my grandmother stayed, it was simply the last one—the one she ran away from.
12. In Miami, this is *pin˙siwamootayi siipiiwi*, which roughly translates to "belly of the wildcat." Wildcat Creek is a major tributary of the Wabash River, one of the main riverways through Miami territory in what is now the state of Indiana.
13. "Taking teachings" is one of the ways Native folks refer to concepts like "learning," but it's not precisely the same. Instead of being understood in either the "banking" or "tools" models common in Western culture, teachings are carried from one teacher to the next. The idea is that all of us exist on a continuum of knowledge production in which we are always carrying, and gifting, teachings. To "take" a teaching, then, is to take responsibility for carrying it and for honoring it.
14. The historical narrative that explains why there are two Miami tribes with nearly identical family and genealogy connections is too complicated to explain here. In brief, when Miamis were removed from the homelands in 1846, some families stayed in Indiana. The Indiana tribe was illegally terminated, so only the Miami Tribe of Oklahoma is currently federally recognized. For more details, see Stewart Rafert's *The Miami Indians of Indiana*

and the websites of the Miami Tribe of Oklahoma (http://www.miamination.com/) and the Miami Nation of Indiana (http://www.miamiindians.org/).

15. Miami University was chartered in 1809 but didn't open its doors to students until 1824—a time when the land it sits on was still primarily occupied by Native peoples, mostly Miamis and Shawnees. It bills itself as a "public ivy" because less than ten percent of its budget comes from state funds, and as "mother Miami" due to the number of fraternities that have been founded ("mothered") there. It is a very specific kind of space with a very specific kind of culture. During my time there, the student population was very white, aggressively upper-middle class, and quite conservative.

16. Coshocton is about 115 miles south and slightly west of what is now Cleveland, Ohio.

17. A year after the Treaty of St. Mary's, which was signed 160 miles west of Coshocton.

18. Notice how the Powells were in Indiana, living on the Eastern edge of the Great Miami Reserve, before that land was turned into allotments in 1872? We all live with the legacies of colonization.

19. Historian Richard White defines the "middle ground" as both a place (the Great Lakes region, 1650–1815) and a process. For him, the middle ground is a space of mutual accommodation and persistent negotiation between traders, settlers, and indigenous populations. For more information, see his *The Middle Ground: Indians, Empires and Republics in the Great Lakes Region 1650–1815*.

20. In colonial parlance, Lenapes are called Delawares. For more information about Lenapes, or how they came to be called "Delawares," see the Official Website of the Delaware Tribe of Indians (http://delawaretribe.org/blog/2013/06/26/faqs/).

21. White Eyes' death in 1778 was reported to be from smallpox, but that report was debated by George Morgan—U.S. Indian Agent and negotiator at the Ft. Pitt treaty—who claimed the Lenape leader was killed by the American militia once they reached Michigan, but that his murder was covered up to prevent the other Lenapes in the party from abandoning the militia before they reached their destination.

22. The spelling of this village differs across colonial and military scribes—*Coshoching, Coshecking, Goshocking*.

23. Ohio became the seventeenth state in 1803.

24. Jennie Dautermann was the composition program director at that time, and was also a member of my committee. Jennie was amazingly supportive during that entire year—an important member of the community of folks who made my initial recovery from my mother's death possible.

25. Here I'm referring to Warrior's *Tribal Secrets*; Vizenor's *Earthdivers, Landfill Meditations*, and *Narrative Chance*; Krupat and Swann's *Recovering the Word*; Krupat's *Ethnocriticism*; Paula Gunn Allen's *The Sacred Hoop* and *Grandmothers of the Light*; and Rayna Green's "The Pocohantas Perplex" and *That's What She Said*.

26. "Cut" beads are called that because a slice of the curve of them is literally cut away to make a flat surface that sparkles in the light.

27. An example of how I managed this rage in my own scholarship can be seen in the shift in tone from my "Blood and Scholarship" (1999) to the "Listening to Ghosts" (2002).

28. "Great Lakes" in Ojibwe.

29. *Wawgawnawkezee* became L'arbre Croche, and marks a swath of land that begins slightly north of Cross Village and runs south along the lake all the way to *Wequitonsing*, which by 1880 had begun to shift from an Odawa settlement to Harbor Springs, a lakeside resort for American capitalists.

WORKS CITED

Allen, Paula Gunn. *Grandmothers of the Light: A Medicine Woman's Sourcebook.* Boston: Beacon P, 1991. Print.

———. *The Sacred Hoop: Recovering the Feminine in American Indian Traditions.* Boston: Beacon P, 1986. Print.

Bedard, Renee. *Peyote Stitch Tutorial Part I.* YouTube, May 27, 2009. Web. June 11, 2016.

Blackbird, Andrew. *Complete Both Early and Late History of the Ottawa and Chippewa Indians of Michigan, a Grammar of Their Language, Personal and Family History of the Author.* Harbor Springs, MI: Babcock and Darling, 1897. Print.

———. *History of the Ottawa and Chippewa Indians of Michigan.* Ypsilanti, MI: The Ypsilanti Printing House, 1887. Print.

———. "The Indian Problem, from the Indian's Standpoint." Ypsilanti, MI: The Women's National Indian Association of Ypsilanti, 1900. Print.

Bonnin, Gertrude (Zitkala-Sa). *American Indian Stories.* Washington, DC: Hayworth P, 1921. Print.

Cameron, James. *A Time of Terror.* Baltimore: Black Classic P, 1993. Print.

The Delaware Tribe of Indians. Official Website. June 11, 2016.

Eastman, Charles Alexander. *From the Deep Woods to Civilization.* Boston: Little, Brown and Co., 1916. Print.

"The Great Lakes in Ojibwe." *The Decolonial Atlas.* December 1, 2014. Web. June 11, 2016.

Green, Rayna, ed. "The Pocohantas Perplex: The Image of Indian Women in American Culture." Eds. Rebecca Kugel and Lucy Eldersveld Murphy. *Native Women's History in Eastern North America Before 1900: A Guide to Research and Writing.* Lincoln: U of Nebraska P, 1975. 7–26. Print.

———. *That's What She Said: Contemporary Poetry and Fiction by Native American Women.* Bloomington: Indiana UP, 1984. Print.

Hopkins, Sarah Winnemucca. *Life among the Piutes: Their Wrongs and Claims.* New York: G. P. Putman and Sons, 1883. Print.

Krupat, Arnold. *Ethnocriticism: Ethnography, History, Literature.* Berkeley: U of California P, 1992. Print.

Krupat, Arnold, and Brian Swann, eds. *Recovering the Word: Essays on Native American Literature.* Berkeley: U of California P, 1987. Print.

The Miami Nation of Indians of Indiana, Inc., Website. June 11, 2016.

Miami Tribe of Oklahoma. Web. June 11, 2016.

Powell, Malea. "Blood and Scholarship: One Mixed-Blood's Story." Ed. Keith Gilyard. *Race, Rhetoric and Composition.* Portsmouth, NH: Boynton/Cook, 1999. 1–16. Print.

———. "Listening to Ghosts: an Alternative (Non)argument." Eds. Chris Schroeder, Helen Fox, Patricia Bizzell. *ALT DIS: Alternative Discourses in the Academy.* Portsmouth, NH: Boynton/Cook, 2002. 11–22. Print.

———. "The Mirror." Unpublished paper, 1989. Print.

———. Private journal, 1996–98. Print.

Rafert, Stewart. *The Miami Indians of Indiana: A Persistent People, 1654–1994.* Indianapolis: Indiana Historical Society P, 1996. Print.

Schutt, Amy C. *Peoples of the River Valleys: The Odyssey of the Delaware Indians*. Philadelphia: U of Pennsylvania P, 2007. Print.

Shuck, Kim. "DHLA:NUWA" and "TALECRUMBS I LEFT MYSELF FOR NAVIGATION." *Clouds Running In*. San Francisco: Taurean Horn P, 2014. Print.

Vizenor, Gerald, ed. *Earthdivers: Tribal Narratives on Mixed Descent*. Minneapolis: U of Minnesota P, 1981. Print.

———. *Landfill Meditation: Crossblood Stories*. Hanover, PA: Wesleyan UP, 1991. Print.

———. *Narrative Chance: Postmodern Discourse on Native American Indian Literatures*. Norman: U of Oklahoma P, 1993. Print.

Warrior, Robert Allen. *Tribal Secrets: Recovering American Indian Intellectual Traditions*. Minneapolis: U of Minnesota P, 1995. Print.

White, Richard. *The Middle Ground: Indians, Empires and Republics in the Great Lakes Region 1650–1815*. New York: Cambridge UP, 1990. Print.

CHAPTER 9

When Depression and Resilience Collide

Might as Well Get Up

JACQUELINE RHODES

> The thing about moving without an established route is that the going is messy. My progression has felt at times like interminable bushwhacking: walking for a while in one direction, and then abruptly changing course. Scratching my legs on raspberry brambles and falling in ditches. But also getting to taste the sweet and wild fruit, and to stumble upon beautiful clearings....
> Which is why I believe there is something distinct about queer time. Queer time is a bushwhacked path, a sled's shaky trail, a web of continual reinvention in many different directions.
> —Lila, "The Pace of Queer Time"

I've structured this *essai* around two questions. The first was posed some thirty years ago when I was hanging out with my friend Katie in her house in Missoula, as we ate gingersnaps and red apples one cold Montana evening. "Who would you be without your melancholy?" she asked. I was silent. Then, as now, it's an impossible question for me, for it requires imagining a self beyond context, in this case the context of chronic depression and remembered violence brought on by nature or nurture or heredity or circumstance. My depression queers my vision of myself in the world. Who would I be without my history? Without the scars, real and virtual, or the overdeveloped hypervigilant Spidey sense about real or imagined danger? As Sara Ahmed writes in *Queer Phenomenology*,

> The body emerges from this history of doing, which is also a history of not doing, of paths not taken, which also involves the loss, impossible to know

or to even register, of what might have followed from such paths. As such, the body is directed as a condition of its arrival, as a direction that gives the body its line. (159)

My student Derek asked the second question over a cigarette downstairs at work, on the topic of queer utopias—in other words, on the topic of *disorientation* becoming *what is given*. "What happens," he asked, "if we construct a world where dominant hegemonic nationalistic principles are nonexistent?" Again I was silent. Another version of "who would you be without your lived context?" To some extent, our current vision of queerness relies on our destabilizing of those hegemonic nationalistic principles. We *make* ourselves through pushing on a door. What happens if the door suddenly opens? Where are we if we've fallen on the floor of our own resistance? In response to Derek, I managed to articulate some queer vision that sees living queer as deeply contextual, deeply rhetorical, marked by impossibility and failure. And again I look to Ahmed, who writes, "We can still ask, what happens if the orientation of the body is not restored? What happens when disorientation cannot simply be overcome by the 'force' of the vertical? What do we do, if disorientation itself becomes worldly or becomes what is given?" (159).

For this chapter, I wanted to tell one story, a clear narrative, but that story was only part of the story. I wanted to write, in an orderly way, about a disorderly lifetime of pushing against and falling through doors with the help of my friends and lovers—my queer kin. I failed. Queer time, queer kin: such time and relations have made my stories possible, have given them structure, such as it is. "Queer time," as J. Jack Halberstam tells us, refers to "those specific models of temporality that emerge within postmodernism once one leaves the temporal frames of bourgeois reproduction and family, longevity, risk/safety, and inheritance" (4). Halberstam points to poet Mark Doty, who writes, in

> his memoir of his lover's death from AIDS, . . . "All my life I've lived with a future which constantly diminishes but never vanishes" (Doty 1996, 4). The constantly diminishing future creates a new emphasis on the here, the present, the now, and while the threat of no future hovers overhead like a storm cloud, the urgency of being also expands the potential of the moment and, as Doty explores, squeezes new possibilities out of the time at hand. . . . Queer time, as it flashes into view in the heart of a crisis, exploits the potential of what Charles-Pierre Baudelaire called in relation to modernism "the transient, the fleeting, the contingent." . . . And yet queer time, even as it emerges from the AIDS crisis, is not only about compression and annihilation; it is also about the potentiality of a life unscripted by the conventions of family, inheritance, and child rearing. (2)

Such potentialities become their own sort of strength, the ability to surf on waves of contingency, to build lives out of our relations with friends and lovers over time—our *families of choice*, as they are sometimes called. Our strength comes through these fractured moments of influence and narrative, fleeting intensities, years of immediacy.

And strength, too, comes from the balancing of choice and chance, of wave and field; in some ways, this balance reminds me of what Susan Miller in *Rescuing the Subject* called "textual subjectivity," that temporary positionality performed by writers in order to write, to resist, and to act. It seems so patently disidentificatory that Jose Esteban Muñoz himself might have drawn on it. The idea of a fictionalized stability, a temporary performativity, if you will, ties Miller strongly to queer theories and subjects. Miller's writing, as she said of all writing, "treats the mixed and unstable confluence of anterior intentions and purposes and posterior 'readings,' 'meanings,' or outcomes *as though* they could be fixed. It is a living fiction of, not an achievement of, stability. Each text evolves indeterminately and multiply at the same time that it is physically and substantially finished" (19–20). So too, we might say, do queer selves "evolve" in queer time.

And in that indeterminate and multiple sense, Miller's textual subjectivity calls to mind the discussion of resilience and agency in *Feminist Rhetorical Resilience*, where editors Elizabeth A. Flynn, Patricia Sotirin, and Ann Brady posit "resilience" as less a matter of individual agency and more a matter of relational and community-based action in the face of adversity. Resilience, the editors write, "suggests attention to choices made in the face of difficult and even impossible challenges" (1). They write that "resilience is transformative not necessarily through effecting a change in circumstances—which may remain bleak or oppressive—but in changing the way a life is lived." In making that change, we exercise our rhetorical agency, an agency "vested in a strategic rhetor marshaling the available means of public action and responding efficaciously to the demands of the circumstances and larger historical-structural forces" (7).

•

Like many from poor white stock in small towns, I wanted to be somebody (and somewhere) else. My family's very existence in Florence, Montana, was "fleeting, transient, contingent," as Baudelaire might say. My three brothers and I were latchkey kids of necessity; my mother was gone working all day, my father was gone drinking and bullshitting with his friends. For most of my growing-up years, our family of six lived off my mom's job as a secretary, my dad's very occasional work, SSD checks from the government, and money from my parents' playing jobs on the weekend (they had a four-piece country-western band). My dad, in his many alcoholic years, had been in a near-fatal car crash in 1969 that left him laid up in a body cast, first in the hospital, then in the front room of our single-wide trailer. It was a foreshadowing of another car crash, many sober years later, which caused so much damage that my father never recovered, dying slowly and painfully over seven years.

But I made it to college, a pre-law political science major, and I paid for it with scholarships and a near full-time job as a typesetter. The first inkling I had that I could be a professor (instead of a lawyer) was during an economics class my second undergraduate year at the University of Montana. John Photiades was telling us about the guns-vs.-butter production/possibility curve, and I was only half-listening. I thought to myself *I could do this*. The thought didn't stay with me; I changed my major six times during my undergraduate years, always with different career paths in mind. In fact, that *professor* thought didn't cross my mind again for six more years.

I was a transient student, psychically speaking, living in my own poverty in order to escape from my family's. Like many first-generation students, I didn't know how to *do* college. I moved in multiple ways at once. Different majors: political science, sociology, communication sciences and disorders, English (linguistics track); English (secondary education track); English literature. Different lovers. Different living spaces. It strikes me, however, that those multiple paths, too, served as queer ways through my five years at UM; my queer time there was "unscripted," as Halberstam would say, by any conventions of straight temporality. It was disorderly and strange, the "constantly diminishing future" indeed hovering like a storm cloud (Halberstam 2), and I found myself living in the moment even as the past interrupted me.

> *At the end of my first year of college, as I came out, I tried to kill myself with an overdose of pills and alcohol. I tell this story in more detail, and better, in* Techne. *Here I will say that it was a long dip into the black moods that still haunt me, self-directed rage and self-harm and a tendency to stay in bed for days. Several years after that time, the smell of wet wood, a trigger. "Why do you shake like that?" Nancy asks. Darkblackcoldblood. I stumble, stutter. "I was raped. Kind of." She stops her van, pulls to the side of the road. "What do you mean, 'kind of?'" When I finally speak, it is the first time I've talked*

about the topic. It had been ten years. Nancy pushed me into therapy for my depression and PTSD. Over the years and three therapists later, I'd say it was a mixed blessing. There is a release in naming and owning experience, but there is also a cost as you structure yourself in a new way. It's healthier, but harder. I cast aside denial and the sickening comfort of silence.

>   Nancy was my lover some thirty years ago. We met in an advanced ASL class at the University of Montana. She taught me to be a lesbian. Women's music: Meg Christian, Therese Edell. Books: Rita Mae Brown. Audre Lorde. Katherine Forrest. She also taught me which fork to use, how to dress in my dyke finery, how to charm (I think). As a Finn, she also got me to appreciate a good sauna. We traveled, we ate, we saw movies. It was my early lesbian education, being mentored into a community of choice, finding kin.

After graduating with a degree in English literature, I had no idea what to do. I moved to southern Idaho with G., my lover at the time, and worked in a graphics studio as a typesetter and occasional tech writer. I wrote stories, all rejected by numerous literary journals. I worked at a group home. I picked up freelance production work at a magazine about fly-fishing. On the weekends, sometimes, G. and I would drive the fifty miles to Pocatello to hang out with Nancy, who was now giving care to her own lover as she recovered from breast cancer. Nancy's lover was a professor at the University of Idaho and encouraged me to go up to Moscow to do a two-week intensive workshop with Marilynne Robinson. I did. I loved Moscow. And soon after, when G. got a job in Spokane, Washington (ninety miles from Moscow), I went to Idaho for my MA.

During my second semester in my MA program at the University of Idaho, the *professor* thought hit me again. I'd been teaching for a semester, still intending to be a fiction writer, and then I took a composition theory class. I converted. I was hooked. It was 1991 and the professor—Evelyn Ashton-Jones—was powerful, eloquent, and the best teacher (at least for formal schooling) I ever had. Evelyn would become my thesis director and, later, my dissertation director at the University of Southern Mississippi. I presented from my thesis at the 1992 CCCC in Cincinnati. I was pure, full of a new convert's zealotry. I felt focused finally. I would be a writing teacher and change the world.

Changing the world through literacy work ended up having to wait. I broke up with G., painfully and dramatically, when I started my first PhD program at the University of Louisville, and it threw me into such an abyss that I couldn't function. As Andrew Solomon writes in *The Noonday Demon*,

> It is not pleasant to experience decay, to find yourself exposed to the ravages of an almost daily rain, and to know that you are turning into something feeble, that more and more of you will blow off with the first strong wind, making you less and less. . . . Depression starts out insipid, fogs the days into a dull color, weakens ordinary actions until their clear shapes are obscured by the effort they require, leaves you tired and bored and self-obsessed. (17)

I dropped out of school and left (I thought) my nascent career. I moved back across the country to Montana to live in my parents' house and went back to typesetting at the local newspaper. I was back to the indeterminacy of my early twenties, convinced of my own weakness, depressed. A circle closing.

Eventually—after three years—I thought I could go back to school. My friend Connie visited me in Montana and because of a bad snowstorm and an even worse block heater, she was stranded with me for a week. *What was your thesis about?* she asked during that visit. As I told her, as I explained, it woke me up. Something mattered again. At the same time, I was plagued with the idea that my depressed brain wouldn't work, that it had somehow snapped under the pressure of the breakup. To stay or go—to pick a path—seemed achingly impossible.

> *What's really painful is that depression is just so damned boring. If you're one of my fellow travelers, you'll understand. To get myself going, I tell myself "might as well." Get up, that is. That's part of my resilience.*

I ended up in a small program in Hattiesburg, Mississippi, ninety miles from New Orleans and thirty-six driving hours from home. Evelyn became my director and mentor, pushing me not only to think but to connect—to network with others in the field, to talk to strangers at conferences, to build a grown-up life in the discipline.

The stories drew me in. What anchored me in composition twenty-five years ago or so, besides the constant *a-ha!* moments in Evelyn's comp theory class, were its stories and people. People knew each other, they were approachable, they had lives and students and desires and dreams. The people in my new and hoped-for home were *real,* a pantheon of scholars who simultaneously wrote incredible work, taught first-year composition, and had lives and failures and successes much like mine. The accessibility of these people's lives and their attachment to their work was my greatest epiphany; I knew that I, too, could do such things, that I could *make my work matter* without giving up my humanity. From hearing these stories on Evelyn's front porch, in her classrooms, and in her office, I learned important lessons about *doing* theory and practice.

> *It was at CCCC in 1996 in Milwaukee that I first met Susan Miller, as she sat in the hotel bar with Gary Olson, surrounded by the South Florida crowd, all leaning in to hear her whispered pronouncements on theory, the field, her wardrobe (she was wearing black leather pants and a white rabbit fur vest), the quality of her drink. Having just emerged from an intense engagement with her written work, I was starstruck. And then I found myself in the elevator with her. She asked what I was presenting on. I said the connections between Vico's contingent logic and Mary Wollstonecraft's rhetorical practice. She was silent. Just before the doors opened and she left, she said "Vico and Wollstonecraft. Interesting." Those four words, especially the last, I took with me as talismanic.*

I did well. I got good grades, presented, published. And then, thanks to choice and chance, I wound up driving cross-country to Southern California to start a tenure-line position in the CSU system.

Evelyn left the field the same year I graduated, and her mentoring of me that year was difficult (for both of us, I suspect). She's now a speech therapist in New Orleans. I hope she's happy. Washing her hands of her old life, she hasn't spoken to me for a dozen years, and I miss her. I feel the loss of mentoring and connection quite keenly, still, now. I sought mentors elsewhere, finding temporaries but looking back to what Evelyn might have said to me about this or that situation. I've stopped that looking, having found help from professional colleagues such as Susan Miller, Cindy Selfe, Beth Flynn, Susan Jarratt; from friends and ex-lovers who, although not in my field, have bolstered my ability to act rhetorically and well, a good "textual subject"; and from people who blend those two categories, like Jonathan Alexander.

> *In Louisville for another CCCC. Susan and I had a dinner that turned into a sort of master class in rhetoric for me. Her* Trust in Texts *had come out a couple of years before, and she insisted that it was a much better book than* Rescuing the Subject. *I didn't disagree, but gently praised the earlier book as*

foundational for a sense of rhetoric as written. She went into minute detail about Trust. She wore a Chanel suit. We split an order of calamari. It's the only time I've ever eaten calamari. The dinner lasted four hours and I was wildly tense, worried that I would say something so stupid that she'd never talk to me again. I felt like Rikki-Tikki-Tavi. In love and adoring, but still the mongoose.

My dissertation became my first book, and an early collaboration with Connie led to my first work with Jonathan, work that has challenged and befuddled and nourished me all at the same time. That work with Connie—an article titled "Risking Queer"—was my first scholarly engagement with queer theory. It was not destiny but, rather, chance that the piece was even written, for when I first encountered queer theory, I resisted it mightily. Connie had to poke me along. First, I didn't want it assumed that just because I was queer, I necessarily did queer theory. Second, and more important, I was suspicious of queer theory's emphasis on play, on resignification, on things that seemed to have less to do with liberatory goals and socioeconomic emancipation than with self-indulgent navel-gazing. As an inveterate navel-gazer with a strong Protestant work ethic, I took queer theory's play personally. *How,* I asked myself, *will this theory—how will I—ever be useful?*

•

My older brother was killed in a truck crash in 2004 in Effingham, Illinois. I was in France at the time. I slipped back into blackness. I stayed in bed staring for days. My wife urged me to therapy, and it saved my life and made me more resilient when my father died five years later.

Claudel
To My Brother Dan, from France

I count but do not recall you,
the contempt held in your fists, secrets
growing sarcomic even now, close under my ribs,
etched into loyalty.

Even now. Late June, you drove truck in Illinois,
hauled beer near Effingham, planned with Mary
on a handheld cell how she'd meet us all, your family,
someday soon when you settled home.

That same day, I was in Chateau Dom Vaysette,
southern France, learning how Camille Claudel,
thought insane, locked away by her own brother
for thirty years, alone, with nothing to sculpt but her own rage.

Imagine their hatred, that pair, and our own.
On the road home to Rabastens—just before the
stateside call announcing your hideous death—
I could imagine it. What I'd never imagined was

the rage, too, of my mother's choked voice, my father's silence,
my other brothers' tears, the way we would stare. Mary,
who we did meet at your funeral, tattooed your name—
black ink, left hip—in memory. My mother asks me
now, *are you ready to go to France again?* It is over
twelve years past. *You must be excited to see all that again,
so soon.*

•

In many ways, my early objections to queer theory mirrored those of Theresa Ebert, who in her 1996 *Ludic Feminism and After* set up an opposition between what she saw as "resistance postmodernism" and "ludic postmodernism." According to Ebert, "resistance postmodernism has as its end a transformative politics, the emancipation that comes from opposition to and freedom from systems of exploitation founded in gender, race, class, and sexual orientation. Ludic postmodernism, on the contrary, is perpetually disrupting and destabilizing" (30). Ebert places queer theory in the ludic and finds it wanting. Ludic postmodernism, because of its deep suspicion of metanarratives, including metanarratives of social transformation, is problematic for those of us who seek such transformation.

And so I was asking with Ebert: does queer theory shift "the site of struggle from socioeconomic emancipation to the sensuous maximizing of bodily pleasures and the libidinal liberation of the individual?" (30) In queering, are we burying our heads in the sand? These questions were more than theoretical for me, in that I was deeply troubled by my own tendency toward libidinal liberation at the expense of my "real" work. I resented my chronic depression (and the therapy for it) as an ongoing interruption of my life. Further, I had interrupted (I thought) too many of my straight paths with thoughts of lovers and friends or my own tendency to play—it was a spin-the-bottle approach to life choices that, to me, seemed the downside of queer time. And yet—I read Nedra

Reynolds, who in "Interrupting Our Way to Agency" writes that "agency is not simply about finding one's own voice but also about intervening in discourses of the everyday and cultivating rhetorical tactics that make interruption and resistance an important part of any conversation" and that interruption combats "discursive exclusion" in those conversations (59–60). Much later, as I worked with Connie (and then with Jonathan), I could see my self-interruptions as twists in the path, queer turns toward unscripted potentialities. My interruptions were my "real" work. My people—my queer kin—rooted me deeply in my own (dis)orderly conduct, and *that was okay* (and even generative).

I had much help from Jonathan, because our promiscuous, playful collaboration has opened up research in ways I couldn't imagine before we started. After ten years of articles, presentations, and multimedia installations together, Jonathan and I wrote *On Multimodality: New Media in Composition Studies*. I was at the height of productivity, career-wise. And yet I struggled; I emailed Erica, my therapist, in the midst of all that work, just a month before *On Multimodality* was published:

> I got out of bed (might as well) because I had to go to work. Today will be hell. I feel awful, like crying, like not holding it together. Raw and tired. And tired of feeling raw and tired and and and I don't know how I can do this. . . . Need to focus somehow. Today is gray to the point of blackness. I'm battling the urge to just shut my office door because talking to people hurts and tires me. Canceled one meeting. Can't get out of others. Have shitloads of things to do and no capacity to do them. That's what it feels like. Isn't it time for this to lift? I am so fucking tired of feeling this way.

It was only in the next couple of years—thanks to Erica and a new cocktail of antidepressants and anxiety meds—that I was able to lift out of that haze and write (with Jonathan), *Techne*. I put denial and silence aside—again, after thirty years—to write *personally* in a professional publication—and this move to bring the personal/political into my work seemed to break some kind of spell.

•

On her blog *Hyperbole and a Half*, Allie Brosh writes:

> The beginning of my depression had been nothing *but* feelings, so the emotional deadening that followed was a welcome relief. I had always wanted to not give a fuck about anything. I viewed feelings as a weakness—annoying obstacles on my quest for total power over myself. And I finally didn't have to feel them anymore. . . .

But my experiences slowly flattened and blended together until it became obvious that there's a huge difference between not giving a fuck and not being *able* to give a fuck. Cognitively, you might know that different things are happening to you, but they don't feel very different.

Which leads to horrible, soul-decaying boredom.

I tried to get out more, but most fun activities just left me existentially confused or frustrated with my inability to enjoy them.

Months oozed by, and I gradually came to accept that maybe enjoyment was not a thing I got to feel anymore. I didn't want anyone to know, though. I was still sort of uncomfortable about how bored and detached I felt around other people, and I was still holding out hope that the whole thing would spontaneously work itself out.

•

In *Techne* I wrote a chapter on a rhizomatic sense of self, looking at inner contradictions that seem to make up a queer life. And those contradictions served in generative ways for me as I wrote for *Techne*. Solomon tells us that "no essential self lies pure as a vein of gold under the chaos of experience and chemistry. The human organism is a sequence of selves that succumb to or choose one another. We are each the sum of certain choices and circumstances; the self exists in the narrow space where the world and our choices come together" (432). In one of those narrow spaces, I wrote. It was deeply theoretical and acutely personal, the telling of an old story mixed with the urgency of moving, if not forward, at least with direction.

Now on the cusp of another cross-country move, my stories and their urgencies re-present themselves in queer time, with its unscripted, exciting moves and vagaries; there isn't necessarily a lesson learned or a narrative closed, but there is a sense of movement in the gaps of selfhood. My "bushwhacked path" in rhetoric and composition, as Lila calls it, has been trod in fits and starts, with my people (lovers and/or beloved) appearing at right moments and wrong moments. I've been productive, yes, and at times it has been a process of wading through psychic mud to find purchase on higher ground. All my kin have had it hard—poverty, car wrecks, death, teen motherhood, court battles, being orphaned young, incest and other sexual assaults, suicides, long-term illnesses, disability. I'm not special. But we persist. Might as well.

WORKS CITED

Ahmed, Sara. *Queer Phenomenology: Orientations, Objects, Others*. Durham, NC: Duke UP, 2006. Print.

Brosh, Allie. "Depression Part Two." *Hyperbole and a Half*. May 2013. Web. June 7, 2016.

Ebert, Teresa L. *Ludic Feminism and After: Postmodernism, Desire, and Labor in Late Capitalism*. Ann Arbor: U of Michigan P, 1996. Print.

Flynn, Elizabeth A., Patricia Sotirin, and Ann Brady, eds. *Feminist Rhetorical Resilience*. Logan: Utah State UP, 2012. Print.

Halberstam, J. Jack. *In a Queer Time and Place: Transgender Bodies, Subcultural Lives*. New York: New York UP, 2005. Print.

Lila. "The Pace of Queer Time." *Autostraddle*. March 16, 2016. Web. June 1, 2016.

Miller, Susan. *Rescuing the Subject: A Critical Introduction to Rhetoric and the Writer*. 2nd ed. Carbondale: Southern Illinois UP, 2004. Print.

———. *Trust in Texts: A Different History of Rhetoric*. Carbondale: Southern Illinois UP, 2008. Print.

Reynolds, Nedra. "Interrupting Our Way to Agency: Feminist Cultural Studies and Composition." *Feminism and Composition Studies: In Other Words*. Ed. Susan C. Jarratt and Lynn Worsham. New York: MLA, 1998. Print. 58–73.

Rhodes, Jacqueline, and Jonathan Alexander. *Techne: Queer Meditations on Writing the Self*. Logan: Computers and Composition Digital Press/Utah State UP, 2015. Web.

Solomon, Andrew. *The Noonday Demon: An Atlas of Depression*. New York: Scribner, 2001. Print.

CHAPTER 10

The Camino

A Pilgrim's Journey of Choice

BETH L. HEWETT

> *In April 2014, I walked a pilgrimage from Valença, Portugal, into the holy city of Santiago de Compostella, Spain, a distance of 100 kilometers. Although we had trained for the walk, my best friend and I encountered significant physical trials. We also struggled emotionally. It was interesting that at times the Camino was a lonely trail through forests and small villages and at other times it wound through business districts and towns. The Camino sometimes intersected the ancient Roman Road. We would follow the Camino/Roman Road for a while and then would be guided by the scallop-shell symbol back to the Camino alone. We met many interesting people along the way, with each interaction ending in the traditional salutation "Buen Camino." This pilgrimage reminded me of my life as a woman, wife, mother, daughter, worker, academic, scholar, bereaved person, and helper to the bereaved; these are my intellectual and my spiritual selves. At times I have walked multiple paths as they intertwined and other times I needed to choose one road or another. These various paths often caused me to feel out of step with the world. I realize now that I am a pilgrim in this world. My life's journey has taken on new meanings. While I have no idea where I'll end up, I know I'm on the right path.*

Being an independent scholar is like a pilgrimage—a journey with unexpected twists and turns, disappointments, and joys. My career journey has been an unusual one inflected deeply by my married life, familial connections, tenacious commitment to certain people and ideas, and dogged determination to see things through to unclear ends. I have experienced a homelessness that comes with being a military spouse and a placelessness that comes with being a scholar independent of an institution. While some of my decisions could be characterized as classically representative of women's concerns, others have come from my own principled nature, vigorous pursuit of practical ideas, and deep desire for authentic relation with others. In almost all cases, these decisions are the result of choices I've made—choices to study what interests me, choices to write what seems necessary, and choices to do what it takes to keep meaningful relationships. While many of the essays in this collection focus on serendipitous occasions, I don't think of my life situations as "happy accidents." There are times of grief and times of joy, but they all resulted from the choices I made to walk this road—I accept the good with the bad, the successes with the failures, recognizing the twisting turns of my life that I illustrate in this chapter.

A FORMIDABLE QUEST

My academic journey began with a major in English/American literature and comparative literature at Western Maryland College (now McDaniel College), a four-year liberal arts institution nestled in north-central Maryland. I starkly recall that although I was taught close reading strategies in literature courses, I was never *taught to write* in my writing classes. My only composition course was multidisciplinary and taught by a theater professor.

> *My first composition paper inexplicably received a "C." If you asked me, I would have told you that I wasn't an average student. I didn't understand what was wrong with the paper or how to do better. When I needed to write my second paper, I despaired. Blocked by fear, each time I sat at my desk to write, I found myself staring at the slug-green dormitory walls. I wrote. I tore up pages. I wrote again. I tore up pages again. Finally, on the night before the dreaded paper was due, anxious and tearful, I talked with my boyfriend, who whispered a secret word in my ear, and my roommate, who encouraged me not to quit. I began writing again. When my hand became tired, I felt afraid. But I fought the fear. For hours I wrote. No pages were torn to pieces. It was finished, and I didn't dare think about it anymore lest my fear return.*

Eventually, I experientially learned to write by constantly writing papers in literature and humanities courses—becoming so good that I could breeze through both course papers and essay exams. By sophomore year, I could write a brief outline of my thoughts and then, as nineteenth-century belletristic rhetorician Samuel P. Newman (1827) would say, I could "look" or think the writing "into shape" (19). A yellow pad, a favorite pencil, and a manual typewriter were the tools that got me from rough ideas to "A" papers, drafted once to avoid typing twice. I loved it: the thinking, the argument building, the knowledge that I'd knocked out another good essay.

What I didn't love was that I didn't know *how* to write on any conscious level. I didn't know *why* I was doing well and *how* to improve. Grades alone taught me to replicate strategy and to avoid risk. Writing seemed to be a combination of luck and mystery. Despite my discomfort—or maybe even because of it—I felt a calling to write more and a desire to teach writing. But how could I teach what I didn't know how to do with awareness and intention?

Driven by a passion to understand the how's and why's of writing, I enrolled in three tutorials, each with a different English professor. I asked each of them to teach me how to write. These tutorials were glorious opportunities. My writing got personal attention, and I learned about audience, content, argumentative strategy, and style. I fell in love with Sheridan Baker's *Complete Stylist and Handbook*—totally awed that there were comprehensible rules for all the grammatical and stylistic infelicities I had been producing and that they were all in one book. Of course, I'd had grammar in high school using the impenetrable *Warriner's*, but now it was beginning to make some sense, a foreign language broken open in my own writing.

A WALKABOUT INTO WRITING INSTRUCTION

Despite my passion about writing, when people asked what I would do with my degree, I had no specific answer. Even though teaching was suggested negatively ("those who can, *do*; those who can't, *teach*"), I decided to earn a teaching certificate. Although the education courses for that certification didn't crack open the secrets of good writing or writing instruction, I did get to interact with students around literature, grammar, and—occasionally—their writing. My practicum taught me that while I didn't choose to work with high school students, I did want to teach writing at the postsecondary level.

> *During practice teaching, I was conducting grammar lessons with the junior year honor's class and asked students for the correct past tense verb for this statement: "I lay/laid the book on the desk." Tommy said, "laid." "Ok," I said. "Tommy, tell me. How did you get laid?" The class roared. I turned towards the chalkboard to blush and laugh. Every class that day snorted when they entered my room.*

Graduate school for my MA in English Literature, Language, and Composition—an innovative focus for 1979—took me to Kansas State University in Manhattan, Kansas. I lived with my new husband Paul, a field artillery officer posted to Ft. Riley. I studied as a teaching assistant (TA) under Donald Stewart and learned by teaching first-year composition courses to traditional day students and night-course multilingual learners, then called ESL students. I most admired a Vietnamese doctor, one of the "boat people," who was a daytime janitor and nighttime English student wanting to be a certified physician in America. His tenacity and humility in learning a new language to regain his chosen profession and doing so from a teacher thirty years his junior humbled me.

Teaching others to write helped me write better, and writing better helped me to teach better. The TA composition pedagogy course taught me such skills as sentence combining and transformational generative grammar. But I most resonated with Robert Zoellner's 1969 monograph, "Talk-Write: A Behavioral Pedagogy for Composition." While I wasn't convinced by the behavioral theory, I was delighted to have Zoellner identify what my essay writing style is and why it likely wouldn't work for my students. My approach was the "think-write" style of the nineteenth-century rhetorical tradition rather than the *talk out your ideas while you write* theory that he promoted. Most important to me was Zoellner's statement that he had never seen a teacher *write spontaneous, original text for the class*, something that teachers of that time and the latter 1970s didn't do. Most don't now. Years before teachers journaled *with* their students, Zoellner dared them to write *for* their students while the students watched—modeling the stops, starts, hesitations, cross-outs, recursion, and general messiness of expert writers.

Zoellner's dare that I write for students—essentially the belief that we should show students how to write and how to get out of problematic writing situations—became the foundation for my teaching life. I have written an original paragraph (on the chalkboard) or an essay (using the computer) for every writing course I have taught for more than thirty-five years. I learned from Zoellner and my students that writing is, indeed, individualized but nonetheless teachable, demonstrable, and learnable when it is personalized by teacher and students doing the job together.

TREKKING INTO THE UNKNOWN

Life happened—multiple times. I graduated from the MA program in December 1980 and moved with Paul to Ft. Sill, Oklahoma. There, I got my first job teaching ESL to Puerto Rican field artillery recruits through Central Texas College. In three-week units, we worked an eight-hour day with various English reading, writing, and speaking skills. If our students didn't succeed, they were sent back to Puerto Rico to find another line of work. The Army—and my work with them—gave them an opportunity to move out of poverty. As rewarding as the work was, the high stakes created great stress, and I decided to leave the position after six months.

Additional teaching would wait until Paul and I moved from Oklahoma to Nürnberg, Bavaria in (then) West Germany. There and later in Stuttgart, Baden-Württemberg, I taught for a variety of postsecondary institutions including the University of Maryland, City Colleges of Chicago, and Temple University. I drove as many as two hours to one school setting, taught soldiers and spouses, earned as little as $800 and as much as $1200 per course, and absolutely loved teaching—not terribly worried about (but aware of) the awful pay. It was the beginning of thirteen happy years of teaching writing wherever and whenever I could.

> *Life happened in Germany, too. I had a son who knew only me during the week and re-met his father each weekend—for nearly the first two years of his life. Green Party terrorism led to barricades around previously open posts and housing areas (called* kasernes). *Once I drove down the mountain from our Stuttgart home and saw a burned-out car on the side of the road with military police and German polizei around it. When I returned about an hour later, there was nothing, not even sparkles of broken glass, to show that the car had been there. My friend, a military policeman, looked at me quizzically when I asked him about a bombed car. "Nothing happened there," he said. Similarly, a baby carriage had been exploded on the grape-vine encircled, mountain path where I daily walked with my son in his own buggy. It wasn't mentioned in the newspaper. In preparation for our return stateside in 1985 and from a need to create, I developed a project called the Dependent ID project, or DID, to teach parents about the possible dangers of child abduction that seemingly was rampant in the States. The goal was to fingerprint, photograph, and offer dog tag IDs for the children. With a slogan of "I DID. DID you?" the program was adopted widely in the local Army area. Both the terrorism and the successful community project influenced me to pay attention to global realities beyond those of the United States and to volunteer wherever I would live.*

Back in the States, we spent four years in Ft. Meade, Maryland—very close to family. I taught regularly for Anne Arundel Community College and was rewarded with promotions and pay increases. My supervisor was a no-nonsense professor who taught me a lot about teaching community college students. She cared enough to tell me I needed a PhD if I wanted a career of teaching writing. The time wasn't right, however, because being and remaining married to an Army officer meant that I had chosen to support him and put our family first. Our stateside tour passed quickly, and we moved back to Germany, this time to Hanau in Hesse.

Paul's work for the VII Army Corps meant less time for me to teach. He assisted with a government-required drawdown, or downsizing, of the U.S. Army in Germany and then applied his skills to the logistics of moving an army corps to a staging area in Saudi Arabia. He left us for Saudi on a tearful New Year's Day in 1991. There, my husband fought a different battle, eventually being returned to us with post-traumatic stress, a damaged sense of self, and a lost career.

> I'll never forget the night that our chaplain's wife came to visit me in our Hanau apartment, a converted WWII barracks that we fondly called the "bowling alley" for its 50' length. It was late, after 9:00 PM. No one calls or visits anyone after 9:00 in the military for fear that the call will be perceived as an emergency, causing a heavily beating heart and unnecessary worry. At the door, I asked her in and offered her tea. Putting the pot on the stove and proceeding to clean the kitchen table, I felt embarrassed that I hadn't done that earlier. As I sponged the table, she told me that Paul was in the hospital and why. I realized that she was my official notification rather than an officer or a telegram. She said her husband had been with him through the breakdown. Time froze. When she left, I sat for a while by my sleeping son. No tears. Then, I went to the computer (the one I had sold a beloved typewriter to buy) and began to write. I did not sleep that night.

When he returned, our lives were irrevocably changed by Paul's war with post-traumatic stress—a conflict that led us all to despair and back.

In 1992, we left the Army and returned to Maryland, where I was fortunate enough to work at the Aberdeen Proving Ground Job Assistance Center (JAC) as a job counselor while Paul searched for work. I taught soldiers and spouses how to write resumes and cover letters and how to interview for jobs. Counseling anxious soldiers and spouses was rewarding, yet painful given that Paul and I were walking in their shoes. I learned a lot about transferable skills particularly since I had to learn to use my own; this job fed our family for nearly a year after Paul left the service.

TOURING SCHOOL—AGAIN

After Paul was employed, I announced that I wanted to get my PhD so I could teach again. I wanted to know what I didn't know about writing. I enrolled in the rhetoric program at The Catholic University of America (CUA) and, having moved to Bowie, Maryland, began as a TA in fall 1993. I found myself in my former JAC clients' shoes when I began graduate school at age thirty-five. Returning to school was crucial for my sense of self and career, yet it put our family at additional risk in an already difficult economic time as it would take me out of the job market for a minimum of five years. Nonetheless, choosing to attend graduate school made me feel lighter and happier than I had in years, and all of us began to enjoy life again.

I loved my CUA classes and the work because I was able to teach with a fuller understanding of rhetoric and composition. At the same time, I struggled with bringing my fully adult self to an environment where I needed to surrender to professors' teachings. My younger classmates overwhelmed me because most had moved straight through from BA to MA to the PhD program. They spoke theory and ideas from our readings that were foreign to me. I needed to learn to read all over again and to absorb new vocabulary. Soon, though, I soared with fresh understanding regarding how theory touches practice. My writing strongly questioned theories with no clear basis in praxis; deconstruction seemed impractical, for example, while reader response and social construction made sense. That's the beauty of applying one's learning as an adult to a real-life context (i.e., *andragogy*): The learner is exponentially enriched with more meaningful learning (Knowles).

At this time, I read an article by Robert Marshak that postulated a middle ground between pedagogy and andragogy. Marshak called this in-between, adolescent-like learning period "adolegogy" to define some characteristics of college learners who crave the independence of an adult yet lean dependently on teachers. Adolegogical learners, who might require explicit instruction about essay content and how to write, may choose to ignore the instruction and write what they'd prefer to write about, for example.

I saw in myself such adolegogical characteristics and, thanks to Marshak, gratefully knew I wasn't alone. I wrote a seminar paper about what is now called *writing about writing* and labeled such writing *metadiscourse*. My professor explained carefully that I couldn't just make words up to fit my meaning; *metadiscourse* already had a different meaning in the field. However, I liked that word to describe my notion and chose to stick with it; I received a slightly lowered grade and a written finger wag. My mixed, not-quite-andragogical learning approach—independent to the point of frustrating my professors, yet dependent on their guidance to the point of my occasional tears—confused us all. I respected them and wanted to learn from them, yet I was intimidated by their superior knowledge. Sometimes, I needed to stand up to them. It was difficult to hold onto my adult self while accepting that to grow intellectually I first needed to bend myself to new ideas and ways of being. Indeed, CUA wasn't the first place I encountered my adolegogical self.

> *When I studied for my MA, I had eighteen months to finish the degree before Paul and I were to move from Kansas. Early in the spring semester, I discussed a possible thesis topic with my advisor. Following that discussion, I conducted my research, wrote my thesis that summer, and presented it complete to my advisor in early October. He looked at me, astonished. "That's not how we do things," he said. "We have a meeting with a committee, you write a proposal, we review and comment on that, and then you can write the thesis." "But, it's done," I said. "But, that's not how we do it," he repeated. "But, it's done," I said again, completely baffled. And it was done and accepted as complete. Nonetheless, I learned that being self-motivated doesn't always lead to having done things the right way in academe.*

Mixed, adolegogical approaches to learning can be somewhat frustrating if teachers don't recognize that becoming an adult learner from a child learner's stance involves testing middle ground in teen-like fits and starts and occasional retreats to more childlike stances. With this understanding, I've become more generous to college students of all ages, guiding them toward levels of educational independence that will serve them well as lifelong learners while overtly teaching them why expected outcomes sometimes trump that independence in college.

A JAUNT INTO NINETEENTH-CENTURY RHETORIC

I frustrated professors in other ways, too. As I studied rhetorical history and online composition, I was surprised to discover that I loved researching both. I couldn't make up my mind which I preferred, and I bounced between professors, which they found irritating. I responded to the program in freeflow, enjoying this, learning that, and generally filling a hungry mind that had resisted the strictures of being an Army spouse and craved intellectual fulfillment.

Hence, when Jean Dietz Moss handed me a copy of Samuel Phillip Newman's *A Practical System of Rhetoric* to analyze, I researched Newman with gusto. He had been severely chastised for being insufficiently innovative. Always a sucker for the underdog, I read Newman's rhetoric and found that there were good reasons that the book had sixty editions and was the first commercially popular text of its time, among them the work's rhetorical currency and the author's strong ethos among students and peers. I've since published four papers about Newman and his influence on nineteenth-century rhetoric.

> *I wonder, who is the underdog, the "minor" rhetorician in our times? I think it is most of us who care about what we're doing—we publish and study and teach and try to make a difference. I remember being a table discussion leader at a Research Network Forum at the Conference on College Composition and Communication (CCCC) convention. One participant said: "I want to study Richard Weaver for my career!" That's admirable, I thought. Weaver was important to twentieth-century American rhetoric. But I couldn't just study Weaver. I want to be a Weaver! This experience revealed to me a desire to be a forward thinker in rhetoric and composition and not one who is content with merely studying others who have gone before me.*

Eventually, I had to decide what I would study for my dissertation and, presumably, for some years after graduation. Reluctantly, I chose to leave Newman and his contemporaries behind for what seemed to me to be a more vital area of research in online composition.

AN EXCURSION INTO COLLABORATION

Collaborative theory as a by-product of social construction was strongly emphasized in graduate school during the mid-1990s, and it fascinated me because I saw the kinds of teaching I did in the JAC as collaboration. While I had used peer response groups and workshops in writing instruction before, reading more about collaboration prompted me to wonder: If peer response groups for undergraduates were supposed to be so powerful, then why weren't we graduate students being asked to participate regularly in peer groups?

> *I asked our professor whether our class could engage in peer reading of our own before papers were due. She and the class agreed to meet during class time for two weekly peer review workshops, and my first major lesson about collaborative reading and writing in academe occurred: Even academics may be reluctant to engage in collaborative peer review. I was the only one prepared with a paper for the class to review. No one else had gotten past an early outline or a*

few paragraphs, and they wouldn't share them; those who brought text to share expressed embarrassment. I was genuinely surprised and felt like my students must feel when they are in peer groups and too few come prepared. I knew that published scholars regularly shared writing for peer assistance before submitting it. I wondered whether my peers' failure to share writing for collaborative discussion was an anomaly or a result of the paper being for a course and not having the exigency of a dissertation or paper/book for publication.

I had another look at collaboration in peer groups for my dissertation research, where I compared oral and online peer response groups' feedback with their writing changes. The findings suggested that the students used their peers' advice, but they used it differently when the group met orally (face to face) and asynchronously online. When they worked orally, they talked a lot about the context and content of their writing and shared their ideas intertextually in the revised writing. Surprisingly, it seemed that students felt free to use each other's ideas more when they worked face to face. They also seemed to generate their own ideas in the context of the conversation. However, when they met online, they appeared to be constrained by the asynchronous, time-delayed threading of the chat; their revisions showed fewer instances of group-generated intertextual and self-generated ideas. I realized that a proscription against plagiarism may discourage online students from using in their own writing the ideas their peer groups generate (*Characteristics* 233; "Characteristics"). This result surprised me because it is completely opposite what educators previously believed about online writing instruction (OWI) and plagiarism.

Twelve years later, Charlotte Robidoux and I coedited *Virtual Collaborative Writing in the Workplace: Computer-Mediated Communication Technologies and Processes*; it focused on collaboration in online workplace settings. I was attracted to this subject because the prevalence of online writing in the global, collaborative work world is ostensibly one reason that we teach students to write in online settings. We invited both rhetoric scholars and technical communication professionals onto our writing team, making everyone's voice equal in the book's overall direction as well as one's own chapter. We used a wiki and an internal listserv, among other collaborative tools. Before long, we encountered significant differences among the writers, who self-identified as "scholar" or "professional" and the held values of these identities. We studied these collaborative processes as the book was written and edited, making the book's final chapter an ethnographic meta-analysis of the collaborative process. Even though initially every writer on the team avowed a commitment to collaborative writing as part of their practiced writing behaviors, we observed that the professional writers were far more collaborative and forthcoming in discussing the direction of their writing, as well as more open to critique. As a whole, the scholars were reluctant even to work in the wiki let alone make word changes to others' texts, citing concern about their own words or meaning being changed or misunderstood. When we began to understand what was happening, Robidoux and I worked to develop a practical rhetoric of trust for virtual collaboration that uses the classical canons refitted to contemporary online collaboration. These experiences taught me that collaboration is an odd concept in academe, and it needs far more attention than the lip service it gets about student peer response group benefits.

SEEKING A ROAD TO COMMUNITY

When I wrote my first dissertation proposal draft in 1996, I went to Martin Buber's "I-Thou" (I-You) philosophy, a belief that genuine relationship is possible yet rare (*I and Thou* "First Part"); this relationship is a communion of sorts. Buber's philosophy of *communion*, which others have used interchangeably with *community*, changed my willingness to use the word *community* in the educational setting. I have experienced the communion he described in certain intimate moments with people who are emotionally open in an especially gifting manner. Every other moment is not community-based in this purest sense, and I want to honor those sacred moments with a term I use nowhere else.

> *There are occasions when people can be genuinely emotionally open, but it takes effort and intention. At times, I have experienced deep connection with my spouse, son, mother, and best friend, as well as a few other people and animals. Such intimate moments are about risking seeing the essence of the Other, who can in turn provide healing acceptance of our very beings, the parts that we fear are completely unacceptable to the world. Such a bridge into community has revealed people's realness and made it possible for me to love others, including my students, more authentically.*

Therefore, I liked Buber's use of the word *association* to describe the far more common, goal-oriented interactions—or transactions—that people have with one another (e.g., 95, 117).

Education is institutionally configured as transactional. Students need to learn; teachers need to teach. Assessments, evaluations, and grades always reveal the false assumption that we are equal (Black). This distinction is why writing centers, peer response groups, and online discussion groups will never be the *pure* community that some believe they can or should be. Similarly, this distinction suggests that OWI *can become* a place of connection among students and teachers because the online setting doesn't interfere with successful community given that such community isn't typically possible in institutional and educational settings (Black 94). By owning transaction in education, a middle ground opens involving not community, not association, but moments of potential connection among students and between and among student/s and teacher, tutee/s and tutor where they might see each other authentically as humans. This forthright, candid approach then enables discussion about what really can happen educationally—especially in the often faceless world of OWI. When we look to what might be achieved realistically without the purity (and impossibility) of community as God term (per Kenneth Burke), we can see the incredible connections that students and teachers actually can and do have in onsite and online settings alike.

→ THIS WAY TO ONLINE WRITING INSTRUCTION

I became interested in OWI in 1994 just as CUA was considering using intranet-based software to network students asynchronously. I wondered why students who lived and took classes on campus would need to meet in classes online. How did this process work and why? In the spirit of answering such questions, I volunteered to head the project. Exploring OWI has enabled me to ask and attempt answers to serious questions affecting hundreds of thousands of college students and their online instructors. After graduate school, my job path became part of my OWI journey, and I sought work in both traditional postsecondary and corporate environments. What started twenty-two years ago continues to be my academic work and my scholarly center.

I accepted a job at a Baltimore community college as WPA, writing center director, and teacher. The anecdotal injunction against taking on WPA or other administration work when untenured is good advice; this job had no tenure to seek, no promotions to grant, and I had no real authority. I worked both as writing program and writing center director, participated in or led seven committees, taught two classes, helped to bring the English department online, and developed a pilot online writing center in eighteen months. I juggled all these balls fairly successfully, but lost sight of the most important ball: being encouraging with and connected to the teachers who needed to adjust quickly to all these changes—and this failure is simultaneously one of my greatest regrets and learning experiences.

I chose to leave this stressful community college job for another stress-filled but exciting position as the Writing Program Director at Smarthinking, Inc. ("Interdependency"). Not only did this job appeal to my belief that online tutoring is helpful for students, but it allowed me to be creative and conduct practical research. In 2001, after nearly two years at Smarthinking, I was offered a job at a branch campus of the Pennsylvania State University (PSU). Finally, I had the tenure-line position of which I had dreamed! To get that sense of place, however, we left our Maryland home of eight years—the longest we had ever lived anywhere. Paul and I moved to Pennsylvania, but he returned to work in his Maryland office weekly. Our son happily began college at Virginia Tech.

At PSU, I immediately began a research project about how online writing students used the instruction they received from instructors (Smarthinking tutors, in this case). No one had studied how student writing actually changed when they received online instruction before, and I was excited to begin that work.

> *I thought I finally was on the right path and in the right place academically, but my journey took some unexpected turns almost immediately. Shortly after we arrived, the terrorist attacks of 9/11 changed Paul's plans to work primarily from Pennsylvania. Thereafter, his work in emergency management required that he stay in Baltimore and Washington, DC, more frequently. I was alone in this new place. At the end of the first semester, after I collected the first part of my research data, I had an initial visit with my dean to explain my research plans. He told me that I needed to stop that work and return to an abandoned piece from years earlier—a study of Newman's rhetorical connections with his student Nathaniel Hawthorne (a paper I decided to revise and publish nearly twenty years later as "Nathaniel Hawthorne" with a coauthor who filled in the gaps regarding Hawthorne's writing). The dean simultaneously was indirect and clear: I wouldn't be tenured with the OWI research.*

Feeling frustrated and uncertain, I learned two days later that my father had died. His death stirred up grief for my older brother's still-excruciating death the previous year. I knew I needed to return to Maryland to help my devastated mother. This decision has since impacted every aspect of my life. I chose to complete my two-year commitment to PSU, so for the next eighteen months, I taught and collected data during the week and drove eight hours round-trip each weekend to care for my bereaved mother.

A FORK IN THE ROAD

Relocating to Maryland in 2003 allowed me to continue to be my mother's companion while taking a new path as an independent scholar. I began consulting with a variety of educational institutions about their OWI programs—from universities to such for-profit companies as Pearson Education and TutorVista. I taught writing for the University of Maryland University College as an Adjunct Associate Professor and worked for seven years as an editor for the online composition journal *Kairos*. Additionally, I continued researching OWI from a passionate desire to understand how writing instruction changes (or must change) in online settings. Most importantly, I began Defend & Publish, LLC, an online, distance-based business for coaching dissertators, scholars, and other professional writers to success. I am proud that since its inception twelve years ago, this company continues to pay special attention to the varied needs of adult writers, and it does so fully online and at a distance.

I've accomplished a lot in researching OWI because I've had a nagging sense that there's something fundamentally different about OWI from traditional writing instruction—a difference engendered by technology that's not just body/face/voice-related. Past theories that guided my teaching and learning have come into play as I've attempted to theorize the online writing center and OWI more generally.

Most recently, I've taken the path of studying how online writing centers (OWLs) mirror and depart from traditional onsite ones. I've been dissecting the difficulties caused by still-current definitions of collaboration and student ownership of writing. My position is that OWLs need to be developed and discussed from a theory-generating stance because I see them as a crucial part of a viable writing program's design. Training tutors, whether peer or professional, for OWL work has its own challenges, and so I have been researching what tutors need and how to offer appropriate training and professional development.

Based on empirical research and observation, I have developed a theory of semantic integrity, which purports there must be fidelity between what teachers and tutors write in their response to online students and what they want those words to mean. Practically speaking, this fidelity requires using straightforward language that is linguistically direct rather than indirect, and foregoing rhetorical and closed questions and conditional, suggestive language. In other words, semantic integrity enacts my belief learned from Zoellner that writing is teachable and that it is necessary to teach writing explicitly in online and text-based settings. We must be more than reader-responders; we also must be teachers who overtly guide by demonstrating and modeling what the student might do next—offering choices but clearly showing what those choices might look like if enacted. My belief that collaboration should be allowable and that it is necessary particularly in online settings means there is no "cheating" in "doing for students" by providing models. Furthermore, semantic integrity theory asks teachers to personalize the response with students' own writing in order to garner trust and interest in what is being taught. Therefore, I have proposed writing problem-centered lessons with a four-step intervention process and an action plan centered on explanation to the online student (see *Online Writing Conference* and *Reading to Learn*).

I've investigated semantic integrity theory further by exploring the cognitive leap that students take with online communication, an issue I wrote about with my son, Russell J. Hewett ("IM Talking about Workplace Literacy"). I believe that the most basic problem of OWI is not one of community unrealized (given that connection can, indeed, occur), but one of *literacy*. One of the major benefits postulated for OWI always has been that students must write much more than in traditional onsite settings (Barker and Kemp; Warnock), which is beneficial for developing fluency. In an OWI setting, even where audio/video content, explanations, or response are offered, the majority of the learning happens *textually* and must be absorbed individually through *reading*. Text-based learning is highly dependent on students' reading and comprehension abilities. Undeniably, as I learned during my years at *Kairos,* alphabetic, text-based literacy remains crucial despite the increasing popularity of digital literacy and maybe even because of it. Text remains part of much multimodal communication even when the rhetorical product is not essayist in nature.

The corollary to that increase in writing is an increase in the number of reading tasks and the general amount and type of reading required (e.g., instruction, content, assignments, their own writing, teacher response, and other students' writing). Students must read even more than they write in online writing courses—hence, the literacy challenge. Nonetheless, it's too easy to place responsibility for OWI-based literacy concerns on students alone. Literacy has two participants: reader and writer. If reading is students' major challenge with OWI, then writing is teachers' and tutors' major problem. Teachers and tutors traditionally have not been taught *to write* their instruction at student vocabulary levels and specifically for student understanding. Instructors need help in writing if they are to assist students with the reading challenges inherent to OWI. *Reading to Learn and Writing to Teach: Literacy Strategies for OWI* engages my long-held understanding of directly teaching and modeling writing, collaboration that allows appropriation, and a sense of association in that the OWI educational venue is transactional but that connection and relationship are attainable.

As the first chair of the CCCC Committee for Effective Practices in OWI, I have had deep association with other scholars. The committee started small with seven original members and grew to twelve active participants and more than twenty experts who supported our work through advice. There, I found a sense of academic place where my interests and skills fit and where others were eager to explore OWI with passion. Beginning in 2007, the committee's goals of empirically researching OWI practices were realized through various published resources, numerous presentations and workshops, an online open forum for showcasing instructors' effective OWI practices, and "A Position Statement of OWI Principles and Effective Practices in OWI" (Committee for Effective Practices). This uniquely rewarding work has led to practical theorizing by some amazing scholars, published in *Foundational Practices in OWI*. By the time I left the chair position in 2014, our committee had done something truly unique in OWI: We purposefully placed *access* at the forefront of our fifteen OWI Principles.

Most recently, my colleagues and I founded the Global Society of Online Literacy Educators (GSOLE), of which I was elected the first president. GSOLE is an international organization dedicated to research and its distribution through professional development mentoring, webinars, conferences, the *Online Literacy Open Resource* (OLOR), and a born-digital, open-access journal *Research in Online Literacy Education* (*ROLE*). We are excited about our progress in developing an international certification for online literacy teachers and tutors. This work will improve quality and accountability as well as bring online literacy education up to twenty-first-century standards.

FINDING A HIGHWAY THROUGH GRIEF

My typical reactions to adversities have been to power through, work harder, and wait for pain to recede—each act stemming from a stubborn, if resilient, nature. However, in the past sixteen years, I have lost two siblings, both parents (my mother having recently died from a traumatic brain injury), both of my in-laws, and a favorite aunt. The griefs from their deaths have been so painful that they required a new response from me: Surrender to the pain, embrace it, and find the healing and grace in life after loss. From my hard work of mourning, I found not only hope but joy. Feeling deep grief and learning how to mourn actively propelled me to learn how to share hope and healing with other bereaved people. My recent work as a certified thanatologist, bereavement trainer, group facilitator, grief coach, and author has brought healing not only to those I serve but also to me.

Working with grief might seem to be an odd direction for a scholar, but grief hits us all, and when it hit me, I needed to do something positive with it. While I was a graduate student at CUA, Lynn Bloom was a visiting speaker. She talked about what would become an influential article: "Why Don't We Write What We Teach? And Publish It?" Her argument, aptly outlined in its title, touched me as a call for rhetoricians and compositionists to enact their craft out of a love of writing and a desire to be authentic. Years later, her words inspired me to write and publish *Good Words: Memorializing Through a Eulogy* as a rhetorically sound guide for a general audience, the people who need just-in-time help in writing eulogies for their deceased loved ones. Later, I published *More Good Words: Practical Activities for Mourning* and, with Richard Ottenstein, *More Good Words: Grief in the Workplace*. Working closely with the bereaved has taught me to listen with ears open, mouth shut, and full presence. That alone is a gift of a lifetime.

WALKING THE *CAMINO*

My pilgrimage to Santiago de Compostella, Spain, left me profoundly changed in some fundamental ways. I learned that when a person has more than one deep interest and a compelling sense of obligation and motivation in different areas, one may never feel complete on any one path. As I review my academic life, I see the many paths I have taken. Of this much I am sure: It is *because* I haven't had the traditional academic journey that I've had such freedom to do what I wanted to do, learn what I needed to learn, and touch lives in meaningful ways. Undoubtedly, even my hardest choices have been the right ones for me although sometimes they didn't feel good and their results seemed upsetting. As I mentioned in the introduction of this chapter, I don't believe my life has been defined by serendipity or chance, but instead, has been about making purposeful choices, like walking a road and acknowledging the forks by choosing which direction to take is one way to live with integrity and to own the journey. Doing so isn't easy, but it can come with unexpected rewards beyond the promise of one job for life. Walking the intentional journey can come with the reward of actually living one's life rather than hoping one's way through it.

Life is a journey. What we do with it is the *way*, the *Camino*. It is the legacy, the destination, and the being—if we actually allow ourselves *to be*. Buen Camino.

WORKS CITED

Baker, Sheridan Warner. *The Complete Stylist and Handbook*. New York, NY: Harper and Row, 1984. Print.

Barker, Thomas T., and Fred O. Kemp. "Network Theory: A Postmodern Pedagogy for the Writing Classroom." *Computers and Community: Teaching Composition in the Twenty-First Century*. Ed. Carolyn Handa. Portsmouth, NH: Boynton/Cook, 1990. 1–27. Print.

Black, Laurel Johnson. *Between Talk and Teaching: Reconsidering the Writing Conference*. Logan: Utah State UP, 1998. Print.

Bloom, Lynn Z. "Why Don't We Write What We Teach? And Publish It?" *Journal of Advanced Composition* 10.1 (1990): 87–100. JAC Article Stable. Web. July 21, 2014.

Buber, Martin. *I and Thou*. Trans. Walter Kaufmann. New York: Scribner, 1965. Print.

Burke, Kenneth. *Burke, 1945, 1969: A Grammar of Motives*. Berkeley: U of California P, 1969. Print.

Committee for Effective Practices in Online Writing Instruction. "A Position Statement of OWI Principles and Effective Practices in OWI." Conference on College Composition and Communication (CCCC), 2013. Web. July 21, 2013.

———. *The Characteristics and Effects of Oral and Computer-Mediated Peer Group Talk on the Argumentative Writing Process*. Diss. The Catholic University of America, 1998. Ann Arbor: UMI, 1998. AAT 9906570. Print.

———. "Characteristics of Interactive Oral and Computer-Mediated Peer Group Talk and Its Influence on Revision." *Computers and Composition* 17 (2000): 265–88. Print.

———. *Good Words: Memorializing Through a Eulogy*. Rev. ed. Bloomington, IN: WestBow P, 2014. Print.

———. *More Good Words: Practical Activities for Mourning*. Rev. ed. Bloomington, IN: WestBow P, 2014. Print.

———. *The Online Writing Conference: A Guide for Teachers and Tutors*. Rev. ed. Boston: Bedford/St. Martin's P, 2015. Print.

———. *Reading to Learn and Writing to Teach: Literacy Strategies for OWI*. Boston: Bedford/St. Martin's P, 2015. Print.

———. "Synchronous Online Conference-Based Instruction: A Study of Whiteboard Interactions and Student Writing." *Computers and Composition* 23.1 (2006): 4–31. Print.

Hewett, Beth L., and Kevin DePew, eds. *Foundational Practices of OWI*. Perspectives on Writing. Santa Barbara, CA: WAC Clearinghouse, 2015. Print.

Hewett, Beth L., and Russell J. Hewett. "IM Talking about Workplace Literacy." *Handbook of Research on Virtual Workplaces and the New Nature of Business Practices*. Eds. Kirk St. Amant and Pavel Zemliansky. New York: Information Science Reference, 2008. 455–72. Print.

Hewett, Beth L., and Richard J. Ottenstein. *More Good Words: Grief in the Workplace*. Omaha, NE: Grief Illustrated P, 2013. Print.

Hewett, Beth L., and Charlotte A. Robidoux, eds. *Virtual Collaborative Writing in the Workplace: Computer-Mediated Communication Technologies and Processes*. Hershey, PA: IGI Global, 2010. Print.

Hewett, Beth L., and Erin Singer. "Nathaniel Hawthorne's Travel Sketches and Samuel P. Newman's *A Practical System of Rhetoric*: A Case of American Belletristic Theory on Praxis." *Advances in the History of Rhetoric* 19.3 (2016): 298–320. Print.

Marshak, Robert. "What's Between Pedagogy and Andragogy?" *Training and Development Journal* (October 1983): 80–81. Print.

Newman, Samuel Phillips. *A Practical System of Rhetoric, or the Principles and Rules of Style, Inferred from Examples of Writing.* Portland, OR: William Hyde, 1827. Print.

Warnock, Scott. *Teaching Writing Online: How and Why.* Urbana, IL: NCTE, 2009. Print.

Warriner, John E. *Warriner's English Grammar and Composition.* New York: Harcourt, Brace, Jovanovich, 1982. Print.

Weaver, Richard. *The Ethics of Rhetoric.* Davis, CA: Hermagoras P, 1985. Print.

Zoellner, Robert. "Talk-Write: A Behavioral Pedagogy for Composition." *College English* 30.4 (1969): 267–320. Print.

CHAPTER 11

Southern Girl Seeks Wide-Open Spaces

My Journey through Academia

TIFFANY BOURELLE

It's a beautiful fall day in Albuquerque, New Mexico, with the aspen trees that line the Rio Grande beginning to turn yellow and orange. I can see the trees dotting the skyline as I sit at my computer, and as I write, I wish I were running along the paved path that winds against the river. I need to do something to clear my head before tackling the big task ahead of me. I'm in my fifth year as an assistant professor at the University of New Mexico, which means I have the daunting assignment of compiling my dossier for my tenure review. The Arts and Sciences website tells me that I'm to include a narrative about my teaching and research, describing what has influenced me the most as a teacher-scholar. I'm also required to include supplemental materials from past mentors and students. This task inadvertently forces me to travel down memory lane, something I don't do very often. I tend to avoid thinking about the past, especially when I have to reflect on my work. I've always thought of my past as being full of mistakes, and I'd rather not think about the difficult times.

In preparation for this compilation of materials, I think about first writing my chapter for this collection, which will help me reflect on what led me to sit right here, in this spot, on the second floor of the humanities building on the UNM campus. I figured I'd probably write about my difficult decision to leave a tenure-track job for a contingent position and the hard road I had to climb to obtain a job at a research-extensive university. But as I start to brainstorm and take notes for this chapter, I realize that most of my decisions were based on opportune chances—kairotic moments—that occurred throughout my life, not just my decision to leave my first tenure-track job. In "Kairos and Rhetoric of Science," Carolyn Miller indicates that a kairotic moment "presents itself at a distinct point in time, manifesting its own requirements, and making demands on the rhetor, which the rhetor must discern in order to succeed" (312). The decisions I've made and the resulting life experiences weren't mistakes; indeed, as Morton Meyers notes in *Happy Accidents: Serendipity in Modern Medical Breakthroughs*, they were "happy accidents" that led me to where I am today. Many paths that have presented themselves in my life seem to have come at just the right moment—kairos and serendipity working conjunctively in my life, demanding new challenges with every situation.

As I draft an outline, my eyes wander over the pictures that line my desk. There's one of me and my husband, Andy, climbing El Capitan at Yosemite, which seems like an appropriate metaphor for the task at hand. There's also another one of an ultrasound with my son, Ben, growing inside my belly around four months prebirth. Another is a picture of me, my husband, and Ben, taken around Ben's eight-month birthday. The last one my gaze falls upon is a picture taken a few years ago of me with Smokey, the mascot for the University of Tennessee. My mom took the picture on my thirty-fourth birthday when I flew home and attended a football game with my parents, hoping to recapture some of my youth with that trip. These pictures remind me of all the twists and turns it took to get me here. But the picture with Smokey is the one that makes me realize—the kairotic opportunities that presented themselves actually occurred earlier than I thought.

MY BLOOD RUNNETH ORANGE

I did my undergraduate work at the University of Tennessee, probably for the wrong reasons. I chose UT because it was close to home and because I was raised on a small farm in Tennessee where the only thing to do on the weekends was watch college football. My love for the Tennessee Volunteers—the boys in orange—ran deep from the time I could understand the rules of football. When I graduated from high school, UT seemed like the obvious choice, and it certainly made my parents proud. I felt like I was headed in the right direction; however, it wasn't as easy as I had expected. I didn't really study in high school and still made excellent grades. Coursework at the university would prove to be much harder.

I wandered aimlessly for a few years at UT, not certain of what I wanted to do with my life. I'm terribly analytical about everything, and my career choice was no different. I went through six majors until, finally, my exasperated mentor who was also my English professor told me, "Just pick something already and stick with it." We talked about how I was good at writing papers in his class, which was a course on Medieval Literature. I loved *The Canterbury Tales, Sir Gawain and the Green Knight,* and *Troilus and Criseyde,* but I just couldn't understand how my love of reading was going to translate into a career. Combine that with the fact that my sister had determined, some years prior, that she was going to obtain a Liberal Arts degree, prompting my dad to ask her why she wanted to flip burgers for the rest of her life. No, literature was not my path.

While taking my mentor's course, I was also enrolled in an Advanced Rhetoric course and was working as a research assistant for a professor who had a dual appointment at the Law School and in the English department. Rhetoric and law seemed to work in conjunction: if rhetoric is the art of persuasion, knowing the skills of rhetoric would help lawyers who were trying to convince a jury or judge. Linda Berger suggests that for law professors, rhetoric offers a way to combine their objects of study (i.e., legal texts that are open to interpretation) with the subject matter of what they are teaching. As she notes, "The professor who uses a rhetorical approach to analyze a judicial opinion will be better able to teach students how to interpret and construct legal arguments because the professor has taken apart the structure of an argument and evaluated the effectiveness of the author's rhetorical choices" (7). Learning to break down these arguments according to their parts could only serve to help future lawyers in structuring their own rhetorically sound arguments. Because rhetoric and law seemed inextricably intertwined, I quickly attached myself to the career path of lawyer. However, while working as a research assistant, I had to sit in on several cases, one of which had enormous impact. I watched a man whom I was certain was guilty escape punishment because of what the jury deemed as lack of evidence. At the moment the verdict was announced, I knew law was not in my future; this would be the first situational context—or kairotic moment—that presented itself and led me to ultimately choose a major.

I was still intrigued by rhetoric, and as a result of my mentor's own use of persuasion to convince me that I was a good writer, I chose English as my major. The university offered different tracks for English degrees, and I decided to focus on technical communication as my emphasis. This may seem like a stray away from rhetoric, but it's quite the opposite. Charles Beck tells us that rhetoric forms the theoretical base for technical communication, as rhetoric informs the process of creating human discourse, both formal and informal, written or spoken; this process includes "thought, language, communication, and purposive action" (781). Similarly, Beck notes, technical communication is concerned with these aspects as well, with a focus on organizational discourse and the collaborative nature of writing. Kelli Cargile Cook calls for the acquisition of rhetorical literacy on the part of a technical communicator, suggesting students need to learn how an audience will shape discourse depending on the purpose of a document and the situation or context for writing. Indeed, students of technical communication must be able to "analyze, evaluate, and employ various invention and writing strategies" based on these decisions (10).

While taking these courses, I still managed to spend Saturdays at Neyland Stadium watching football. In fact, my love of football is what inadvertently influenced my decision to go to graduate school. In 1998, the Tennessee Volunteers had their "Year of Destiny" where it seemed they just couldn't lose. They made it all the way to the national championship that year, and people lined up outside the student union to register for the lottery that would give away tickets. With 40,000 students attending UT that year, it seemed unlikely that I would win. And I didn't. But my best friend did, and as she passed her extra ticket over to my greedy hands, we determined that we were somehow going to the game. We didn't have a car that could make it all the way to Arizona where the game would be played, so we asked a couple of friends if they wanted to road trip the 2000 miles from Knoxville to Tempe. Luckily, they said yes, and we set off—my first time past the Mississippi River. On our way, we stopped in Flagstaff, and I felt something I hadn't felt before. I somehow knew I was supposed to come back to Flag—as the locals call it—and live there. I was awestruck by the wide-open spaces, specifically by how the San Francisco Peaks jutted out of the land in an unexpected way, seemingly strangers in the barren desert land that stretches for miles and miles on Interstate 40. After arriving back home, I researched Northern Arizona University, the only university in town, and discovered they offered a master's in Rhetoric and Composition. I applied to no other graduate programs except NAU, and, fortunately, I was admitted. I would start my master's in Rhetoric and Composition in the fall of 2001. After graduating from UT, I packed up my bags, told my parents goodbye, and headed out West to start my new life.

GETTING MY KICKS ON ROUTE 66

I became a serious student at NAU, and although I was admitted without a traditional Teaching Assistantship the first year, the chair of the English department found a position for me as a writing consultant for the Forestry Department. I coached undergraduate and graduate students through the process of writing, from brainstorming down to the final editing stage. Because of my background in technical communication, I could easily help them with their lab reports, memos, and management plans. During my first semester at NAU, I also took a class on ethnography, and I was assigned to write an ethnographic research paper on a group of my choice within Flagstaff. I chose the forestry students as my group, and I focused on learning their most evident writing issues or problems; this study included assessing student papers according to a rubric used by the forestry professors to grade papers. My two-year study allowed me to look at their papers across several semesters, illuminating students' progression or regression in writing skills. I also did follow-up interviews with the students to learn what impacted the fluctuation in assessment scores, asking them to discuss their needs in terms of what the department could do to better serve them and why they felt their writing had progressed or regressed (i.e., life factors, particular classes, etc.). The results of this study would help future writing consultants, as well as professors and instructors, learn how to best address students' problems in writing, and perhaps more importantly, their needs in terms of curriculum and overall degree trajectory.

The study I describe evolved into my thesis project, and while researching over the two years, I became heavily entrenched in Writing-Across-the-Curriculum (WAC) theory and practices. I was influenced by the initial work of Art Young and Toby Fulwiler in *Writing across the Disciplines: Research into Practice,* especially the idea that students are capable of learning in a variety of ways, including hands-on experience, memorization, or other techniques. In addition, WAC seeks to help instructors across campus learn to incorporate writing into their assignments, especially when they are new to the "writing-to-learn" approach that WAC promotes. As Writing Consultant, I hosted several workshops for teachers and students alike, helping instructors develop writing-intensive assignments and lesson plans and assisting students in learning the genre conventions of the documents they were creating in their majors. In other words, I was already doing the work of WAC, I just didn't know it or have the theory to support it. The theory—and the kairotic moment to apply what I learned in my experiences as Writing Consultant—would present itself in Reno, Nevada, where I would go on to obtain my PhD and work in a WAC-based writing center.

THE BIGGEST LITTLE DECISION

To simply say I moved to Reno is drastically skimming over the difficult decision to leave Flagstaff. I did visit Reno, and while sitting in a park with a friend who made the trip with me, I couldn't help but notice how the city seemed dilapidated. The university sits right at the end of downtown, and as a tourist visiting campus, I stayed in a casino hotel because it was cheap. To get to the school, you have to walk through downtown and see the city in all of its glory. There were numerous pawn shops, bars on the windows of store fronts, and McDonald's food bags lining the streets. If I'm not painting a pretty picture, that's because my first impression of Reno wasn't a good one. And it wouldn't improve after I moved there, with strippers living across the street and a known drug dealer two houses down. My life was bleak as I reminisced about the Coconino National Forest, daydreaming about my daily hikes up Mt. Humphrey, the majestic mountain that serves as backdrop to the quiet little hippie town of Flagstaff.

It didn't help matters that I felt like a fraud in all of my classes at my new university. Like most new PhD students, I felt I didn't belong at that level. It took me several years to find an idea for my dissertation, which I now realize is somewhat normal for graduate students. At the time, however, I felt like a failure, especially when the students around me seemed to know what they were doing. I would soon understand that my peers' ideas would change and evolve, or even be thrown out for entirely new ones. I went through several iterations of the dissertation, starting one draft after another, but nothing really intrigued me. I was the Assistant Director at the writing center for three years while at UNR, under the direction of Dr. Mark Waldo, but I really had no intention of getting a job with a writing center after graduating; therefore, I didn't think that a writing center dissertation was in the cards. However, a conversation with a tutor made me start to think about how to connect my master's work to my doctoral work.

As Assistant Director, it was my job to train the tutors, and this training consisted of observing them and offering feedback. I had just observed one tutor, Barrie, and she and I were having a conversation about what she could do to improve her tutoring. She asked me if there was a list of common errors that students came to writing centers for help with, and was there any scholarship surrounding how to approach these issues in writing. I asked Waldo, and he led me to rhetoric and composition scholars such as Andrea Lunsford, Robert Connors, and Franklin Eugene Horowitz who outline common errors made by first-year writers in their handbook, *EasyWriter*. Or other scholars, like Paula Gillespie and Neal Lerner, who suggest specifically that tutors in writing centers often see problems with thesis development, support for arguments, and appropriate levels of critical thinking. As I read more scholarship, an idea began to form, but I wasn't exactly able to pinpoint what it was.

While working in the center, I took a graduate seminar from Waldo during my third year, and we read Mary Field Belenky et al.'s important work,

Women's Ways of Knowing. Belenky et al. posit that a great number of women feel silenced and remain that way until a catalyst for change influences them to help find their voices. In an effort to prove that women's learning styles are different from those of men, the authors interview several women, ranging from students receiving formal education to women who received their education from "invisible colleges," what they describe as agencies providing services to mothers. In choosing these women from the "invisible colleges," Belenky et al. shed light on less well-known strategies for promoting women's developmental practices in out-of-school settings (13). Through interviewing these women, Belenky et al. outline five levels of development, the first of which is silence. The youngest of the women interviewed had not yet found their voices; they lacked the ability to express or develop thought. Feeling passive without a voice, they turned to authorities as knowers. I could relate to this stage—I hadn't yet found my voice in academia and often stayed silent in seminars. And I definitely recognized a pattern in turning to authorities for guidance, especially my professors, and I almost always let their advice guide my decisions.

But I also realized that these authorities—my many mentors in undergraduate and graduate school, not to mention my mother—had guided me to find my own voice and to make my own decisions. As Belenky et al. suggest, these mentors showed me understanding and acceptance, and many times they encouraged collaboration and dialogue to help me work through my collegiate issues. I wanted to do something similar with the students who came into the writing center. Instead of teaching my tutors to impose their own expectations and arbitrary requirements, I could teach them to "encourage students to evolve their own patterns of work based on the problems they are pursuing" (Belenky et al. 229). I started by researching gendered patterns in writing, discovering that scholars before me had outlined these patterns for me. While researching these patterns, I found my topic: I would study gender patterns in writing, focusing on the first-year composition students who used the center's services.

Specifically, I observed tutoring sessions between UNR's writing center tutors and first-year composition classes (ENG 098, ENG 101, and ENG 102). After observation, I then transcribed and analyzed the language used by the tutors and the first-year students in the session through discourse analysis techniques. I analyzed every word in the transcriptions, noting areas where the tutor paid attention to gendered issues in writing. In certain cases where the tutor acknowledged issues or patterns but didn't get the student to see or make those changes, I commented on how the session could have been more effective. I used this commentary to make my argument that sessions could be improved if tutors knew what to look for and how to respond accordingly. My main argument was that if tutors could know what patterns to look for, they could help the students work through their issues and ultimately find their voices, at least in terms of writing.

I passed my defense, but I didn't know that was the easy part. Now I had job interviews and campus visits. Like any doctoral student, I anticipated the job market, afraid that I wouldn't be qualified for any jobs, or if I did, those jobs would all be in strange locations. But the real issue was that my boyfriend was also seeking tenure-track positions in Rhetoric and Composition. This factor would make it even harder to find jobs together, as one would probably have to negotiate a position for the other. My anxiety mounted as my cousin, a former academic, told me that we would never find tenure-track jobs together because most universities were afraid of nepotism. He was (mostly) right, and as I'll talk about throughout the remainder of this essay, it was nearly impossible to find the perfect situation, which in my eyes was two tenure-track jobs in a Western state.

Our plan, collaboratively, was to finish our dissertations and enter lecturer jobs that were available for graduates of UNR who weren't really ready to go on the job market for one reason or another. I took my time with my dissertation my fifth year, figuring that we would be in Reno for another year (or even three) in those lecturer positions. I now loved Reno for all of its outdoor opportunities, and I didn't want to leave. I loved it so much that I put down roots, buying a house, complete with a chocolate Lab and a view of the Sierras—it would take an earthquake to make me leave. Until we learned the English department lost its funding for the lecturer jobs, and there would be a hiring freeze. This meant I had to start looking at the job list in the spring, where the number of tenure-track jobs is considerably lighter. This particular spring was no exception. There were a few jobs that matched my qualifications, and I applied to five.

As luck would have it, a small school in rural Montana expressed interest. The chair of the Montana department informed me that the hiring committee wanted to set up a phone interview. After the phone interview, they asked me to fly up for a campus visit. Three days into my visit, I became unsure about the position and the location. The load was a three-three with little expectation to publish. The university was on the block system, which meant each professor taught courses for four hours, five days a week, for 3 ½ weeks in length. Students could only take one course at a time, allowing them to focus and put all of their effort toward mastering the course outcomes. Professors received one block off where they could focus on their own research and other projects. The five faculty in the English department were collegial and friendly, leading me to accept the job when the provost called. Truthfully, although I was nervous, I was also excited to start my career. Unfortunately, my previously mentioned boyfriend, who was now my husband, was only offered adjunct work, but that was better than what he could negotiate for me when he was offered a tenure-track job elsewhere. We were newly married in the summer of 2009, so we decided we couldn't live apart. We made the difficult decision to take the jobs in Montana, and we moved to Big Sky Country.

BIG SKY COUNTRY = BIG SHOCK TO THE SYSTEM

When I first started my career as an Assistant Professor at the University of Montana Western, I became interested in experiential learning, as the university used a method called "Experience One," where every teacher was encouraged to use hands-on learning methods. This teaching method was based on John Dewey's work, which suggests that placing students in real-world or authentic learning situations allows them to learn from the experience and apply that knowledge to future situations. I quickly recognized the benefits that experiential learning can provide. As students become engaged in real-world situations both in and outside the classroom, they actively participate in the construction of meaning, acknowledging their roles and responsibilities in the learning process.

I taught a Women and Literature course where I partnered with the local women's shelter; the students in the course were required to read literature such as Inga Muscio's *Cunt: A Declaration of Independence,* Betty Friedan's *The Feminine Mystique,* and Susan Faludi's *Backlash: The Undeclared War against American Women,* but they were also required to volunteer with the shelter. Although they couldn't work directly with the victims of abuse, they were able to create an informational brochure to place in the community where residents would know of their services, and they were also required to find, read, and annotate feminist-based books they could donate to the shelter at the end of the course, creating a library of resources for the shelter's residents. Finally, we held a mini-conference where students would choose an issue related to women (i.e., female contraceptives, teen pregnancy, and ecosensitive period accessories like the Diva Cup, an alternative to tampons), write a paper on that topic, create a poster presentation and marketing materials to give the audience, and present their papers to an audience. We invited members of the local community to the conference, based on bell hooks's idea in *Feminist Theory* that these feminist ideas should not be reserved only for academics, but rather, should be available to the community at large.

While I enjoyed teaching students who had never been exposed to such texts as *Cunt*, during my first semester, I taught three straight blocks, and by my "off" block, I was exhausted. The duration of each course was around four hours a day for twenty-seven days, not to mention office hours and committee meetings. This schedule day in and day out for three months can take a toll on anyone, and I used the off block to recover and discover my new town. There were only 4,500 people in the town of Dillon, Montana, which was approximately two hundred miles from any major city. Dillon's small population meant that the city had little cultural offerings in terms of museums or art. In addition, the cold winter weather led many of the restaurants in town to close their doors for months at a time. Generally, it was hard to find extracurricular activities that interested me. I love camping and hiking, but every day was freezing cold, and the winters in Montana are long and bleak. Between the block system and trying to adjust to rural life, I was mentally drained.

I was also worried because I was not keeping up with my writing. I hadn't published anything since graduate school, and I was afraid that this lull would be a trend, mostly because the block system seemed so intense. I am certain that the block system works for students and professors alike; however, it was not an environment in which I thrived. A few of my colleagues felt the same way, although they had been at the university for several decades. They urged me to leave while I could, speaking from experience. I feared becoming stuck in Montana, and I frantically searched for other jobs. Again, I was searching the job market in the spring, so there were few options. One that caught my eye was a contingent position at Arizona State University, a step down in pay and in rank from my tenure-track position. I decided to cut my losses and accept the job when it was offered to me. The words "career suicide" not only rang in my head but also in the hallways; although some colleagues advised me to leave, most thought I was crazy. In my heart, I was afraid that I was dooming my career, but I knew I had to leave. Andy was also willing to leave, and ASU seemed smart, as we would have the opportunity to work with numerous scholars in our field, which would hopefully increase our chances of someday obtaining two tenure-track jobs together. We packed up our rental house and headed to Arizona, determined that a change of venue would make all the difference.

FROM EXTREME COLD TO EXTREME HEAT

During my short year at Montana Western, my classroom pedagogy became largely influenced by the work of Ira Shor and his discussion of the democratic classroom in *Empowering Education: Critical Teaching for Social Change*. I began experimenting with assignments that challenged students to become active "thinkers, communicators, and citizens" (10). Adopting a critical pedagogy, as Henry Giroux defines in *On Critical Pedagogy*, I prompted "students to take risks, act on their sense of social responsibility, and engage in the world as an object of both critical analysis and hopeful transformation" (14). I designed entire semesters around service-learning projects—a natural progression from experiential learning—where students would work with nonprofits to effect change in their communities. I often incorporated service-learning projects into my technical communication courses—projects that asked students to engage in Thomas Deans's idea of writing *for* the community (his emphasis), where they interact and collaborate with outside organizations to produce documents. For instance, in many of my technical communication courses, I typically divided the classes into "businesses," where students offered their writing services to local nonprofit organizations. Throughout the semester, students designed and wrote a myriad of documents, including fundraiser proposals, desktop publishing materials, and new media. At the end of the semester, students presented their ideas to the nonprofits, assisted the organizations with implementing the fundraisers, and reflected on their learning experiences. This type of civic engagement provided an authentic learning opportunity for the students, as they clearly saw the impact their writing had on their world. And surprisingly enough, I was using the skills learned in my bachelor's degree to structure these courses.

    I became well versed in the theory behind experiential learning and service-learning, recognizing that students' experiences outside the classroom should shape what happens *inside* the classroom as well. Within my service projects, the organizations asked students to create documents such as brochures, websites, and other content that used various modes beyond the written text. So why was I still assigning traditional text-based essays in most of my classes? In my office at ASU, I told a colleague and friend that I was struggling with this dilemma, and she suggested I look into multimodal composition as an extension of my service-learning pedagogy. I quickly discovered that other scholars such as Takayoshi and Selfe incorporate multimodal projects, or projects using more than written text to communicate, believing that these projects are the outside "experience" students need to cultivate in an academic setting. In other words, because students communicate every day beyond the traditional text-based essay, they should also be asked to create these projects within the classroom. Believing in Glynda Hull and Mark Nelson's claim in "Locating the Semiotic Power of Multimodality," which states that students can experience a sense of power by learning and communicating multimodally in my first-year writing courses, I began to challenge students to become critical thinkers and communicators in our digital world, prompting them to develop projects such as blogs, videos, and podcasts.

The purpose of integrating these projects into first-year courses is not to teach students how to use "cool" technology but to learn to examine what Claire Lauer calls the "rhetorical context for writing," as they identify "who the audience for a particular text will be, what the purpose is, and which modes or combination of modes might best suit the communicative event" (236). These critical rhetorical considerations of audience and purpose (i.e., critical thinking skills) would be beneficial for life beyond academia, no matter what field they enter (Takayoshi and Selfe 4). The choices students learn to make help them learn the important outcome of rhetorical knowledge, as they determine how context can influence their overall message; at the same time, the freedom to make these choices embodies Shor's idea of active and empowering education. Indeed, multimodal composition is grounded in rhetoric, even though the students may not grasp how the foundational principles as developed by Aristotle can be relevant today. In my multimodal classes, I teach them Aristotle's argument that a good rhetor learns to address and persuade audiences by using all available means. Resources have certainly changed since Aristotle's day, so it is my job to teach them how to use available technological means to convince or persuade their audiences.

My work with multimodality helped me obtain a higher position at ASU, where I worked as a lecturer under Dr. Duane Roen to develop the Writers' Studio, a fully online first-year writing program that attended to twenty-first-century literacies in an online environment. Multimodal composition seemed like a natural fit for the online world, which is inherently multimodal by nature. Additionally, research indicates that online students need to be engaged in order to succeed in the online environment, and multimodal composition provides the active learning distance students need to keep them motivated (Simpson 5). The Writers' Studio was also a chance for me to ensure that distance education students were receiving comparable experiences to their face-to-face counterparts, which is important as the number of online students currently surpasses seven million (Allen and Seaman 11).

Our ENG 101, 102, and 105 (advanced composition) courses within the Writers' Studio were designed based on a heavy process model, with students producing multiple drafts for each project. Students created multimodal projects such as blogs, videos, podcasts, and an electronic portfolio where they showcased their work and reflected on course outcomes. A feature of the model included the incorporation of Instructional Assistants (IAs), or embedded tutors, and I learned how to train these tutors to provide feedback to students during the composing process. I also taught several courses in the model and served as an administrator of the program, which involved hiring, training, and mentoring other faculty. My colleagues and I won the President's Award for Curriculum Innovation, and before leaving ASU, I trained faculty to teach the courses and maintain the program. Our work at ASU is detailed in various articles and chapters in edited collections (see Works Cited).

My career seemed to be finally taking off, as I was teaching classes I loved and somehow managing to continue my scholarly publication record. I really liked Phoenix, and I enjoyed working for ASU, a much bigger university than I was used to. However, something inside kept nagging me, probably my ego, reminding me that I only had a contingent job where I signed a year-to-year contract. I craved the stability of a tenure-track job. I wanted to start a family, and my husband and I constantly stressed about where our careers were headed. In our second year at ASU, we started looking for tenure-track jobs. Again, we would be searching for two tenure-track positions, making it that much harder. We weren't terribly optimistic. This might be putting it mildly—most of the discussions we had revolved around not feeling "relevant" in our field anymore. We had the sneaking suspicion that if we didn't find tenure-track jobs that year, we were probably destined to live as lecturers, which wouldn't be that bad. We liked our jobs, our boss, ASU, and even Phoenix. But I still felt something wasn't quite right.

MAKING A LEFT TURN AT ALBUQUERQUE

In the fall of 2011, I started looking at the MLA Job List. I applied to only a few jobs, including one at The University of New Mexico. The Dean of Arts and Sciences at UNM heard of the success of the Writers' Studio and hired me as an Assistant Professor to establish a similar online first-year writing program. As luck would have it, I was able to negotiate for my husband, who once again received a tenure-track job offer elsewhere but had to turn it down because the school couldn't offer me more than a chance to interview for an instructor position. Luckily, Andy was also involved in the Writers' Studio project, and the Dean offered him a lecturer position at UNM with the chance to apply for an assistant professorship in his second year. We visited Albuquerque, made our peace with leaving Phoenix, and accepted the positions. After one short year, the university did offer my husband the tenure-track job, and now we're both working as assistant professors. We had bounced around a bit, but we finally achieved our goal.

Together, Andy and I developed eComp (short for Electronic Composition). Like the Writers' Studio, the new program emphasizes multimodality and heavy process (students produce multiple drafts for each project), but I have added an extensive training component for instructors. I believe that many instructors remain unsure of how to teach and assess multimodal projects (Takayoshi and Selfe 4), and the added element of the online format may pose an even greater challenge. Thus, the eComp program encourages teacher training in both multimodality and online course design. I currently teach a seminar entitled ENGL 532: Multimodal and Online Pedagogies, which informs graduate students of the theory and practice behind multimodal composition and online teaching, and I help facilitate the development of the online courses they create and oversee their online teaching efforts in subsequent semesters. As an administrator, I provide mentorship to all eComp instructors (including adjuncts, lecturers, and professors) by offering program orientations, technology workshops, and opportunities to meet one-on-one throughout the semester. This inclusion of multimodality and teacher education ensures both UNM students and instructors can succeed in the online environment. In fact, the eComp program has proven so successful at UNM that Andy and I were prompted to design a similar program for our sophomore-level online technical communication courses, called eTC (short for Electronic Technical Communication). In this sense, my undergraduate studies and my work now have come full circle: I am using my technical communication degree to influence the curriculum development of the eTC classes.

Many of my decisions are still influenced by my mentors, and my teaching is often grounded in the theory I read as suggested by other teacher-scholars in the field. Michael Potter and Erika Kustra define these practices as scholarly teaching, or "teaching grounded in critical reflection using systematically and strategically gathered evidence, related and explained by well-reasoned theory and philosophical understanding, with the goal of maximizing learning through effective teaching" (3). My research is heavily influenced by the classes I teach: I try new ideas, study my students' reactions to or their actual work within projects, and share my results in peer-reviewed publications. Potter and Kustra define these practices as the scholarship of teaching, or "information intended to be *publicly shared for critique and use by an appropriate community*, generally as some sort of product—a conference presentation, a book, a paper, an internet resource, a documentary" (2, their emphasis).

The authors suggest that scholarly teaching and the scholarship of teaching are two distinct concepts—an instructor can be a scholarly teacher without publishing results just by reading theory, developing curriculua around that theory, reflecting on classroom results, and making changes to future curriculua. While the distinction between the two concepts is clear, they can be combined, or rather, scholarly teaching can lead to the scholarship of teaching. My experiences and career moves have undoubtedly led me to be the scholar I am today. And while I still turn to past experiences and the voices of mentors, I think I have finally found my voice; if I'm lucky, this voice will continue to guide me, no matter what the future holds.

ROADS? WHERE WE'RE GOING, WE DON'T NEED ROADS

All of these academic adventures led me to this moment, right back to the dreaded tenure review. Through writing this chapter, I recognize that my career moves have caused me to be on a slower path to tenure. Most of the friends and colleagues I graduated with at UNR have already gone up and passed. Once again, I could feel as if I'm the one left behind—that I don't have it all quite figured out like everyone else. But I take all of these so-called "mistakes" made over the course of academic life and remember: I made my own choices. Sometimes they seemed random, but they were still my own. In "Technologies of Serendipity," Paul Fyfe suggests that we all have random instances that occur throughout our life, but serendipity requires recognizing these encounters for their meaning. Together, kairos and serendipity were at play in my life; opportune moments presented themselves at the right times, prompting me to make decisions and change the course of my life at various points. Ultimately, these two concepts have helped me finally find meaning for all of the random occurrences I've experienced to get here—home, at the unlikeliest of places, in Albuquerque, New Mexico.

While I may feel settled in this relatively new role, I recognize that kairotic moments will probably open up roads that lead to a future I can't yet imagine. The wanderlust inside me will pull me in different directions. For instance, I am always challenged to take on interesting projects—even when I don't have the time to take anything new, I can't help myself. This openness, however, helped shape my career path and my research to get to this point, so I can't really say it is a negative character trait. After reading the other chapters in this collection, I recognize that my career is relatively young, and that recognition encourages me to remain open. Sometimes it seems like I've lived a full life because I have moved a lot to advance my career; however, I'm also willing to accept that I could be just getting started. As I write this, I have taken on new projects; for instance, my colleagues and I are studying how usability testing, a common technical communication practice, can be used to train faculty to develop their online courses and improve their multimodal curricula in composition classes. Again I find my life and research intertwined and pushing me in a new direction. For now, I'm learning to channel my wanderlust and kairotic moments into something meaningful—as ways to guide my research.

From writing this chapter, I also recognize that my family has always been a large influence in my life and will continue to be. Andy and I moved around a lot in order to find jobs together and not live apart. I was not going to live without him at any point, no matter how great the job might seem. My parents, who have always been a big influence in my life, moved out to Albuquerque when my son was born, and they continue to help me with the push and pull of being a mom and a teacher-scholar. The importance of family has been made even clearer to me, as my husband and I have recently had another baby. My son, Ben, is now three, and since I wrote the first draft of this chapter, I have had a baby girl, Aubrey, who is now almost a year old. Many people probably thought I was crazy getting pregnant in the first year of my tenure-track job at UNM and then having a second before tenure. I remember once that a friend of mine told me that I couldn't get tenure and have a family—the two just didn't mix. I don't believe this to be true, and I'm working toward proving her wrong. While I wrestle every day with wanting to be a prolific scholar in the field or wanting to be a mother instead, I look at other women in the field, especially the ones in this collection like Elizabeth A. Flynn and Beth Hewett, scholars who have influenced my own work, and know that it *is* possible to reside in both worlds. I don't have to choose between my work and motherhood. I can do both equally well.

As I finish this chapter, I start digging through drawers to find a zip drive that might have documents I can use for my tenure files. I come across a picture that was tucked away that has an image of Andy and me at our wedding, heading up a little worn path toward the top of the mountain where we were married. The wedding was only days after we defended our PhDs, and we thought we had our entire future mapped out, starting with the move to Montana. Little did we know that the path we were taking would fork off many times and take us in unexpected directions—a life ultimately defined by the concept of kairos. At the time, we didn't worry about the uncertainties of the future. I have no intention of taking my tenure lightly; however, I think I can learn from this picture, too. My path from here may be uncertain, but as I work toward tenure and beyond, I recognize that my family, mentors, and friends will help me continue on this road, wherever it might lead. On that note, I think I'll take a break and go pick up my kids from my parents' house. I'll spend a little time with them—my greatest accomplishments—and come back to the tenure file tomorrow.

WORKS CITED

Allen, I. Elaine, and Jeff Seaman. "Grade Change: Tracking Online Education in the United States, 2013." *Babson Survey Research Group and Quahog Research Group, LLC.* 3.5 (2014): 1–40. Web. March 3, 2015.

Beck, Charles E. "Rhetoric and the Collaborative Nature of Technical Communication." *Technical Communication* (1993): 781–85. Print.

Belenky, Mary Field, Blythe Mcvicker Clinchy, Nancy Rule Goldberger, and Jill Mattuck Tarule. *Women's Ways of Knowing: The Development of Self, Voice, and Mind.* New York: Basic Books, 1986. Print.

Berger, Linda L. "Studying and Teaching Law as Rhetoric: A Place to Stand." *Legal Writing: J. Legal Writing Inst.* 16 (2010): 3–66. Print.

Bourelle, Tiffany, Andrew Bourelle, and Sherry Rankins-Robertson. "Teaching with Instructional Assistants: Enhancing Student Learning in Online Classes." *Computers and Composition* 37 (2015): 90–103. Print.

Cook, Kelli Cargile. "Layered Literacies: A Theoretical Frame for Technical Communication Pedagogy." *Technical Communication Quarterly* 11.1 (2002): 5–29. Print.

Dewey, John. *Experience and Education.* New York: Touchstone, 1938. Print.

———. *How We Think.* New York: Courier Dover Publications, 1997. Print.

Faludi, Susan. *Backlash: The Undeclared War against American Women.* New York: Broadway Books, 2009. Print.

Friedan, Betty. *The Feminine Mystique.* New York: W. W. Norton and Company, 2010. Print.

Fyfe, Paul. "Technologies of Serendipity." *Victorian Periodicals Review* 48.2 (2015): 261–66. Print.

Gillespie, Paula, and Neal Lerner. *The Allyn and Bacon Guide to Peer Tutoring.* Boston: Allyn and Bacon, 2000. Print.

Giroux, Henry A. *On Critical Pedagogy.* New York: Bloomsbury Publishing, 2011. Print.

hooks, bell. *Feminist Theory: From Margin to Center.* London: Pluto Press, 2000. Print.

Hull, Glynda A., and Mark Evan Nelson. "Locating the Semiotic Power of Multimodality." *Written Communication* 22.2 (2005): 224–61. Print.

Lauer, Claire. "Contending with Terms: 'Multimodal' and 'Multimedia' in the Academic and Public Spheres." *Computers and Composition* 26.4 (2009): 225–39. Print.

Lunsford, Andrea A., Connors, Robert, and Franklin Eugene Horowitz. *EasyWriter: A Pocket Guide.* New York, NY: St. Martin's Press, 1997. Print.

Meyers, Morton A. *Happy Accidents: Serendipity in Major Medical Breakthroughs in the Twentieth Century.* New York: Arcade Publishing, 2007. Print.

Miller, Carolyn. "Kairos and the Rhetoric of Science." *The Rhetoric of Doing: Essays on Written Discourse in Honor of James L. Kinneavy.* Eds. Stephen Witte, Neil Nakadate, and Roger D. Cherry. Carbondale: Southern Illinois UP, 1992. 310–27. Print.

Muscio, Inga. *Cunt: A Declaration of Independence.* Berkeley: Seal Press, 2002. Print.

Potter, Michael K., and Erika Kustra. "The Relationship Between Scholarly Teaching and SoTL Models, Distinctions, and Clarifications." *International Journal for the Scholarship of Teaching and Learning* 5.1 (2011): 23. Print.

Shor, Ira. *Empowering Education: Critical Teaching for Social Change*. Chicago: U of Chicago P, 2012. Print.

Simpson, Ormond. *Supporting Students in Online Open and Distance Learning*. New York: Routledge, 2013. Print.

Takayoshi, Pamela, and Cynthia L. Selfe. "Thinking about Multimodality." *Multimodal Composition: Resources for Teachers*. Ed. Cynthia Selfe. Boston: Bedford St. Martin's. 2007. 1–12. Print.

Young, Art, and Toby Fulwiler. *Writing across the Disciplines: Research into Practice*. Portsmouth, NH: Boynton/Cook Publishers, Inc., 1986. Print.

CHAPTER 12

My Kismet in the Making

Navigating the Profession "alla Turca"

IKLIM GOKSEL

WHY ALLA TURCA?

Born in Turkey and raised in all things Turkish, the notion of kismet has always reinforced agency and resilience in my life, obscuring ambivalence and any impulse to deviate from my scholarly pursuits and interests. From the standpoint of those who live in Turkey and the wider Middle East and North Africa region, "kismet" departs from a fatalistic philosophy and appropriates a particular view of life that creates an affinity between human individual agency, tolerance, humility, resilience, reason, and choice. This insight extended into my professional life and ran parallel to the development of my moral actions, ethical values, and intellectual skills in the academic path I decided to invest myself in. I reflect here in this essay upon the notion of kismet to convey how non-Western notions of self and identity have allowed me to navigate our field. My goal will be to share how my background in non-Western emotional and linguistic thought helped me in making choices and taking chances. I hope that my discussion will recognize women's alternative forms of knowledge-making practices in academia and will draw attention to how giving voice to women's non-Western forms of linguistic and cultural rhetorical choices can enrich our understandings of the diversity of women's experiences in our field.

As a woman and an immigrant from Turkey, resilience played a crucial role in building my kismet and my career. To quote Elizabeth A. Flynn, Patricia

Sotirin, and Ann Brady, my resilience was not merely tied to the strength of my psychological qualities but was rather a move toward "resilient rhetorical action" and "recreating meaningfulness" (8). In an unfamiliar sociocultural context, the making of my kismet entailed "rhetorically engaging with material circumstances and situational exigencies" (7). Hence, throughout the process of this remaking, I drew on the philosophical and cultural influences of figures such as Rumi, Yunus Emre, Omar Khayyam, and Mustafa Kemal Atatürk. For example, Rumi's teachings methodically treat the human capacity for resilience, choice, and empowerment, which are summed up in his call to humanity "to come as one is." Rumi's call is not only an invitation toward traversing limitations and adversities, but it is also the embodiment of human agency and resilience. Within this framework Rumi's philosophy encompasses the call toward breaking free from constraints and conventions to be able to make choices and take chances. In critically considering my career path and at the same time nurturing my passion for a successful teaching and research career in academia, Khayyam's philosophy furthermore reminded me of putting my mind to the present. By ignoring the regrets of the past and the concerns for the future, I have always had the opportunity to seize serendipitous moments to effect change and bring about happiness in my life. As Yunus Emre says, we should love and be loved, and also make life easy on ourselves because the earth shall be left to no one. To me, this view of life was particularly important as it allowed me to challenge societal expectations, seek alternatives to conventions, and create kairotic moments that were central in my intellectual growth and scholarship in rhetorical and composition studies. As the title of my essay implies, kismet does not represent a ready-made world but rather entails a remaking that suggests inquiry, capability, resilience, choice, chance, and serendipity. In the Turkish sociocultural context in which Atatürk's principles play a foundational role in the minds of many individuals, a world that was ready-made has always appeared arbitrary to me. Denying absolute knowledge and fatalism, Atatürk recognized and discussed in his Great Speech (*Nutuk*) that nations and peoples made their own history by forging their own movements and struggles. To his modern critics, his philosophy presented a limited and an absolutist perception of reality. However, those who recognized his far-reaching ideals, which triumphed against colonialism and founded a secular nation based on *laïcité*, took them as the groundwork for knowledge-making and for envisioning the social, political, and economic future of the young Turkish nation-state.

I was deeply invested in these theories when I completed the social sciences line in a Swedish gymnasium[1] in Stockholm, Sweden. At the time, I did not recognize it, but my education had already started to prepare me for a career in rhetoric. I had arrived in Sweden due to my mother's job transfer and had chosen the social sciences line as opposed to the International Baccalaureate line, which trained students in the natural sciences. Against the popular notion and advice in my social circle that an International Baccalaureate diploma in the natural sciences would open more doors for me, I followed my intuition and the wisdom of Yunus Emre to study what I enjoyed and to be happy. Years later, I discovered that my choice had been uniquely useful in providing the foundation and knowledge base toward my education in the liberal arts, including the completion of my doctoral degree in rhetorical studies. Amenable to my interests, my classes in the social sciences line were comprised of subjects such as world religions and history, world philosophies, literature and languages, social movements and political theories, and fine arts. However, my choice was telling in how much risk I had taken against the expectations of my social circle. Hence by looking back, I am constantly reminded of how choice and chance converged in the early stages of my career in the humanist tradition to create the platform that would prevent me from losing sight of what was important to me and to be able to respond to Rumi's call to come as one is and to be true to myself. In my native Turkey, it was a serendipitous occurrence when I earned a place in the English Literature department rather than in the vocationally oriented Translation and Interpretation program. In the Turkish university entrance examination system, students are matched with programs of study that they select according to their examination scores. The Translation and Interpretation program was on my list to prevent the risk of being unmatched. I completed my undergraduate studies in English literature in three years with highest honors by increasing my course load each academic semester. My choice in making the three-year plan was based on my financial circumstances and on my need to quickly enter the workforce. It was a serendipitous moment and my way of bringing happiness into my life when the department of Modern Languages at the Middle East Technical University in Ankara surprisingly announced job openings several months before my graduation. After passing a series of written and oral examinations administered by the university, my career in teaching English and writing began.

BUILDING ON KISMET

When I returned from Sweden to Turkey in 1990 for my undergraduate studies, a favorite part of my daily routine was riding the *dolmuş*. In Turkey, *dolmuş* is a shared taxi ride in minibuses that have set routes within a city. Just like stopping a taxi cab, people hail their hands to ride them. It is also possible to wait for them at designated *dolmuş* stops, but the more conventional way of riding them is by hailing them with one's hand. Getting off of the *dolmuş* is also very convenient; passengers shout to the driver that they would like to get off by saying "*inecek var*" (someone wants to get off). At that moment, the *dolmuş* driver quickly spots a convenient location and pulls to the right to let the passenger out. To me, the *dolmuş* has always represented a site of culture, history, socialization, debate, humor, meeting, laughter, fright, and excitement. It is a place where people from all walks of life converge and later part. However, it is consistently the site where one enters the fabric of Turkish life. There is fright because the driver will ignore all traffic rules and will speed until you can no longer hold your breath. And, there is also laughter because it is always funny to watch people's heads move up and down due to the bumpy ride. More importantly, it is in the *dolmuş* that one often engages in unexpected conversations in terms of their content and intensity. In one *dolmuş* ride, it is not uncommon to find oneself listening to a woman complain about her daughter-in-law. On the next ride, the conversation with the person sitting next to you might be about how the phone company made an error in his billing and suspended the service. During some other ride on a different day, the conversation may take a turn toward politics. Hence, it is in the *dolmuş* that serendipitous moments emerge that present the individual with random encounters, new opportunities, and unlikely friendships. The process of building on my kismet resembled these *dolmuş* rides where my resilience and serendipity converged, and I followed my aspirations in spite of a social and intellectual milieu that was at odds with my intellectual pursuits. This was because the 1990s in Turkey was a time when neoliberal free-market policies, private sector development, and entrepreneurial activities were introduced and promoted to society as markers of progress and success. Academic disciplines such as business administration, finance, and management studies were the fields that students were encouraged to pursue. Nevertheless, I was immersed in my teaching and in the process of discovering the possibilities it afforded in the writing classroom. I was in particular aspiring to be a teacher along the lines of John Keating, the English teacher in the film *Dead Poet's Society*, who taught his students to read and write the world in the Freirean tradition. The choices I had made due to my resilience, such as prioritizing my desire to be happy, following my heart and returning to Turkey to study English literature, were slowly taking me away from the limitations of a business-oriented cultural milieu, allowing me to remake my kismet toward invention and new forms of self-expression. I had taken a stance against societal pressures and norms for success by publicly voicing my desire to be happy and to pursue my own academic interests in the midst of unfavorable financial circumstances. I find this to be similar to what Gloria Anzaldúa defines as her *mestiza* consciousness, a move beyond binaries in the remaking of the self and the assertion of her agency. With much authorial power, Anzaldúa's agency lies within her ability to establish her own way of writing against the demands of conventions, which allows her to cross boundaries and to find her own voice.

WHEN SERENDIPITY AND RESILIENCE INTERSECT

My bumpy but rewarding *dolmuş* ride changed its course with crossing the Atlantic and beginning my graduate studies in Rhetoric and Composition in the United States. My geographic shift was swift and so was my candidacy for the doctoral degree. By the fall of 2001, I was composing my dissertation proposal in the Language, Literacy, and Rhetoric program at the University of Illinois at Chicago. Although my preliminary examinations coincided with the very sad, traumatic, and turbulent times of the weeks of 9/11, I found peace and solace in my teaching and in the academic community I was a member of. In my scholarly work, I was interested in how I might contribute to conversations on global rhetorics and how my social and cultural background would allow me to attend to larger questions of making connections between the classroom and local and global communities outside of the academia. My goals of cultivating critical inquiry and global citizenship materialized during this important time toward thinking about the possibilities of exploring and introducing alternative and non-Western rhetorical models, specifically Turkish and Middle Eastern, to students in the writing classroom. I wrote a paper titled "Rhetorical Traditions in Turkey: Implications for Teaching Composition in the U.S. Classroom" to be presented at the Conference on College Composition and Communication (CCCC) in the spring of 2003 in New York City. Unfortunately, due to several flight cancellations on the day of my departure for New York City, I missed my panel and the opportunity to present my very first paper as a graduate student at a national conference. Coming to grips with missing the opportunity for an intellectual dialogue about my project was not easy, but I decided that I would have more time to develop a theoretical approach in addressing alternative forms of rhetorical engagements in the writing classroom. My interest in promoting awareness of international contexts in making meaning and considering non-Western literacies to prepare students for public and civic life was similar to Sharon Crowley's examination of how individuals may engage in rhetorical exchange and public argument for critical citizenship and civic discourse. My goals for global rhetorics in the composition classroom drew on these ideas, which seek for ways to make the exchange of ideas in the civic sphere possible. Whereas Crowley frames her inquiry around the notion of stasis, I looked for ways to create new classroom experiences based on the understanding of communities not as "clashing" in the Huntingtonian sense but rather as connecting. My study proliferated into two more papers titled "Resistance, Silence and Fear: Challenges in Teaching Writing as a Social Action" for the CCCC in 2005 and "On Literacy and the *Kemalist* Rhetorics of 1928" for the CCCC in 2006. My studies also gave fruition to a collaborative work titled "Teaching Turkish Rhetoric through Atatürk's *Nutuk*" for the Deep Rewards and Serious Risks: Working through International Higher Education Writing Research Exchanges workshop sponsored by the CCCC Globalization Committee in 2015. The project finally blossomed into a collaborative book project on Turkish rhetorical tradition and into a journal article on the pedagogical implications of introducing non-Western rhetorics into the U.S. classroom.

My ability to reconfigure a missed opportunity into several meaningful projects was empowering and helped me in cultivating my voice and forming new alliances in my academic work. This constructive outcome motivated me to take on other projects regardless of the amount of time it took to complete them. This experience also taught me to convert unanticipated disruptions in my academic work into new meaningful projects and reflectively negotiate my expectations of the ideal outcome of a project. Instead of aiming for a seamless path toward building a career, I focused on Khayyams's philosophy of putting my mind to the present and opted for a tentative and revisable research agenda that would enfranchise me to be persistent and engaged in my work. I find this approach to be a good example of resilience and feminist rhetorical agency that is, in the words of Flynn, Sotirin, and Brady, a responsiveness to contexts, and "creating and animating capacities and possibilities" (8) so that with dynamic creativity opportunities are reshaped. In my department, opportunities for academic growth were well established, and the tools to build the foundation for a successful career path were available. My teaching responsibilities were enriching and conducive to professional development. My first year as a teaching assistant in the doctoral program entailed teaching two classes of English Composition per academic semester. In the following years, our course load was reduced from a 2/2 load to a 2/1 load, which facilitated additional opportunities for fulfilling other academic responsibilities. Hence, although attending training seminars, preparing lesson plans, grading essays, and providing students with individualized attention for their academic needs could occasionally leave less time for my own graduate course work, I nevertheless embraced the intellectual and collaborative milieu I had found myself in.

TOWARD ETHNOGRAPHY AND FEMINIST RHETORICAL SCHOLARSHIP

Looking back on the ways my scholarship in rhetoric and composition started to take new shapes in the English department at UIC, I would argue that working with Ralph Cintron, who later would become my dissertation chair, and Marcia Farr expanded my vision of intellectual and pedagogical venues by introducing me to practices of ethnography in language, literacy, and rhetorical studies. And, in new and compelling ways working with Judith Gardiner allowed me to make deeper connections between feminist scholarship, rhetoric, and ethnography. In thinking about my own work, I know that I was able to weave these threads to build my career and to be able to seek other effective means of pursuing my intellectual interests without losing sight of the goal of being happy. As Rumi puts it, joy comes when things are done from one's soul. I consider my determination to obtain joy from my academic work to be a feminist rhetorical response in "changing the way a life is lived" (Flynn, Sotirin, and Brady 7) with hope and imagination in relation to my surroundings and circumstances. Instead of viewing myself as a goal-oriented, competitive, and self-sufficient academic, achieving happiness and joy for me defined my academic identity and primarily involved a collaborative attitude. My willingness and readiness to collaborate did not only entail coauthoring my academic work but also becoming an audience and an avid listener in the academic community to be able to engage in dialogue with my colleagues. This relationality involved asking for advice, building knowledge through collaborative work, staying attuned to the needs of my students and colleagues, and forming alliances through empathy. Among many other things, receiving a thank you card from a student or taking over and teaching a class for a colleague in need always bring joy and are extremely fulfilling.

This relationality and outlook played a crucial role in my perspective on rhetoric and writing and in the ways in which I might achieve other effective means of success and happiness in my career. Marcia Farr's class discussions of language use and literacy practices of individuals of Mexican origin in Chicago gave me a useful direction in how to engage in rhetorical and anthropological inquiry in the field so that I would be able to create a sense of community without objectifying or othering my informants. I learned that applying ethnographic methods by means of a community-based research meant building respect and trust relationships in the field without essentializing the cultural practices and social contexts of individuals. For example, Farr's description of a literate Mexican man refusing to read aloud in class at a local community organization and claiming to be illiterate taught me specifically about cultural sensitivity and contextualizing the field site for an understanding of social relationships. In Farr's description, this individual's refusal to admit his literacy was due to refusing to "respond positively to a program that placed a high value on promoting individuals at the expense of relationships within the family and the social network" (43). This and similar ethnographic accounts of field sites gave me an understanding of designing socially and culturally sensitive research practices that also take into consideration issues of gender, class, and race. The study of literacy practices of the everyday in the private and public spaces and the diversity of their patterns through rhetorical moves further sparked my interest in combining my training in rhetoric and composition with ethnographic inquiry. Ralph Cintron's ethnography of the rhetorics of the everyday in a mid-sized town in the Midwest helped me shape the way I could bring together rhetoric and ethnography to explore discursive and non-discursive rhetorical practices in a variety of settings. For example, in reading about one of Cintron's ethnographic narratives about a boy and his bedroom walls, I gained an understanding of how everyday rhetorical performances manifest themselves in myriad ways and how an ethnographer with training in rhetorical studies can interact with them to explore a set of notions and assumptions in rhetorical theory such as ethos and logos. In his analysis of spaces, places, and events in this boy's life, Cintron also looks at relations of power and alternative ways of asserting one's individuality. According to Cintron, this sometimes can be in the form of hanging various correspondence cards on one's wall to claim one's identity. I found it fascinating to be able to explore through ethnographic methods a rhetorical move toward identity formation and performance. An inquiry into the use of the imagination to rhetorically subvert social constraints and in order to create acknowledgement had a significant impact on the direction I would take toward the completion of my doctoral degree. Naturally, the ethnographic studies of other scholars encouraged me as well in designing a research proposal for my dissertation. The ethnography of Beverly Moss in African American churches to explore literacy events and rhetorical practices in nonacademic settings and Elizabeth Chiseri-Strater's ethnographic research on women students' ways of knowing and learning allowed me to recognize the ways in which I could utilize rhetoric and ethnography within a feminist framework in my studies.

Indeed, my journey in the field of rhetoric and composition has been similar to riding the *dolmuş*. My beginnings with teaching writing and my turn toward ethnography, feminist scholarship, and interdisciplinarity was like a bumpy *dolmuş* ride, not knowing who I would encounter and where my conversations would take me. And a flat tire is almost always an inevitable outcome of a bumpy *dolmuş* ride. For example, my decision to merge my studies in rhetoric and composition with ethnography necessitated Institutional

Review Board (IRB) reviews and approval. Through extensive training and certification, I familiarized myself with IRB procedures and principles. The approval process lasted for one year with extensive correspondence with the IRB committee until permission for my ethnographic research was granted. Two years went by after passing the preliminary examinations before my dissertation prospectus received both departmental and IRB approvals. I considered this to be a significant loss of time in terms of the progress I wanted to make toward the completion of my degree. However, I was in full realization that I had taken on an ambitious project that involved challenge and risk. My committee included faculty members from the English, Anthropology, Political Science, and Sociology departments. This interdisciplinary nature of the project brought excitement and changed the course of my career. Hence, I regard this moment in my career as the opportune or kairotic moment; a time when I made the choice of moving forward with my project while conditions were right. In spite of the delays and challenges, my professors were willing to work with me. As implied in the introduction of this book, "success" may often be essentialized within binaries in the academy to connote fixed meanings. However, a feminist outlook and rhetorical resilience always have the potential of neutralizing and blurring these binaries to make new meanings. In my case, I was motivated by the ideal of creating a dissertation project that I would enjoy and learn from. Through the collaborative efforts of an interdisciplinary committee, I accomplished my goals in remaking my kismet, and with the help of my peers and colleagues, I collaboratively created the means to get a hold of resources. Over the years, the opportunities for interdisciplinarity also culminated in writing monthly columns for a publication of the American Anthropological Association as well as an entrée into Turkish Studies and presenting my work at the meetings of the Middle East Studies Association (MESA), American Anthropological Association (AAA), and the Association for the Study of Nationalities (ASN) at the Harriman Institute of Columbia University in New York City.

THE VIEW FROM THE *DOLMUŞ*

While writing my dissertation, I followed my husband to a small town in northern Indiana. Having completed his fellowship at the University of Vermont, he was excited to accept a job offer to work as a hematologist/oncologist at a newly opened cancer center that he would build. The close proximity of 120 miles to Chicago appealed to me. I determined that I could easily travel to Chicago often to meet with my committee and defend my dissertation. Also, being in a small town afforded a low cost of living, which would allow us to quickly pay off our student loans.

My initiation into the world of adjunctship took place while writing my dissertation in this corner of the world. I found an opportunity to teach English composition at the local community college. The transition from an urban research university to a rural community college was a valuable learning experience. I did my best to provide the students with a safe and comfortable environment to write and to "read the world" in the Freirean sense. After teaching three sections of English composition for one semester, I was nominated for a teaching award by the students. This was a humbling experience that was priceless, and I remember my time there fondly. Following this rewarding experience, I decided to travel forty-five miles each way to the Indiana University Purdue University Fort Wayne (IPFW) campus to continue teaching English composition. However, as my dissertation defense date approached, I discontinued my travels to the IPFW campus.

Following my doctoral defense, many people were interested in knowing whether I might consider starting a family. Did this mean that since I had no job prospects due to my geographic location, the next available means of giving meaning to my life was the adoption of the role of motherhood? Thanks to my long-standing decision to remain child-free, I had the vantage point of observing these discourses from the perspective of my studies in rhetoric and composition. And, it was refreshing that it foregrounded a global but often overlooked conceptual model of patriarchy at work that organized gender roles and power relations in society. It was a discourse cognate with complicating and gendering the public and private spaces women occupied by assigning specific roles to them. And, it was an attestation to the ways in which fixed notions of sex and gender expand beyond our imagination to occupy capacious horizons. These discourses are consistently recognizable in varying degrees and always motivate me toward considering the ways in which they animate the very conditions that feminist ideologies try to evade.

Currently an adjunct faculty member in the Women's Studies Program at IPFW, I find the experience of teaching part-time valuable because I have time to embark on new projects to write and publish so that I can be an active participant in the conversations and dialogues of the academy. In pedagogical terms, my teaching and classroom experiences continue to provide me with a broad repertoire of teaching competencies and practices. My teaching allows me to build bridges between my academic work in Turkish and Middle East Studies, rhetoric and composition, and the classroom. For example, many of the writing assignments I integrate into my Women's Studies syllabi are based on my scholarship in rhetoric and composition theory. All of this thus makes my academic life productive, marking an alternative presence in the academy until I have the means to modify my geographic location. Sometimes "success" can be a trope to impose and sustain fixed and absolute notions that silence voices and erase subjectivities. Hence, our true voices can always emanate from our minds and hearts for a truthful feminist rhetorical resilience so that we can remake our kismet. In my case, I continue to do so my way, or alla Turca!

The story of my kismet, then, is a portrayal of how choice, chance, and serendipity converged in my life and allowed me to move forward in my career in some very bumpy *dolmuş* rides. For those scholars joining the conversation from non-Western contexts, it is an attempt to open up a platform to include their stories and to animate discussions about how we may further give voice to lesser known stories in our field. My narrative considers how the cultural and intellectual histories that I have grown up with bore significantly on the choices I made throughout my academic path and allowed me to take risks. My decisions to forego studies in the natural sciences and business-oriented programs, or my determination to write an interdisciplinary dissertation were certainly risks that I took. However, serendipity played a crucial role in allowing me to build on my background in the social sciences and humanities and to undertake a new career path in rhetoric and composition. Furthermore, I was able to widen this career path with ethnographic studies, feminist scholarship, and a new scholarly pursuit in the Turkish rhetorical tradition. Although these choices did not always offer optimal circumstances, they were my way of remaking my kismet toward invention and new forms of self-expression. I hope that my quest in seeking harmony in my professional life and in navigating difficulties as an immigrant will expand the conversations on women's ways of being in the academy.

NOTE

1. Schools in Germany and Scandinavian countries that emphasize academic learning and provide advanced secondary education.

WORKS CITED

Anzaldúa, Gloria. *Borderlands: La Frontera: The New Mestiza*. San Francisco, CA: Aunt Lute Books, 1987. Print.

Atatürk, Mustafa Kemal. *Nutuk: 1919–1927.* Ed. Hıfzı Veldet Velidedeoğlu. İstanbul: Cumhuriyet Kitapları, 2002. Print.

Chiseri-Strater, Elizabeth. *Academic Literacies: The Public and Private Discourse of University Students*. Portsmouth, NH: Heinemann/Boyton-Cook, 1991. Print.

Cintron, Ralph. *Angel's Town: Chero Ways, Gang Life, and Rhetorics of the Everyday*. Boston: Beacon P, 1997. Print.

Crowley, Sharon. *Toward a Civil Discourse: Rhetoric and Fundamentalism*. Pittsburgh, PA: U of Pittsburgh P, 2006. Print.

Emre, Yunus. "Hak Cihana Doludur." *Yunus Emre Divanı—Seçmeler*. İstanbul: Altın Kitaplar, 2005. Print.

Farr, Marcia. "En Los Dos Idiomas: Literacy Practices among Chicano Mexicanos." *Literacy across Communities*. Ed. Beverly J. Moss. Cresskill, NJ: Hampton, 1994. 9–47. Print.

Flynn, Elizabeth A., Patricia Sotirin, and Ann Brady, eds. *Feminist Rhetorical Resilience*. Logan: Utah State UP, 2012. Print.

Goksel, Iklim, and Elif Guler. "The Pedagogical Implications of Teaching 'Atatürk's Address to the Youth' for Global Rhetorics and Civic Action in the U.S. Writing Classroom." *Reflections: A Journal of Public Rhetoric, Civic Writing, and Service Learning*. Forthcoming.

———. *Turkish Rhetorical Tradition: Perspectives and Practices from the Pre-Islamic to the Republican Era*. Foreword by David Metzger. Under review by Southern Illinois UP.

Khayyam, Omar. "Geçmiş olan dünden hiç yad etme." *Ömer Hayyam Rubailer*. İstanbul: Çağrı Yayınları, 2012. Print.

Moss, Beverly. "Creating a Community: Literacy Events in African-American Churches." *Literacy across Communities*. Ed. Beverly J. Moss. Cresskill, NJ: Hampton, 1994. Print.

Rumi. "Gel." *Mesneviden Seçmeler*. İstanbul: İnkılap Kitabevi, 2012. Print.

CHAPTER 13

My Life in Composition Studies
Serendipity, Shame, Status Anxiety, and Trusting My Instincts

IRENE PAPOULIS

I've spent way too much time feeling like a failure when it comes to my professional life in composition, even though by many measures I'm doing fine. I've taught at Trinity College in Hartford for twenty years; I've given many talks at the Conference on College Composition and Communication (CCCC); I've published a few essays. And yet, in the company of people like my sister-authors in this collection, I sometimes have felt ashamed that I haven't been more of a "success" professionally. I haven't had the well-placed academic positions I've longed for, and I don't have the recognition I want as a public thinker. I haven't published enough. And I'm also ashamed of complaining about all that.

As I think about this I can see myself squeezed in somewhere on the proverbial imaginary ladder, between the scores of people above and below, not the best and also not the worst. We in the academic world, of course, know that the idea of a hierarchical ladder is ridiculously simplistic, and we're even suspect of concepts like "above" and "below." But we can't help it: we compare ourselves to others all the time, and most of us, no matter where we are, have felt shame at some point about not being *better*.

Alain de Botton, in *Status Anxiety*, explores the kind of shame many of us feel if we think we somehow don't live up to certain standards of "status." He points out that we determine our sense of how much social "wealth or esteem" we deserve "by comparing our condition with that of a reference group, a set of people who we believe resemble us" (25). Yes, the sense of failure I've felt is connected to my identification with the shapers of the field of composition, including many of the women in this collection.

That's somewhat presumptuous—we can't all be important people in the field. And I also know that my personal psychology has played an inevitable role in my relation to achievement: strict father, passive mother, and all that. But my goal in this essay is to explore how the social realities of the field of composition fueled my status anxiety. At the same time, I want to acknowledge the serendipitous set of experiences that have helped me come to terms with, and ultimately transcend, the discomforts I've felt at not being "successful" in someone else's terms.

HOW I GOT INTO COMPOSITION STUDIES

My goal from a young age was to be a writer, and I majored in English and creative writing at Binghamton University. After that, in the late 1970s, I worked as a secretary in New York City, imagining that I would quickly find a market for my writing. That didn't magically happen, so I decided to go back to school, getting an MFA in fiction writing from Columbia University. My intense shyness prevented me from networking while I was there, so I left with some decent writing but no connections or mentors. From my little apartment, I sent out a few short stories, but I got debilitated by rejection, which prevented me from nurturing my own writing. I completed a novel, but having my query for it rejected by a few agents felt so awful that I put the book in a drawer, ashamed. I let chance take over: my college boyfriend had begun graduate school in literature at Stony Brook University and, lured by the comfort of a teaching scholarship, I followed him.

In graduate school, I overcame my shyness and became the outspoken, social person I'd always known was the real me. I loved literary studies, and decided I was on my way to a job as a professor of English. Like many graduate students in the '80s, I was politically minded—I believed in enfranchising the marginalized other and dissolving binaries, and I loved learning about concepts like "Orientalism" and "the female gaze." I passionately believed that such ideas could help change the world for the better, and I was hopeful about joining the larger conversation about them. I began writing my dissertation on Virginia Woolf's aesthetic techniques as an enactment of the ideas of feminist theorists like Nancy Chodorow and Hélène Cixous.

At the same time, I was vaguely disturbed by the disjunction between the theories I was reading and the context in which I read them: my professors lived contented lives of economic and social privilege, apparently never seriously questioning their place in the hierarchy even as they theorized about the destructiveness of hierarchies.

Of course, theorizing itself, I reflected with friends, is doing something. It stirs things up and influences action, if not by theorists then by readers and people the readers come in contact with. Theories trickle down, right? "Yes," we reassured each other, "studying theories that point us beyond hierarchies is something. When such theories get out into the world, things inevitably shift."

True. But what was my best purpose, I wondered? To study and write theories? My modicum of doubt about that grew. I loved reading and talking about ideas, and I loved Virginia Woolf, but the life of a literary scholar didn't call to me as much as I knew it should. I loved teaching, but I wanted to be more of an activist, outspoken beyond the academic world. I wanted to write out my ideas and send them into the public sphere for general readers. Why didn't I? I was busy with classes and teaching, yes, but I was also plagued by a secret but insistent inner voice saying, "No one really cares about your ideas."

Swatting that voice away, I continued to study and write about literature, fantasizing about the job I would soon have as a respected professor. Once I got that job, went my fantasy, I would certainly become a public intellectual.

But serendipity intervened in my plans: in my fourth year of graduate school, after I had finished my coursework and begun my dissertation, Peter Elbow became the director of the writing program at Stony Brook.

Up to that point, none of us graduate students in literature had heard of Elbow, and we saw the teaching of writing as simply a necessary chore we did to earn our graduate fellowships. To us, the main function of a writing teacher was to "correct" unsophisticated or resistant students. We lectured in our English 101 classes about how to write an argument, and we dug up "controversial issues," like the death penalty or abortion, for students to argue about. This yielded, for the most part, mind-numbing essays that we procrastinated grading.

Elbow astonished us from day one. He instituted regular workshops for graduate-student composition teachers in which he made us sit in a circle and write together, and he even wrote with us. He quickly managed to convince most of us that the teaching of writing could not only be fun and exciting, it could actually give us a practical way to enact the nonhierarchical academic theories we believed in. Instead of talking about the marginalized other in abstract terms, we could insist on equal participation by all, and thus invite the marginalized other in our classrooms to become part of the conversation!

Now, of course, I scoff a bit at that. Certainly the "marginalized other" was not a person who would find her way to a classroom at Stony Brook

University, right? But wait: traditional teaching—lecturing, or simply posing discussion questions to which only a handful of students respond—can allow some students to remain throughout the semester as "other," perhaps with inner shaming narratives like mine in their heads. Elbow's methods—sitting in a circle, writing together, hearing from everyone in various ways—gave us practical strategies for attending to, and incorporating, all perspectives.

As I became fluent in such methods I began to rethink my academic interest in literary studies. Could I become a compositionist? I was torn; in spite of my theoretical resistance to hierarchies, it mattered to me that literature was far more respected in the academic world than composition. But during the two years it took me to finish my thesis, I attended a reading group on composition theory that Elbow convened; I learned about Ken Bruffee's ideas on collaborative learning; and in addition to Elbow I read compositionists like Ken Macrorie, Donald Murray, Tom Newkirk, and Sondra Perl. I came to believe that composition pedagogy could be a force to change peoples' consciousness, a real-world application of the theories that had always interested me in literary studies.

That belief ultimately caused me to change my career path and move into composition. Little did I know that as soon as I left graduate school I would slowly lose my resilient self-confidence as I confronted three powerful, shame-inducing realities in the discipline.

EXTERNAL REALITY #1: BEING A LECTURER

As graduate school ended, I sent out many letters of application for tenure-line jobs all over the United States. I got only a few nibbles back, and began to fret until I heard of a job in Santa Barbara. My friend Carl had completed his degree at Stony Brook a year earlier and gotten a job there; another position like his—lecturer, not a tenure-line position—was available in the University of California's writing program, which was staffed exclusively by lecturers, most of whom had PhDs in English, and a few graduate students.

I was overwhelmed by Santa Barbara's sunny and exuberant beauty when I first saw it in January of 1986. It was the middle of winter, and yet I wore red shorts as Carl and his wife Stella showed me the grounds of the beautiful Santa Barbara courthouse. As I stood under a palm tree, after a super-healthy lunch in a funky downtown restaurant, the thought of being able to live in Santa Barbara seemed too good to be true. I happily breathed in the sunny, sea-breeze-and-eucalyptus scented air, energized by my certainty that even though the job could never be tenure-line, I would take it if I got the chance.

And so I did. I packed up my aging car and drove across the country, and I found a beautiful log cabin to rent—a ten-minute walk, through a dry mesa, to the top of a spectacular cliff with a stairway down to the Pacific. Sure, I was disappointed that my job wasn't tenure-track, but this would be fun for a couple of years, I told myself; I could get a "real job" somewhere else later on. I was thirty-one.

I loved my students and my work in classes. But being a lecturer was more painful than I had imagined in terms of my sense of having a place in the university. To my surprise, lecturers were not members of the faculty senate at UC Santa Barbara. We taught more courses than professors did, because we were not expected to spend much time exploring theories, traveling to conferences, and writing books—our focus was supposed to be on our classrooms.

That was fine, in a way—I liked teaching. But I also wanted to write about it, go to conferences, and publish. And I was especially disturbed that most of the "real" faculty, tenured and tenure-line, did not take us lecturers seriously as colleagues. I went to many interesting talks and meetings on campus, sponsored by various academic departments. All but a few faculty at those, it seemed to me, would interact with me only until they discovered I was a lecturer. "Oh," they'd say dismissively when I told them I was in the writing program. Then they would nod patronizingly at whatever I was trying to say about the lecture and look for a way to escape from our conversation. Was that my imagination? I wasn't sure. Nevertheless, shame at my lowly status secretly built up in me.

Of course, my study of feminist theory had given me a framework from which to analyze the position of "lecturer." In my first year at Santa Barbara, I wrote an essay applying Simone de Beauvoir's concepts in *The Second Sex* of "immanent"—in the house; belonging to women—and "transcendent"—out in society; belonging to men—to academic teaching. No matter our gender, we lecturers in composition were doing "immanent" work since we were training the "children," first-year students, so they could leave us and go out in the world to engage with the manly (no matter the gender of their professor) and "transcendent" experiences of enculturation in the disciplines. I sent my essay to the now-defunct journal called *Freshman English News*, and it became my first academic publication. Seeing my name in print was exhilarating, and I wanted more.

Viewing the disparagement of composition teachers' work as a version of patriarchy's suppression of women made me realize that I shouldn't take it personally. But it bothered me on a personal level anyway. I wanted to be a "real" professor, with all the attendant glory that I imagined such a position would earn. I developed a hangdog feeling around campus, a vague, perpetual sense of shame, as though I had a scarlet letter "L" affixed to my chest: lecturer, not professor, not an equal or worthy colleague, someone to be dismissed.

EXTERNAL REALITY #2: COMPOSITION STUDIES ITSELF

My being a lecturer was partly connected to another fact: the shaming that the study of writing itself often suffers in the academy. In those days, Rhetoric and Composition was a very young field, but in the United States, interest in the teaching of writing in higher education was burgeoning. English departments were granting PhDs for writing specialists, and some colleges and universities were forming writing programs unaffiliated with literary studies. Nevertheless, in many academic circles the stigmatization of writing as a field was unexamined and sometimes vicious. Plenty of literature departments insisted that their writing faculty were "contingent"—untenurable and always peripheral—even if they published regularly, were great teachers, and were hired in national searches.

Most people inside and outside our field now agree that writing is a rich subject of study. But even now Rhetoric and Composition still sometimes struggles to assert itself as a legitimate discipline. Plenty of academics, along with much of the general public, still have not even heard of our field, in spite of its tens of thousands of practitioners. Classes in academic writing still sometimes hold the stigma of what used to be called "bonehead English"— the tedious-to-teach class for students who can't write. And some faculty still slide their eyes away with disdain when discovering that a colleague teaches in a writing program. Lecturers are sensitive to that attitude; it fosters shame.

EXTERNAL REALITY #3: EXPRESSIVISM

The first two realities—being a lecturer, and being in composition—felt shameful enough, but within a few weeks of starting at Santa Barbara, I confronted yet another difficult reality, one not visible to outsiders but very strong within composition at the time.

Having been hired by Sheridan Blau, whose ideas were similar to Elbow's and my own, I was shocked to discover that some of the other lecturers in Santa Barbara's large composition program vehemently disagreed with the pedagogy I believed in, which I had mistakenly assumed was central to the field of composition as a whole. Later deemed, sometimes pejoratively, "expressivist," that pedagogy was grounded in the idea that we could teach academic discourse by helping students gain access to, and explore the nuances of, their own unique responses to ideas and texts. In contrast, those on the other side, most often called "social constructionists," scoffed at the idea of "empowering" students as a goal in itself. To them, a writing teacher's job, as defined by David Bartholomae in "Inventing the University," was to get students to put aside their personal reactions in order to adopt a new, alien language—academic discourse. That meant drawing attention to how their own ideas and language, along with everyone else's, were socially constructed by the various voices they had internalized from the outside.

It seems almost laughable now to remember how vehement the "Elbow vs. Bartholomae" debate between those two positions was in the late '80s and into the '90s. Their gigantic divide bifurcated college writing teachers all over the United States in spite of the fact that both sides had the same ultimate goal: to help students write more effectively in the academy. People on each side tended to view the other with contempt, leaving both sides feeling unfairly stereotyped and vilified.

I didn't see it so clearly at the time. Instead, I became dug into my own position, angry at the suggestion that my desire to "empower" students was naïve. "NO, it's the opposite of naïve!" I said to friends, "Teaching students to examine and articulate their own inner voices helps them confront external forces much more effectively!"

But along with my defensiveness, doubt grew, shaking the resilience I had developed in graduate school. I'd always thought I was an iconoclast, resisting the status quo, but looking at myself through my nonexpressivist colleagues' eyes I saw a naïve, touchy-feely do-gooder who wasn't sophisticated enough to truly appreciate the harsh political realities she claimed to want to disrupt! Could it be that my insistence that students articulate "authentic" perspectives was preventing them from understanding how they had been indoctrinated by a multitude of cultural voices? It was a horrifying thought, and my faith in expressivist pedagogy wavered under it.

Motivated by shame, I began altering my pedagogy to prove that I too had "social constructionist" credentials. At a conference, I heard Patricia Bizzell seeming to sneer at writing teachers who focused on "craft" at the expense of theory, and I fretted that she—whose writing I both admired for its thoughtfulness and resisted for its seeming contempt for people like me—would think my classroom practices lacked rigor. I began to insist that my Santa Barbara students eschew personal stories and analyze their received knowledge, and I chose *Ways of Reading* as a textbook for the next quarter because of its emphasis on difficult texts.

Going over an essay in that book with a struggling student one day, though, I paused. He was a sweet student with a quirky perspective, and he was striving to do whatever I told him to with John Berger's theories. I realized that our conversation was pulling him farther and farther from his own reactions to the text, and thus I was undermining the thing I could do best as a teacher: getting people to articulate their own most unique ideas and then explore the evolution of those ideas in interactions with outside material. I didn't want the student to pretend to know more than he knew; I wanted him to write his subjective story of how he thought about the material. I was an inveterate expressivist, I realized, I couldn't help it, and trying to transform myself into another kind of teacher was backfiring on me. Although Bizzell might criticize me for perpetuating hierarchical systems if I didn't critique them explicitly enough in class, I felt that it was in the "craft," the pedagogy of "begin with your own personal reaction," that I could have the most impact on students. Yes, "empowering students" was a disparaged cliché, but it was still what I wanted to do.

Luckily, the fact that I'd had Elbow as a model helped get me past my habit of succumbing to the shaming idea that something was wrong with me for being "nice" and nurturing students. I knew I was tough and critical as well, even if it didn't look like that on the surface. I strove to make better use of Elbow's example: the diffidence and indecisiveness he sometimes displays on the surface masks a powerful and textured intellect, and he too suffers from shaming when he is lumped in with "subjective" and "touchy-feely" perspectives. No! "Touchy-feely" can be a terrible insult in the academic world, because it implies a lack of rigor. Elbow, though, along with expressivism itself, insists that we reconsider our notions of what "rigor" means. Can learning how to cultivate, articulate, rethink, and share one's at-first-vaguely-defined instincts be rigorous? Of course it can, and it does. I want to resist the inner as well as outer voices that try to tell me otherwise.

Things have changed dramatically in the field of composition since the '80s, of course. Most of us have adopted a both/and perspective when it comes to the old "expressivist vs. social constructionist" debate. "Of course a writer's own ideas are important," we now say, "and of course our language grows out of the received voices that surround us." We know it's absurd to argue either that the self is unique or that an individual's own perspective consists solely of heard voices. And yet the shame of being accused of "not rigorous enough" when we encourage self-exploration can linger.

A LONG LULL IN MY CAREER

In spite of my eagerness to be active and productive, those three shame-inducing realities—being a lecturer, being in composition, and being on the expressivist side of a debate in composition—continued to get in my way. After four years in Santa Barbara, I was restless. My lecturer position, while endlessly renewable, would never lead to tenure, and I wanted to publish more so I could get a tenure-line position. Like so many busy teachers, I imagined that if I had time off I would work for hours each day on a sustained and wonderful project. I had saved enough money to live for about a year, and my boyfriend was tired of his job at a Santa Barbara think tank and wanted to get a PhD in Computer Science and enter the academic world. He decided to go to the University of Massachusetts in Amherst, and I decided to move East, too, to New York City. My plan was to write a bit and live on my savings, publish, and within a year or so, I was sure, secure a sparkling job as a tenure-track professor.

But like many people who imagine that all they need is a sudden space of free time to start disciplined writing for hours each day, I had trouble getting focused. I loved being in the city, but while I sent out a few job application letters and writings, I couldn't seem to get myself established. Bizzell's "Beyond Anti-Foundationalism to Rhetorical Authority: Problems Defining 'Cultural Literacy'" came out in *College English* that fall of 1990 and deeply inspired me. She was looking for a way to rescue "foundationalism" while also honoring antifoundationalist philosophies, which is what I felt I too wanted to do. I sat in my apartment writing out my thoughts, longing to take my place next to Bizzell as an important thinker in composition theory. But my ideas were fragmented; I couldn't push them as far as they needed to go; and that made me ashamed.

An unsympathetic inner voice kept interrupting me. "What's wrong with you? You should have written a book by now! Get a job, and send essays out for publication!" Yes, in my four years in Santa Barbara, I had published two essays on teaching and one on Woolf that grew out of my dissertation. That wasn't so bad, I tried to reassure myself. I began quite a few pieces—essays about expressivism, personal reflections on teaching and life, fiction—and sent a few of them out. But even though I knew I shouldn't be, I was debilitated by rejections; one would stifle me for months or more. I held onto my desire to write a book—books—but that nagging inner shaming voice was relentless. "No one wants to hear your thinking. You don't have a job; you have no credibility." I knew exactly what I needed to do in response—just keep going! write!—but shame was a powerful obstacle.

And then, in February of 1991, my mother, only sixty years old, unexpectedly died of a heart attack. Partly out of shock and sadness, and partly out of sympathy for my father, I moved out of my city apartment and back to Long Island to live with him. I set up a desk for my computer and books, thinking I'd have no choice but to write.

No go. My resilience drained out of me, and I reverted to the person I had been in that house in high school—moody, frustrated, and berating myself for being stuck. Meanwhile, like Woolf's Mr. Ramsay, my father walked, dazed, around the house with his arms outstretched. Also like Mr. Ramsay he had once seemed to have all the power in our family—he was loud and dominant, he traveled around Europe and the United States giving lectures in electrical engineering, and he had seemed intensely independent. We had thought of my mother as the weak one, the underling, the "touchy-feely" person with little power who could never really understand him. But like so many powerful men, it turned out, my father was terrible at taking care of his own quotidian needs. My mother, I saw, had been Mrs. Ramsay, the buttress for him even as he believed, and led her and others to believe, that he didn't need her.

As I cooked the Greek foods my father liked, and served them to him as he liked—always with salad, bread, and olives on the table—I reflected on my mother's life as Mrs. Ramsay, the unacknowledged ground for my father's life. My father could be delightful: fun and engaging. But clearly his unspoken demand for emotional support—in the form of listening to him, validating his ideas, and never contradicting him for long—could only be fully satisfied if I abandoned myself entirely and gave up my own aspirations, as those Victorian daughters, and "good" eldest daughters everywhere, had done. My training in feminist theory helped me to determine that I had to get away.

Summer approached, and I was lucky to find some more serendipity. Thanks to my friend Lynn Hammond from Santa Barbara, along with the fact that I knew Peter Elbow, I got invited to teach in the three-week August program required for all entering first-year students at Bard College. Elbow had initiated the program, for which teachers came from colleges all over the United States.

The institute woke me up. For five hours each weekday, we each taught a small class of incoming Bard students, and each evening we teachers collaborated intensively in our faculty dormitory about readings and classroom plans. In doing so, we got to know each other very well, both as people and as thinkers. The pedagogical framework of the institute was very much in keeping with the approaches I had learned both from Elbow and in Santa Barbara's branch of the National Writing Project. Entering that professional space, where I could be more of myself, was exhilarating. By the time my first three weeks were over, all forty or so teachers were a new sort of family for me.

During that summer, my boyfriend and I decided to get married. Thus, in my modern version of a Victorian woman's journey, I avoided "spinsterhood" at age thirty-six by moving from my father's house to my husband's in Amherst, Massachusetts. We wanted to have a baby, and after so many years of striving to prevent pregnancy, I thought, surely I could easily do so anytime, simply because I wanted to.

But it took four years. And to my great shame, I couldn't get a full-time job at any of the colleges in the orbit of Amherst. I ended up going "backward"—instead of getting a full-time job, I began teaching adjunct courses for a couple of thousand dollars per course, just as I had in graduate school. This time it was at Western New England College, in Springfield, Massachusetts.

My career-shame intensified further, and my "lecturer" job in Santa Barbara began to look dazzlingly successful by comparison with my current professional life. How could I have left it? How stupid I'd been, I told myself, to pursue the fantasy of moving to a better position! Where were those books I was so convinced I could write? I did write, fitfully, but I didn't have any effective plan for sending my writing out, or even finishing most of it. On some irrational level, I seethed with impotent bitterness and shame about my lack of social status. Those feelings stifled my attempts to organize my writing or get a job, and the certainty that it was my own damn fault twisted within me. Try harder! I told myself.

During my five academic years in Amherst, I continued to teach day-, weekend-, or week-long workshops for teachers with the Institute for Writing and Thinking, in addition to my annual work in Bard's summer program for incoming students. Thus, I matched my husband's graduate-fellow salary, and we got by. Leading those workshops a few times a year gave me a chance to develop new skills and continue to develop a professional identity: I loved working with teachers, and the positive feedback I got from them helped me fight my persistent shame.

That shame continually reminded me, though, that those years, my late thirties, were supposed to be the time during which I was establishing myself firmly in a career. Being untethered to any institution was humiliating, especially when anyone asked, "What do you do?" But at the same time, of course, in some ways it was great to be free and living again in a graduate-student world, especially because of another important serendipitous fact: Peter Elbow was by then teaching at UMass. I began sitting in on his classes and talking with him in depth about composition studies. We read James Berlin's *Rhetoric and Reality* in one of his classes, which allowed us to contemplate what we saw as a deeply wrong characterization of "expressionism." I read Elizabeth A. Flynn's "Composing as a Woman" and then "Composing 'Composing as a Woman'" with admiration and envy: I wanted to be out there with her, speaking and arguing.

I began attending CCCC each year, presenting papers with Elbow and/or my good friend Jane Danielewicz, whom I'd met in Santa Barbara. Those conferences buoyed me. Presenting my ideas and experiencing others'; walking through hotel lobbies and running into people I knew in the field; and going to dinners with composition friends, often including Elbow and other prominent writers—these things were great enemies to my shame. At least once a year, I was a valid member of the field in spite of my lack of bona fide credentials: I was confident speaking to conference audiences, relaxed and assertive in conversations with well-known scholars, and sharply aware of the fluid and burgeoning ideas in our field. But secretly I knew my membership in the field was superficial. No job, no book, no name recognition: I might be someone worth chatting with over dinner, but I didn't really belong.

After four years in Amherst I finally got pregnant, and for a while I didn't think about my career at all. I was lucky that my husband and I were still in our graduate-student apartment, which meant that I could shift my focus to the pleasures of pregnancy and childbirth without worrying too much about income.

While pregnant and nursing I continued to lead whatever occasional workshops I could get through the Institute for Writing and Thinking. I kept sending out letters looking for jobs, knowing I was competing with scores of well-qualified applicants. I learned never to fantasize about moving to the many institutions I applied to, since the chances of rejection were so high. When my son was almost four months old, I was surprised by two offers of interviews: one was at Trinity College in Hartford, for a full-time job teaching writing! I got a new blazer, packed my manual breast pump, secretly pumped milk in the bathroom during my day-long interview, and got the job. The director of the writing program, Beverly Wall, explained that I would have all the benefits of regular professors—in terms of course load, voting membership in the faculty, travel funds, and so on—but that since the college didn't see writing as a legitimate academic discipline, it would never make our jobs tenure-track. "Will the fact that it isn't a tenure-line position be a problem for you?" she asked.

"Not at all!" I said. I wasn't lying—it really didn't seem like a big deal at the time, since by that point the thought of finally being able to answer the question, "What do you do?" without shame was such a relief. There was a childcare center on campus, and my husband had finished everything in his graduate program except his dissertation. He wanted time to finish his dissertation before he, too, applied for jobs, and so in the summer of 1996 we moved seventy-five minutes on a busy highway away from Amherst to Hartford, thinking we would only stay there for a little while.

TRINITY AND STATUS ANXIETY: HARTFORD, CT, 1996–THE PRESENT

Once I got settled into my job at Trinity, though, the reality hit me. A lecturer, again! I felt it as soon as the first faculty member I was introduced to asked me what department I was in. The writing program was referred to on campus as "the writing center." It was in fact a program, with a respectable number of courses at various levels. However, the fact that everyone at the college called it "the writing center" inevitably made many people think that the four of us who taught in it full-time simply did clean-up work for students' writing. More than once, upon hearing what I did, my faculty colleagues began talking about their students' atrocious grammar. I wanted to say, "No, no, I have a PhD in literature; I was hired on a national search; the teaching of writing is a discipline; it is not about correcting people's grammar; okay, grammar is an important subject of study, but it's much more complicated than whether students have learned grammatical rules, and . . ." I did try to say those things, at first, but somehow my words seemed to disappear into the air, unacknowledged in the firm reality of the slot that most of my colleagues placed me in. I learned to smile politely and murmur assent—"Yes, students' syntax is quite sloppy."

I never got rid of the flicker of shame I felt every time I introduced myself as a lecturer. Even people outside the academic world, on hearing that I taught at Trinity, would follow, "So, you have three months off every summer?" with "Do you have tenure?" "No," I'd mutter apologetically, "my job gets renewed in multiyear contracts." "Oh," they'd say, disenchanted. Of course, lots of people would be delighted to have my job. I knew that. But if I had been better as an academic, I felt, I would surely have a more impressive job.

In spite of all that, I continued to believe in myself as a member of the field of composition. I began writing about my teaching, and I continued presenting papers each year at the CCCC and other conferences. I grew fascinated with emotions in the classroom, and at first I wrote about the tension between thinking and feeling in argumentative writing, then about students' fear of their own ideas, and eventually about my own emotions as a teacher.

My CCCC papers over the following years explored shame, anger, and fear in either my students or myself. I strove to write as honestly as I could, and I loved the attention I got from audiences. I wanted more. But while I continued to present various aspects of my ideas at conferences, I rarely sent anything out for publication. Occasionally I would get it together and send something out, maybe even get it accepted. But not enough. I coedited a book on teaching literature and composition with a graduate school friend, Michelle Tokarczyk, and I also read extensively in the area of emotions and cognition, but nevertheless, in a larger sense of myself as an academic I felt stuck, embarrassed that my computer was filled only with notes and half-chapters, and with the nagging awareness that I was simply a lecturer.

But fed by my knowledge that the writing strategies I had learned from Elbow could transform lives including my own, I didn't give up. I eventually found a therapist who helped me look back at my life not as a failure, but as a series of clues about myself. That led me to view my status anxiety differently: could I have been resisting the notion that there was something about being an outsider of sorts that ultimately suited me?

Yes. I'm still at Trinity now, finally able to enjoy my status as both part of and separate from the tenure system. Since I feel less pressure to produce academic work, I can focus very productively on my students. I can also continue to present my thoughts at CCCC, and also publish essays and op-eds on any topics that interest me. I serve on faculty committees; I'm a commentator on a Connecticut National Public Radio show; and I've finished a draft of a memoir.

The connections I've made with others, and the serendipitous moments that have nurtured the person I intuitively knew myself to be, have helped me to emerge from the gloom of my status anxiety and honor my own achievements. As I do so, it becomes easier to be more comfortably productive. It also helps me to realize how many people in the academic world struggle with their own versions of "scarlet-L" shame when their status isn't perceived as up to par. Perhaps women, especially those of us with unconventional routes to achievement, feel it more often, but the ladder of success can potentially shame everyone, and it's a terrible feeling for people on every rung. Associate professors can feel ashamed for not being full, and full professors can feel ashamed for not producing more, or not being recognized widely enough, and it goes on and on.

The antidotes to academic shame begin with acknowledging what the feeling is and how our institutions foster it. Shame thrives when it is private and hidden, and it has economic as well as social causes and consequences. Bringing it into the open and connecting with others can allow us both to see that we're in fact not alone in feeling shame, and to honor what we *have* achieved more than what we *haven't*. That can be the best route away from shame and toward productivity and contentment.

WORKS CITED

Bartholomae, David. "Inventing the University." *Journal of Basic Writing* 5.1 (1986): 4–23. Print.

Bartholomae, David, and Anthony Petrosky. *Ways of Reading: An Anthology for Writers*. Boston, MA: Bedford St. Martin's, 2008. Print.

Beauvoir, Simone de. *The Second Sex*. New York: Bantam, 1970. Print.

Berlin, James. *Rhetoric and Reality: Writing Instruction in American Colleges, 1900–1985*. Carbondale: Southern Illinois UP, 1987. Print.

Bizzell, Patricia. "Beyond Anti-Foundationalism to Rhetorical Authority: Problems Defining 'Cultural Literacy.'" *College English* 52.6 (October 1990): 661–75. Print.

Bruffee, Kenneth A. "Collaborative Learning and the 'Conversation of Mankind.'" *College English* 46.7 (November 1984): 635–52. Print.

de Botton, Alain. *Status Anxiety.* London: Hamish Hamilton, 2004. Print.

Flynn, Elizabeth A. "Composing as a Woman." *College Composition and Communication* 39.4 (1988): 423–35. Print.

———."Composing 'Composing as a Woman.'" *College Composition and Communication* 41.1 (1990): 83–89. Print.

Woolf, Virginia. *To the Lighthouse.* London: Harcourt, 1981. Print.

CHAPTER 14

Empowerment through Change and Resilience

A Technical Communicator's Tale

NATASHA N. JONES

One of my fondest childhood memories is of my father jumping rope in our family sunroom. My younger sister and I would lie flat on our tummies at the top of the short flight of stairs that led down into the wood-paneled room. We were always silent as we watched the rope flip over my dad's head, under his feet, and crisscross in front of him. Even if we wanted to talk to each other, we wouldn't have been able to hear each other's words. Dad would always have Stevie Wonder blasting at the highest volume. "Isn't she lovely? Isn't she wonderful?" Stevie would croon. To this day, that song always makes me feel valued, empowered, and strong. These are the traits that I have carried with me throughout my academic career as a technical communicator interested in social justice, through undergraduate and graduate school, and into my current position as an assistant professor. At times, I did not have the words to explain why I took a path that I did or why I felt compelled to research what I researched. However, retrospectively, I understand that I have always been concerned with how people are valued, with empowerment, with resilience, and with making changes in order to promote the democratic ideals of justice and equality.

I understand that empowerment requires resilience and transformation—a movement toward a goal or an ideal. Empowerment, resilience, and transformation go hand in hand and have clearly shaped my personal and professional experiences. As I see it, change is fueled by the actions of those who embrace individual agency and promote agency in others, a resilient spirit coupled with the desire to rise above adverse circumstances. Academically and personally, I see transformation and growth at points where I felt most empowered, where I embraced the idea that I had the power (the agency and the desire) to create for myself (and for those around me) a space for action and make a deliberate move from the "here and now" toward the "where I want to be." This retrospective essay identifies transformative, yet empowering points in my life, emphasizing empowerment, agency, and resiliency as themes that significantly impacted my academic trajectory and personal life, and more specifically, shaped my academic identity as a scholar interested in issues of social justice. The moments of transformation, resilience, and empowerment in my life sometimes occurred without my fully understanding that they were important for my academic life. Often, I saw these transformative, empowering moments as only personal and intimate. Some of these transformative moments were small and hard-won. Some were big deals, and I recognized almost immediately that I would remember those moments for years to come. All of these moments, however, reflect how inextricably intertwined my personal life is with who I am in my academic life.

TRANSFORMATION 1: THE WONDER YEARS

For about the first ten years of my life, I only wanted to be Tina Turner. Then, in fifth grade, I made the all-A honor roll. I was ecstatic. My dad bought me a bright pink big-girl bicycle with colorful streamers tacked onto the handlebars. It was beautiful. It was lovely and wonderful. My dad reminded me that there are rewards for excelling in school, for hard work, and for determination. He explained that being intelligent, smart, and motivated was important, something that, as a young black woman, I couldn't afford to take for granted. My father grew up in the '50s and '60s. He was very much proeducation as a way for blacks to attempt to level the playing field. But, as my dad warned me, even my education would not be enough to save me from an unjust and unequal society. But, education could give me a better chance. However, because of my gender and skin color, I couldn't afford to be mediocre. I remember my father telling me that I had to be the best, the brightest, and the quickest. People wouldn't expect (and sometimes not respect) my intelligence, but it gave me an advantage, and it gave me a fighting chance. When I made the honor roll in fifth grade, earning one of the highest class averages of my classmates, my father beamed! He was proud of me. He reminded me of my value, my strength, and my potential. And, just like that, I felt powerful.

A change occurred in me that year. I began to see myself as smart, a scholar (as far as my ten-year-old mind understood the word). I wallowed in the praise that my father rained down upon me, but I also heeded his words and decided it was time to have a more serious focus on my education. I decided that I would be a lawyer—lovely, wonderful, successful lawyer like Claire Huxtable. In my small and limited frame of reference (mostly '80s television shows like *Matlock*), lawyers were powerful. Lawyers made a difference in people's lives. Lawyers represented justice, a voice for victims. This would become especially important to me as I grew older and began to research social justice issues in technical communication. As a graduate student, I became interested in the ways that lawyers sought justice for disenfranchised and marginalized populations. Specifically, the Innocence Project (a network of activist-lawyers who work toward criminal justice reform via exoneration and legislation), and the social justice work that was being undertaken by lawyers and volunteers within the Innocence Project and related organizations would become a foundation for my research. But, before I was even aware of the Innocence Project and similar organizations, I was interested in how lawyers could serve as agents of change and transformation, as empowering individuals.

I completed high school and enrolled at a large state university. I decided that I would major in English and prepare to become a lawyer. Starting college was like beginning a new life. I had developed a deep love of learning. Being in the classroom, listening to lectures, engaging in discussions was all very invigorating for me. I became passionate about my education, and I excelled. But one thing stood out for me during the early years of my undergraduate program—there were so few African American professors. There were even fewer African American women professors—women who looked like me. In the four years of my undergraduate program, I could count on one hand the number of black women professors that I had the opportunity to interact with—two. According to Harris and Gonzalez in 2007, six years after my undergraduate graduation, "women of color held only 7.5 percent of full-time faculty positions" (1). Further, Ryu notes that "the percentage of women of color declined steadily with rising academic rank. Women of color comprised 10.4 percent of instructors and lecturers, 9.9 percent of assistant professors, 6.6 percent of associate professors, and only 3.4 percent of full professors" (qtd. in Harris and Gonzalez 1). I was surprised at the limited number of black women scholars. The university that I attended was located in a very diverse, large metropolitan city. The student body included a large number of minorities and international students. I wanted to see more faculty members who looked like me! As fate would have it, I found a black woman scholar at my university who ended up being one of my most impactful mentors.

During my second year, I was assigned as a student assistant to a professor in the Communications Department. She was a commanding presence. She was tall, thin, and wore traditional African attire. She embodied resilience, having won hard fought battles in her personal life in relation to her health and in her academic life and her area of study. I remember our first meeting. I was completely intimidated and fully in awe. During that year, we worked on organizing and logging books in her small cluttered office. A playwright, she studied African American theater, film, and performing arts. She introduced me to Ntozake Shange's *For Colored Girls Who Have Considered Suicide/When the Rainbow is Enuf*. From her, I learned about Toni Morrison and Sweet Honey in the Rock. It was while working with her that I began to see how writing, literature, and performing arts could make a difference in people's lived experiences. I had always been a decent writer. Even in elementary school, I would write short stories and read them to my family. In high school, I began writing poetry. I even wrote a couple of short plays. But, I never really thought about how writing and telling stories through text, images, and music, could change the storyteller as well as those who listened to the stories. I was fascinated. I changed my major from English to print journalism and began taking courses that I felt would allow me to write creatively, but also would have a voice in the way that people and issues were presented in the media. I felt that print journalism would help me extend my reach, be heard by more people, and empower me to effect change on a greater scale.

I did well in my print journalism classes. I realized that I loved research, and I thoroughly enjoyed the challenge of piecing together an article or an essay. I continued to work with my mentor. She encouraged me to think of my work beyond the classroom and beyond academia. During my senior year, I landed an internship at a historically black newspaper. I authored a few articles featuring arts in the black community around the city. Seeing my byline in print was exhilarating, and I just knew I was doing exactly what I was meant to do. I continued with print journalism and graduated with honors. It took only a few short months before I started my first job as an editorial assistant at a small magazine. In my mind, this would be only the first step in my long and successful career as a journalist, writer, and publisher. I was on my way!

Soon after I began my job as an editorial assistant, I found out that I was pregnant. Of course, I was terrified. But, even then, a part of me knew that there was a purpose for this unexpected change of events. I had graduated within four years with my bachelor's degree, landed my dream job, and begun making a way for myself as an adult. I had never considered having children at this point. I was adamant about my success. Little did I know, the success that I would eventually achieve would look quite a bit different from the success I was reaching for at the time. Almost a year to the date of my college graduation, I found myself giving birth to an amazing baby girl, and my life and my goals changed in an instant!

TRANSFORMATION 2: BABY MAKES TWO

I never saw myself as a motherly type. Moreover, I didn't see myself ever being a single mother. It was clear from the day that I found out that I was pregnant that my daughter's father was not interested in sticking around, even though at the time, I thought that this person whom I had known since high school would always be there for me. Sometimes things just don't turn out how you envision them. Having a daughter, and knowing that I would have to raise her on my own, pushed me to make some hard decisions and changes. Again, this transformation required resilience and a determination that I did not know that I possessed.

I was aware of and, almost immediately, confronted with the stereotypes about black, single mothers and the challenges that I would face because of the gendered and racialized perceptions that are entrenched in our society. As Kennelly demonstrates in her study of how black, single mothers were perceived in the workplace, black women are often seen as laden with family responsibilities and less educated. Kennelly quotes an interviewee as stating:

> It goes back to just education issues that a lot of Blacks are maybe only getting through high school. And whether it is because of economic issues or whether they just don't have the drive, or y'know, a variety of factors. But they don't pursue, I guess, y'know, being more educated than just being able to get by. (177)

As a young mother-to-be, I had to begin negotiating and dealing with stereotypes like the one illustrated above. One particular instance stands out to me: I had scheduled an appointment with a doctor whom I hoped would deliver my daughter. I arrived on time for the appointment, and the receptionist provided me with a new patient questionnaire. As the receptionist prepared paperwork for my appointment she inquired, "What grade of high school have you completed?" Shocked and angry, I informed her that I had not only completed high school, but I also held a bachelor's degree in print journalism. This was a low point in my life. I realized that, as my father had warned so many years before, my education did not "save" me from being impacted by issues of race and gender. I began to question myself and my ability to make any significant change in my own life, let alone the lives of others. I allowed a microaggression to impact the way that I thought about myself. Then, unfortunately, within months, my life took an unrecognizable turn. The magazine for which I had worked for only a couple of months let me go, with the human resources manager asking me, "How did you let that happen?" when I explained to her that I was expecting. Still in my probationary period, I had no recourse. Without a job, I ended the lease on my apartment, moved in with my best friend, and took a part-time retail position in a local mall. I worked a handful of hours each week and waited for my daughter to be born. I felt powerless. I felt trapped. I found it hard to conjure up the resilience that I had discovered during my undergraduate years. The only thing that I looked forward to was being a mother—something I had not considered seriously before. But, at the time, I longed for the change that I knew motherhood would bring—a change that would push me to be strong because I had someone who would be completely dependent on my strength.

After my daughter was born, I took some time to nurse my wounds and retreated from my aspirations of making a difference. I moved closer to my parents, and I focused on my daughter, an amazingly bright and curious child. I doted on her and I embraced motherhood with all of myself. Eventually, I took an office job that paid well and offered great benefits. For a while, I was content. Then, after a few years and a couple of promotions, I couldn't ignore that I knew I was supposed to do something else. I missed writing. I missed having my voice heard. I missed feeling like I had the potential to make any sort of real difference. I had to make a change. I knew I couldn't stay where I was.

At the same time that I was having an existential epiphany, my younger sister had enrolled in a master's program in clinical psychology at Auburn University. I complained to her that I needed a change, that I missed school, and that I wanted to do something different. I also told her how I did not think that I could pursue print journalism at this point, but I still loved research, writing, and editing, and felt that I needed a job that allowed me to do those things and still make enough money to support my daughter. My sister told me that I should check out a technical communication program at Auburn.

I had no idea what technical communication was and had never even heard of the field of study. But, I decided that I had nothing to lose and began researching the program. Auburn University's Masters of Technical and Professional Communication (MTPC) degree program seemed to be an answer to my prayers. Having been out of school for a few years, I struggled through drafting a personal statement. My undergraduate mentor wrote a glowing letter of recommendation. I completed the application with little time to spare before the deadline. Mailing off the application made me realize that I not only wanted change, I *needed* change more than I had allowed myself to believe in the previous few years. Applying for the MTPC program put the power back in my hands. I felt like I was doing something about the direction my life was taking instead of sitting back and being pushed along. It's funny, now that I look back, how much of an impact an academic program had on my personal life. After acceptance into the program, my daughter and I moved into my sister's spare bedroom, and I braced myself once again for change.

The MTPC program at Auburn was a perfect fit for me. The first semester was challenging, but exciting! It was invigorating to be back on a university campus. But, my experience this time around was drastically different from my undergraduate years. Now, I was a single mom with little disposable income or time. I had to "learn" how to read theoretical texts (something I was never pushed to do in my undergraduate program), often using dictionaries, university databases, and reading articles that texts referenced in order to gain a full understanding of a work that I was reading.

At the time, my daughter was in preschool. She was full of energy and curiosity. Figuring out how to balance being the mother of a preschooler, a full-time student, and a teaching assistant was hard, but my sister and her husband were generous with their time and space. Sometimes, they would take my daughter out to play while I studied. Other times, I would try to squeeze in as much work as possible during the day while my daughter was away at preschool. A few times, my teaching and course schedule presented difficulties and spilled over into the evening. I had to rely on my sister or her husband to pick up my daughter from school. Money was tight, and I had taken out loans to supplement my living expenses and pay for my daughter's preschool tuition. However, I was able to contribute rent and groceries, and I cleaned the house. This was a far cry from my undergraduate days of house parties and hanging out with friends, but I was happy! I slowly began to realize my strength and my value again. I had let the hardships of the previous few years strip away my sense of agency, but I found voice again during my days at Auburn. I slowly began to feel more empowered.

In addition to changes in my personal life, my academic life began to shift and develop. As part of my financial aid, I was offered a teaching assistantship and would work in the writing center on campus. I had never taught before, and I had never considered teaching. At first, I was immensely more comfortable working in the writing center as a tutor than I was standing in front of twenty-four freshmen every Monday, Wednesday, and Friday morning. But eventually I came to love being in the classroom. My first semester at Auburn, I took a composition pedagogy course. This is where I first learned of liberatory teaching approaches touted by scholars like bell hooks and began to read the works of expressivist, Peter Elbow. Elbow, who encourages a focus on voice, and hooks, who asks educators to value our students' experiences and voices, became the foundation for my approach to teaching. At Auburn, my teaching philosophy sprouted to life. My liberatory, expressivist philosophy was evident in the first iterations of a written philosophy of education statement that I developed. I wrote:

> It is essential that instructors come to the realization that their sphere of influence extends far beyond the classroom or university. As a technical communication instructor and composition teacher, I understand that my job is not only to assist students in developing the skills needed to construct a well-written piece of writing, but I am also helping to shape lives. By encouraging students to express themselves and tap into their own voices, I am able to raise students' confidence and capability in academic writing and communication and ensure that my instruction adheres to the tenets of student-centered teaching.

I began to infuse in my teaching approaches the practice of allowing a space for students to speak in their own voices on their own terms, celebrating different ways of learning, knowing, and understanding, and encouraging students to approach technical communication and composition from their unique, individual perspectives. My teaching practices included requiring my students (even my technical communication students) to keep a journal about their experiences with writing and communication. I invited my students to bring examples of writing and communication that they were able to engage with or connect to their personal lives. I shared pop culture references with my students. I listened carefully to what my students had to say about my course content, about my teaching practices, and about me. In my mind, this encourages a more just and equitable approach to communication analysis and design, and promotes the agency of individuals.

Even as I was seeking ways to promote agency in my students, I began to better understand my own agency as a researcher. For me, my focus on agency was grounded in my refusal to allow my circumstances to get the best of me. I funneled that determination into my academic pursuits. I took practical courses in technical editing, grant and proposal writing, and information design. Even though my courses were very different from the print journalism courses that I had taken during my undergraduate program, I was given the opportunity to stretch my writing muscles in a very different way. Technical communication provided a way for me to significantly contribute to the design of a text. Slack et al. address the issue of the agency of technical communicators, positing that "to communicate is to exercise power" (19) and that technical communicators, as authors, are also expert mediators of meaning as transmitted to readers and users (30). Further, the authors note that the work of technical communicators is not apolitical or neutral (Slack et al. 30). Moreover, "no contribution is really transparent; it is only rendered transparent in relation to power. So, just as the power of the technical communicators is recognized (as they are empowered), so too must they be held responsible" (Slack et al. 30). The texts that I engaged with in my technical communication courses pushed me to think more carefully about how people actually use texts in their lived experiences. I was obligated to think not only about my own agency but also the way I enacted that agency and the impact of that enactment in the texts that I created. It forced me to think about texts in a new way—as tools that can help or hinder individuals and as mediating artifacts that had the potential to shape the nature of work and people's understanding of large-scale ideas like science literacy or social justice. As a technical communicator, I understood that I acted as an advocate for those who read and used the texts that I created (Dawson). This positionality as an advocate was exactly what I had been searching for through journalism and creative writing. I began to see technical communication as a way of providing a voice for the marginalized and disenfranchised, and empowering those that are often least valued, but I understood that advocacy was only part of the puzzle. My focus shifted to social justice in technical communication. In her article, "Mapping the Research Questions in Technical Communication," Rude asserts that, as a field, technical communication has the knowledge and expertise necessary for influencing and contributing to the creation of a more democratic and socially just society (267). Other scholars were researching and exploring the need for social justice in technical communication. For instance, Haas examines technical communication pedagogy and issues of race and technology. Williams, who would later serve as an important mentor, studies how policy and regulative writing impacted black populations in Texas. Inspired by the work of scholars such as these, a focus on social justice began to provide a foundation for (and continues to ground) how I perceived my work as a scholar and researcher.

TRANSFORMATION 3: IF YOU CAN'T BE ONE, RESEARCH ONE

It was during the MTPC program that I truly began to understand the work of a scholar. I was mentored by the director of composition at that time. Though she was the director of composition, she also taught some technical communication courses. One semester, she taught a technical communication course that focused on biotechnology. I had my reservations about signing up for the course because I couldn't immediately make the connection between two seemingly very different fields of study. The course was enlightening. We studied how discourse about advancements in biotechnology (like nanotechnology, stem cell research, genetically modified foods and animals, and DNA forensics) and genetics impacts individuals in increasingly social, political, and ethical ways. My mentor offered me the opportunity to coauthor my first article with her based on our experiences (mine as a student and hers as an instructor) in the course. In the article, "Genetic Interfaces: Representing Science and Enacting Public Discourse in Online Spaces," we note that during the course,

> we came to see that genetic discourse and public policy necessitated more than scientific knowledge—it involved an understanding of audiences' social, economic, and health conditions as well as their ability to engage multiple scientific and technological resources. Moreover, students came to understand that public policy has the potential to disempower and marginalize certain peoples while at the same time advancing scientific knowledge and human understanding. (Sidler and Jones 29)

My work on this article emphasized for me the power that is wielded with words and texts. More specifically, examining the ways in which public policy about science and technology revealed to me the inherently political nature of large-scale societal ideals like the benefit of science, the nature of crime and punishment, and the usefulness of information communication technologies. As we examined two civic action or advocacy groups (The Genetic Alliance and the Innocence Project) that promoted the use of biotechnology for health and social purposes, I began to appreciate how technical communication requires skilled communicators to "marry factual scientific knowledge with cultural and emotional rhetorics while providing an interface for multiple stakeholders in public policy change" (Sidler and Jones 29). In other words, technical communicators are in the ideal position to promote the use of communication and information communication technologies as tools for social action. This is what I believed, and this is what I wanted to do as a technical communicator.

While my mentor examined The Genetic Alliance group, I focused more closely on the Innocence Project. I was fascinated by this network of lawyers working pro bono to reform the justice system and exonerate wrongfully convicted individuals. I was reminded of years before when I realized that lawyers could work for the creation of a more just and equitable society. I remembered being ten years old and deciding that I wanted to be a lawyer, wanting to strive for justice and equity. Even though life took me in a different direction, I embraced the opportunity to study the work of the Innocence Project. If I wasn't going to be a lawyer, at least I could research lawyers!

My initial research about the Innocence Project investigated how the organization used their website to communicate complex scientific information about DNA forensics and exoneration. I examined how the Innocence Project's website interface provided access to scientific and public policy information through a design that promoted the "cultural empowerment" and civic engagement of the users (Sidler and Jones 41). Moreover, we argue that "with thoughtful consideration, technical communicators can design interface technologies that not only encourage citizen participation in public policy discourse and creation, but also assist in helping to create more informed and knowledgeable citizens that are capable of navigating the political and ethical agendas inherent in public policy issues" (Sidler and Jones 47). This article, my first scholarly publication, brought me a sense of accomplishment in both personal and academic ways. For me, it proved that I could use my scholarship, which lies at the intersections of technical communication, human-centered design, social justice, and rhetoric, to interrogate ways that I could empower others. It also reinforced my personal desire to transform my own lived experience and the lived experience of the marginalized and disenfranchised.

TRANSFORMATION 4: COMMITMENT TO EMPOWERMENT

My commitment to empowerment and social justice through my scholarship did not end with my master's program. In fact, my mentor encouraged me to apply for doctoral programs in technical communication, and in 2007, I was accepted to the Technical Communication Department (now the Department of Human Centered Design and Engineering) at the University of Washington. Having lived my entire life in the Southeast, I was anxious about moving to the Pacific Northwest where I had no family and no friends. As a single mother, I did not know what to expect. How would I make ends meet financially? Who would pick my daughter up from school if I were running late? Did I want to live so far away from my community and circle of friends? Eventually, I pushed past my fear and realized that in order to achieve the goals that I had set for myself, I had to, once again, embrace change and move forward.

My doctoral program was rigorous and required me to adapt in both personal and academic ways. I learned to build a network of people who could help me when I needed childcare or when my car failed. I was careful with my time, relishing the moments I spent with my daughter after school and during meal times, and then studying and reading late into the night after her bedtime. As with any doctoral program, there were moments when I felt defeated and tired, but overwhelmingly my experience was empowering. During the course of the program, I was surrounded by new friends who supported me and faculty members who pushed me to not only succeed, but excel. Even more, I was able to further develop my skills as a researcher and cultivate my examinations of the potential for technical communication to impact issues of social justice and inclusion.

As a doctoral student, I worked with amazing scholars in technical communication, including my dissertation advisor, Mark Zachry, and the then-department chair, Jan Spyridakis. In fact, my second published scholarly article was the result of a research group that Dr. Spyridakis facilitated. She helped me learn to design and implement a research study, and I was able to lead-author an article based on the study that our small group of graduate students conducted. This study was unlike any other research that I had done because we used a mixed methods approach, featuring quantitative data and also qualitative data gathered from focus groups and surveys. The study examined the impact of employing specific plain language techniques on the comprehension and perception of readers of environmental impact statements. This article, like the article I had written during my master's program, investigated ways that public policy can be impacted by discourse. Our study indicates that the use of plain language guidelines (like using personal pronouns and headings) and considering document design features (like the inclusion of relevant images and use of white space), can "affect readers of environmental policy documents" (Jones et al. 364). Broader implications of our study emphasize the political and rhetorical impact that the textual and visual design of text can have on public policy that affects large groups of individuals.

Also, during my doctoral program, I was able to revisit my research on the Innocence Project. I learned that there was an Innocence Project organization located on the University of Washington (UW) campus, and I knew that my dissertation project had to incorporate the work of this group. My dissertation examined the Innocence Project Northwest as a site of activism, investigating how the small group of lawyers, volunteers, and a paralegals communicated with each other and with other stakeholders as they worked toward the social goals of reformation and exoneration. My ethnographic field study required that I use the skills and tools that I had studied in a qualitative research methods/ethnographic research methods course that I had taken one semester from Dr. Charlotte Lee at UW. Ethnographic research methods allowed me to focus on lived experiences. As I note in my dissertation,

> using ethnographic research methods in my study pushed me to take into account what individuals were actually faced with as they completed work. This focus was not based on what I thought participants may do (an "idealized image"), but it was grounded in what I actually saw participants do—how they used technology, how they communicated, how they coordinated—and the outcomes of their communicative actions. (Jones 64)

Ethnographic methods quickly became the manner in which I committed to conducting research because ethnography, if done right, affords a researcher the opportunity to build an understanding with a group of people. "Actively participating in another way of life, the ethnographer learns what is required to become a member of that world, to experience events and hence to understand what they mean and portend to others" (Emerson 21). Understanding how people actually communicated and actually lived and understanding their experiences is key to designing texts and interfaces that empower and encourage agency. Without a clear understanding of how individuals experience and communicate in the world around them, technical communicators and designers can only assume. These assumptions can often disempower and fail to address the true needs of individuals. As I came to this realization, my research necessarily extended to consider not only the analysis of but also the design of texts and interfaces, and the consideration of how issues of social justice and equity could be addressed through thoughtful, critical design.

TRANSFORMATION 5: TEXTS, INTERFACES, AND SOCIAL JUSTICE

I graduated with my PhD in 2012 from the University of Washington's Human Centered Design and Engineering Program. Since then, I have been careful to continue to nurture my academic profile as a researcher dedicated to the consideration of ways that technical communication and design can engage issues of inclusion and social justice. I continue to argue for an understanding and celebration of technical communicators' capabilities to use texts to interrogate issues of justice and equity and then intervene to pragmatically create texts that encourage individuals' agency. To help develop this research perspective, I argue in a 2016 article that our field should integrate social justice into its theory and pedagogy. Currently, the field of technical communication has much work to do in order to fully consider justice and inclusion in our work. Williams and Pimentel lament the "reticence" of scholars in technical and professional communication to directly engage with issues of race and ethnicity. However, because of our role as authors, mediators, and meaning-makers, we cannot afford to ignore issues of equity. As Savage and Mattson note, a "commitment to diversity is now vital to sustained relevance for our field. Our field is deeply involved in the complex process of globalization, a process that not only entails opportunities and benefits for business, professions, and human lives but that also often sweeps through cultural, social, environmental, and economic domains in destructive ways" (5). Technical communicators possess the knowledge, the agency, and the opportunity to make a real difference, and some scholars are taking on the challenge to effect real change (see for example: Haas, 2012; Williams, 2010 and 2013; Williams and Pimentel, 2014; Sapp, Savage, and Mattson, 2013; and Moore, 2013). However, there is much more work to be done.

At the 2014 Conference on College Composition and Communication (CCCC), I had the opportunity to hear Dr. Angela Davis, a brilliant scholar and activist, speak. She called scholars in composition, technical communication, and related fields to action by asking us how we were engaging issues of social justice, inclusion, and equality in our research and in our pedagogy. It is my full intention to answer Dr. Davis's call in my own instruction and scholarship, focusing on the empowerment of others through my work, both academically and personally, recognizing that my academic life has been shaped, formed, and transformed by my personal experiences.

CONCLUSION: MY STORY IN BLACK AND WHITE

When I was a kid, I was fond of a cartoon called *Transformers*. The cartoon featured unassuming cars, trucks, and vehicles that could transform into super-hero, larger-than-life robots that fought for truth and justice. The motto of the autobots (the good guys) was, "Transformers: More Than Meets the

Eye." I love the meaning that the phrase invokes. For me, this phrase suggests that change sometimes comes when you least expect it, from people who may seem unimpressive and less than powerful. But, change is coconstructed with empowerment. Change and empowerment can have a symbiotic and dialectical relationship, where one builds on the other and both become reborn. This also holds true for the symbiotic and dialectical connection between my academic and personal life.

I have changed a lot since my days of lying on my belly, watching my dad jump rope as Stevie Wonder's voice pulsates in my ears. But maybe my academic career really began there, on the top step of the stairs leading down into the family sunroom. Or maybe it began later, as I watched Martin Luther King speeches on the television with my sisters, my dad having taken us out of school for the day to celebrate the not-yet national holiday in his own quiet act of protest. Or maybe it was as an undergraduate, listening to my mentor talk passionately about Ntozake Shange's *For Colored Girls* in her small, cluttered office at the end of the long hallway. Perhaps my academic career began when I found myself eight months pregnant working a part-time job in the mall, or when I gave up my decent office job to head back to school and live in my sister's spare bedroom. Either way, my academic career, my personal journey, is marked with experiences and people that changed me, transformed me, that pushed me to be resilient and strong, that made me feel empowered and valued. Sometimes this empowerment, resilience, and transformation came from places and people that I purposefully turned to for strength. Sometimes, my strength was wrenched from the hands of an adversarial or difficult situation, times when my full-on Taurean stubbornness kicked in and I just wouldn't back down. Other times, change and strength came on quietly, and it wasn't until I looked back that I saw a difference.

My story, in black and white, at its most basic level, is simply that my personal and academic career goals are one in the same—to embrace change and to empower others and myself to be resilient and strong. Academically, I can do this by investigating, interrogating, and intervening to understand and create texts and interfaces that are more inclusive and socially just. In my personal life, I believe that it is my responsibility to be conscious and aware of issues of social justice and inclusion and to make a commitment to address these concerns in my career, through my interactions with students, in my social engagements with friends and families, in political and civic participation, and in the way that I raise my daughter. As an academic and as an individual, I am a black woman, a single mother, and a scholar—parts of a whole that cannot be separated out.

WORKS CITED

Dawson, Joseph A. "Advocacy Work in Technical Communication: Technical Communicators on Different Sides of the Environmental Sustainability Debate." Professional Communication Conference (IPCC), IEEE International, Cincinnati, OH. IEEE International, October 2011. Web. March 13, 2016.

Elbow, Peter. "Closing My Eyes as I Speak: An Argument for Ignoring Audience." *College English* 49.1 (1987): 50–69. Web. March 13, 2016.

Emerson, Robert M. *Contemporary Field Research: Perspectives and Formulations.* Long Grove, IL: Waveland Press, Inc. 2001. Print.

Haas, Angela M. "Race, Rhetoric, and Technology: A Case Study of Decolonial Technical Communication Theory, Methodology, and Pedagogy." *Journal of Business and Technical Communication* 26.3 (2012): 277–310. Print.

Harris, Angela P., and Gonzalez, Carmen G. "Introduction." *Presumed Incompetent: The Intersections of Race and Class for Women in Academia.* Eds. Gabriella Gutiérrez y Muhs, Yolanda Flores Niemann, Carmen G. González, and Angela P. Harris. Boulder, CO: U of Colorado P, 2012. 1–7. Web. March 13, 2016.

hooks, bell. *Teaching to Transgress: Education as the Practice of Freedom.* New York: Routlege, 1994. Print.

Jones, Natasha N. *Mediation, Motives, and Goals: Identifying the Networked Nature of Contemporary Activism.* University of Washington, Diss. 2012. Print.

———. "The Technical Communicator as Advocate: Integrating a Social Justice Approach in Technical Communication." *Journal of Technical Writing and Communication* 46.3 (2016): 342–61. Print.

Jones, Natasha N., Justin McDavid, Katie Derthick, Randy Dowell, and Jan Spyridakis. "Plain Language in Environmental Policy Documents: An Assessment of Reader Comprehension and Perceptions." *Journal of Technical Writing and Communication* 42.4 (2012): 331–71. Print.

Kennelly, Ivy. "That Single-Mother Element. How White Employers Typify Black Women." *Gender and Society* 12.2 (1999): 168–92. Web. March 13, 2016.

Moore, Kristen. "Exposing Hidden Relations: Storytelling, Pedagogy, and the Study of Policy." *Journal of Technical Writing and Communication* 43.1 (2013): 63–78. Web. November 19, 2014.

Rude, Carolyn D. "Introduction to the Special Issue on Business and Technical Communication in the Public Sphere Learning to Have Impact." *Journal of Business and Technical Communication* 22.3 (2008): 267–71. Web. November 19, 2014.

———. "Mapping the Research Questions in Technical Communication." *Journal of Business and Technical Communication* 23.2 (2009): 174–215. Web. November 19, 2014.

Ryu, Mikyung. "Minorities in Higher Education: Twenty-Fourth Status Report." *Washington, DC: American Council on Education.* (2010). Web. March 13, 2016.

Sapp, David Alan, Gerald Savage and Kyle Mattson. After the International Bill of Human Rights (IBHR): Introduction to Special Issue on Human Rights and Professional Communication. *Rhetoric, Professional Communication, and Globalization* 4.1 (2013): 1–12.

Savage, Gerald, and Kyle Mattson. "Perceptions of Racial and Ethnic Diversity in Technical Communication Programs." *Programmatic Perspectives* 3.1 (2011): 5–57. Web. November 19, 2014.

Shange, Ntozake. *"For Colored Girls Who Have Considered Suicide/When the Rainbow is Enuf."* New York: Simon and Schuster, 2010. Print.

Sidler, Michelle, and Natasha N. Jones. "Genetics Interfaces: Representing Science and Enacting Public Discourse in Online Spaces." *Technical Communication Quarterly* 18.1 (2008): 28–48. Print.

Slack, Jennifer Daryl, David Miller, and Jeff Doak. "The Technical Communicator as Author Meaning, Power, Authority." *Journal of Business and Technical Communication* 7.1 (1993): 12–36. Web. November 19, 2014.

Williams, Miriam F. *"From Black Codes to Recodification: Removing the Veil from Regulatory Writing."* Amityville, NY: Baywood, 2010. Print.

———. "A Survey of Emerging Research: Debunking the Fallacy of Colorblind Technical Communication." *Programmatic Perspectives* 5.1 (2013): 86–93. Web. November 19, 2014.

Williams, Miriam F., and Octavio Pimentel, eds. *Communicating Race, Ethnicity, and Identity in Technical Communication*. Amityville, NY: Baywood, 2014. Print.

Williams, Miriam F., and Octavio Pimentel. "Introduction: Race, Ethnicity, and Technical Communication." *Journal of Business and Technical Communication* 26.3 (2012): 271–76. Web. November 19, 2014.

CHAPTER 15

What I Learned about Teaching, Administration, and Scholarship from Singing with the Scottsdale Chorus

SHIRLEY ROSE

Five years ago, I began attending weekly rehearsals of the Scottsdale Chorus, a group of 120-some women who constitute a chapter of the International Sweet Adelines, an organization devoted to music education and the promotion of "barbershop" harmony through competitive quartet and chorus performances as well as entertaining audiences in public and private shows. Though I could not have anticipated it at the time, my weekly decisions to attend those first few rehearsals—decisions that seemed to be small choices at the time—turned out to be a critical contributor to what I now recognize as a turning point in my personal, professional, and intellectual lives. Unlike the critical decisions recounted by many contributors to this collection, this turning point came relatively late in my professional career. As I detail in what follows, joining the Chorus turned out to be an important decision point in my professional life, though it was initially intended to take me a few steps away from a singular focus on professional concerns.

I started visiting Chorus rehearsals in late September of 2011 after hearing and seeing the group perform at an educational program about American Musical Traditions on the Tempe campus of Arizona State University, where I teach and direct the Writing Programs. At first, I was just interested in hearing more of their music. I loved the barbershop harmony, and the women in the Chorus were obviously having fun performing. I thought I might want to join, but I wasn't ready to commit to it, and I didn't have any idea whether I would be able to pass an audition.

After about a month of just visiting, I officially started the audition cycle, which lasted around twelve weeks for me and involved a couple of practice vocal auditions prior to a formal audition where I sang the two songs the chorus had chosen for their upcoming regional competition in the spring. The vocal audition was followed by several weeks of learning the choreography for one of the songs and also learning how to use my eyes and upper facial muscles to communicate emotion. Except for occasionally singing along with the radio in the car or singing hymns in church, I hadn't sung since I was in my small college choir as a first-year student, and barbershop-style singing was new for me. The Scottsdale Chorus is a very high-level performing group, winning five International Sweet Adelines championships in the past fifty-one years and never placing lower than third in any international competition. We won the gold medal for our most recent international competition in Las Vegas in November 2015.

Sometimes it is difficult to trace big changes in our lives back to a single critical decision or turning point. Often we do not recognize a decision for what it is. We are unaware we've made a choice because we didn't see other alternatives or don't appreciate the potential magnitude of what seems, at the time, to be low stakes. There were a couple of weeks at the start of my journey with the Scottsdale Chorus when I was conscious of making a choice about whether to go back to another rehearsal and just watch. If I hadn't been captivated by the process of learning I was observing, I wouldn't have continued going only to listen, although I enjoyed the music very much.

There are also times, long after making an important decision, when we can, looking back, identify reasons for our choices that we weren't quite aware of at the time we initially made them. That doesn't mean that we invented the retrospective rationale after the fact, just that it was perhaps one that we couldn't understand or recognize at the time. When I initially declared my intentions as a prospective member of the Chorus, I was asked about my reasons for joining, and I explained, "I don't have enough time in my life for this. So I am going to do it—if I pass my audition—because I need to make time in my life for something just for me." I had struggled with being a "workaholic" for my entire career. As an academic, there has always been more I could see that I could do as a teacher, scholar, and WPA. I've received many more indications of what I've left undone than cues that I've done enough.

That's what I understood about my reasons then.

In retrospect, I can identify other, serendipitous outcomes of joining, ones I could not initially have anticipated. My Chorus experience was and is fulfilling needs I hadn't identified at the outset, but could recognize only as they began to be met. One of these serendipitous outcomes is that through singing with the Chorus I am meeting and interacting with a diversity of people I never would have otherwise known. Our chorus includes women from ages eighteen to eighty-some years, with sometimes radically opposing politics, living in different economic circumstances and having different aspirations from mine, though we all love to sing and want to become better singers. I hadn't realized how homogeneous my circle of acquaintances—not just my circle of friends and colleagues—had become until I met these women. It's been a great personal gift to me to observe how women who are ten and fifteen years older than I are maturing not just gracefully but joyfully. Getting to know the college-aged women in the Chorus has helped me to recognize that I can learn from them as well, while it also reminds me how much more is going on in my students' lives than I can know from our brief time in classes. Most of my professional colleagues share my political views. I can't say the same about my fellow Chorus members. We don't discuss politics at Chorus activities, but I am Facebook friends with around forty other Scottsdale members, and I've inevitably realized that people I know to be good and smart can hold very different opinions concerning Arizona politics than I do.

Another serendipitous outcome of joining the Scottsdale Chorus that I didn't anticipate at the outset was my realization that I needed more "followership" experience. As a senior faculty member and an experienced Writing Program Administrator (WPA), I have had plenty of leadership experience. In my current role as Director of Writing Programs at Arizona State University, I provide leadership for a unit that includes over two hundred teachers and several full-time administrative staff. I have also been President of the Council of Writing Program Administrators, a national organization of several hundred directors of college-level writing programs and writing centers, and others who are interested in issues in writing program administration, and I am the current Director of the WPA Consultant-Evaluator Service. At my home institution, I am currently President-elect of the Tempe Assembly of the ASU Senate. In addition to serving in these organizational leadership roles, I have published scholarship about issues in writing program administration such as writing teacher preparation, curriculum development, writing program research, and writing program archives over my thirty-year post-PhD career and have taught thousands of students in classes ranging from first-year composition through PhD seminars. As a result, in my professional life I've become pretty accustomed to having people listen to me, defer to me, and follow my instructions.

I'm in a much different position as a Chorus member, however. Becoming a member of the Chorus has given me a chance to put in some extended time listening to others, following instructions, letting others make the decisions, and trying to simply be competent enough to do as I'm told. For example, far from having any say in what music we perform or what our visual plan for a song might be, my role is simply to follow the plan. At this stage of my development as a singer, I'm happy enough just to be able to recognize that there is a plan. The same is true with nonmusical management work for the Chorus: one of my jobs as a Chorus member has been to bring bottled water to sell at rehearsals as a money-making project for the Chorus. One month a year, I also take a turn at setting up the risers for rehearsal. I am not in charge, and I enjoy not being in charge in my Chorus activities, but I'm learning some unexpected but valuable lessons about how I can be better at being in charge in my professional life. For example, I've learned about the importance of getting detailed, specific feedback so that I know when I am doing something wrong and receiving reinforcement for what I have learned and encouragement for my willingness to keep on learning. I learned about the need for repetition of lessons in order for me to learn them, as I was not always ready to grasp particular points or understand specific vocabulary I was hearing for the first time . . . or even for the second or third time. I've had to have "plus notes" explained to me several times in several different ways before I began to understand what they were or why they were important to barbershop harmony. With each explanation, there was a little more I understood, because I had a little more context and a little more experience to connect with. I learned that I need to have patience with myself and to persist even when I cannot see progress. I have also become aware of how important my own metacognition is to my long-term retention of what I learn. Thinking about what I was learning, recognizing when I was using new skills, along with the occasions and purposes for using them, helped me to remember them better and have a stronger sense of command over them. This is true for me as a writer as well, but I had forgotten how long it took me to begin using my writing skills consciously and strategically—and how I continue to learn that over and over with each new writing challenge. These are lessons about providing leadership that I did not set out to learn from singing.

It is sometimes difficult for me as a learner to tell how far I am from realizing a goal, even though I can see how much I have improved. When I began singing with the Chorus, I often could not hear the difference between what was identified as "ok" vocal production and what was identified as "good" or "excellent" vocal production. A typical strategy during a Chorus coaching session is for the coach to ask us to sing a note or phrase, then instruct us in how to sing it differently—to change the shape of our lips or to change our posture—then to ask us whether we can hear the difference, and if we can hear it, whether we can appreciate that it is a change for the better, and if we can appreciate that it's better, whether we can understand why it is better. When I started singing with the Chorus, I often could not even hear the difference in the two versions of the note or phrase. More and more frequently now I can hear it, appreciate it, understand it—and actually produce that different sound myself. My struggles with learning as a singer have helped me to appreciate the difficulties that developing writers—whether they are first-year college students, graduate students, or senior scholars such as myself—encounter when they are learning new forms of writing. Often, they cannot see the differences between "good" and "bad" writing that seem obvious to more experienced writers, and even when they can recognize those differences, they may have difficulty appreciating why one is valued over the other. Learning how to recognize and appreciate those differences is a process of not just education but acculturation that takes time and takes practice. I appreciate this principle better now that I am experiencing it in my own development as a singer.

Sometimes when I am singing with the Chorus, I think I am getting it right, but when I listen to my own voice on a self-recording, I realize that it's the person next to me whose voice is so strong and beautiful. Sometimes, I literally cannot tell that it is someone else's song I am hearing. On one level, this lack of distinction between voices is wondrous and beautiful; after all, perfect blending is what we strive to achieve. On another level, however, my fledgling ability to distinguish voices makes evaluating my own performance even more difficult, so I have had to learn ways to monitor my singing, such as recording myself while I am singing in rehearsal or singing along to a recording of the whole chorus. I listen through earphones plugged into one device while I record my own voice singing on another device, then I can listen to how I sound without the other hundred-some voices singing along with me. My writing students have similar difficulties with really hearing their own voices when they write, and I find myself returning to some of the practices advocated by Donald Murray and Peter Elbow—pedagogical theorists I had last read decades ago—who encourage students to read aloud their own writing in order to hear what they are actually saying, not what they mean to say.

I've learned some lessons too about how to understand students' questions and to be more patient with questions I think I've answered already. As I go through the process of learning about how to improve my singing, I am not always able to understand information when it's first given to me. Many Chorus members learn more quickly than I do because they have more formal music training, or because they've been singing barbershop longer, or because their minds are more agile. And, furthermore, I need to be reminded of things even after I have learned them once already. I might forget what I've just learned about shaping vowels when I'm struggling to train my mouth to sing a tongue-twisting phrase like "and right away watch Lady Luck pay you a call"—with the right notes and the right syncopation at the right tempo. All of this has reminded me how hard it is to learn to write and that the process of learning to write is never finished.

When our Chorus learns a new song, we draw on skills we've developed from mastering other songs in the past, but it's sometimes necessary for our director and coaches to point out to us what those transferable lessons are. For example, mastering the diphthongs in "springtime" and "snow" in one song will help us with the diphthongs in "smile" and "only" in a new song. I understand the concept of transfer in learning to write much better, now that I'm aware of how I have experienced transfer of learning in my singing. And I understand better what my role as a teacher is in helping my students to develop a conscious practice of identifying what they already know about writing that they can bring to new writing tasks, just as our Chorus Director helps us to develop our practice of transfer of musical skill by making connections explicit for us.

When I first joined the Chorus, I didn't anticipate that it would change the way I think about feedback and assessment. Because the Sweet Adelines organization requires member choruses to regularly compete and be evaluated, our Chorus understands very well the benefits we derive from the detailed feedback we are provided for every competition performance. I began attending Chorus rehearsals near the end of a year that the Scottsdale Chorus was the reigning international champion and was preparing to sing their "swan song" at the upcoming annual competition. Initially all of the discussion of competition and explicit discussion of how to earn points was surprising, puzzling, and even a little off-putting for me. But I've had a chance since then to understand competition differently. As an A+-level chorus, we might seem a little too obsessed with how to earn points in one category or another, but that point system, while subjective, reminds us of the differences between a good performance and an excellent one. One of the pleasures of singing in a competition is knowing that our audience of fellow competitors is made up of people who recognize, appreciate, and understand those differences too, who will want to acknowledge and reward our performance. The organization has developed a very detailed rubric that makes it possible to train judges to score consistently with attention to shared criteria with agreed-upon differentiated weights. These criteria, like a rubric for evaluating writing, help ensure fair judging, of course, but more important in the long term, they help ensure that the organization is actively and strategically cultivating and promoting the kind and quality of music it values most highly.

It also is enormously helpful to me to have immediate feedback on my singing when I have a personal vocal instruction session with a fellow chorus member or when I'm singing for qualification to perform a new song, when we're singing in sectionals, or even once in a while getting direct specific personal feedback from the Director during rehearsal. I know my writing students can also benefit from direct and immediate feedback, so I try to find ways to give it and accompany that feedback with positive support for what they are demonstrating they are learning, even if it means something very direct and very specific to a particular student. Getting feedback on my performance from Chorus teachers is helpful, but there's another kind of feedback that is qualitatively different, and that's the feedback from the audience. The audience's physical reaction to Chorus performances, whether it is to cry when we sing a ballad or to jump from their seats when we ring a chord in the "tag" of a lively up-tune, is unlike anything else I have experienced in my life. No feedback or response I have received as a teacher, as a writer, or in any other aspect of my professional life has been so immediate and so strong and so unequivocally positive as a standing ovation for a chorus performance that I have sung in. As an academic, I have received whatever response readers might have had to my scholarship long after I first wrote it. As a teacher, I know that my students will not know how to evaluate the quality or usefulness of much of what I have taught them or the experiences I have designed for them until months or years after my classes. When I have been reviewed by my peers for tenure and promotion, much of that review has been done confidentially and behind closed doors, and while I may know the outcome, for the most part I did not witness the response of these audiences to my scholarly performance. When I sing with the Chorus, I do not have to wait to know the outcome or learn about it secondhand. The applause is immediate, and I can hear it.

One of the most important lessons I've learned is about singing out, even when it means risking singing a sour note very loudly. While it's still a challenge for me, I've received only supportive feedback and encouragement from our Chorus Director, from our section leaders, and from the Chorus member who teaches me during "personal vocal instruction" and listens to me when I attempt to qualify on new music, or even from our visual evaluators. Because I know I have much further to go before I can sing well, I often hesitate to sing out boldly because I don't want my shortcomings as a singer to be obvious. But it's that very temerity itself that so often undercuts the quality of my voice and makes it less resonant and more out of tune. This experience has helped me appreciate how student writers often have similar problems: lacking the courage to speak out, afraid of offending or appearing foolish, they don't believe that only when they let their true voices ring out will they find an audience. Though I wrote about this aspect of "voice" in student writing early in my academic career, I have returned to this lesson with new understanding as I learn it with my singer's voice as well as my writer's voice. I also see that I'm becoming bolder in areas of my life besides singing, thanks to the confidence my Chorus experience has given me.

My participation in the Chorus has provided the occasion for other serendipitous discoveries that help me understand writing, teaching, and administering a writing program in new ways. My understanding of performance is much altered as I've come to understand that not only can performance be authentic, authenticity itself is a performance. Performance is not pretense but a conscious effort to manage emotions and behavior for a purpose, particularly to have an effect on an audience. That is, performance is rhetorical. I can sing about being happy and send a sincere message about being happy that can affect my audience without having to actually *be* happy in some existential sense. The same is true in my professional work. I can perform calmness even when I am frustrated, angry, or anxious without being untrue to myself. In fact, performing whatever emotion or state of mind the situation requires is how I can have agency and best realize myself. Even so, I've also learned that singing about being happy actually does lift my spirits, and I am very grateful to our Chorus music team for choosing songs with positive messages. There's a world of difference between singing "Whistle a tune of gladness. Gloom never was in style!" and "What'll I do when you are far away and I am blue?" week after week of rehearsal.

I don't want to overstate how much my joining the Chorus has influenced my professional and intellectual life. I've had my postgraduate career for three decades now, and I've been a member of the Scottsdale Chorus for only five years. There have been other activities that have served as hobbies from which I've learned life lessons and gained professional insights, such as refinishing furniture, gardening, and needlework. And there have been other pastimes that have given me a big break from work stress, like reading all of Agatha Christie's mysteries.

Since I've been involved in the Chorus for only five years, it hasn't set an entirely new direction for my career in any significant way at this point. But it might be helping me to see the way to what comes next. Do I wish that I had found the Chorus sooner? I don't know whether I could have. For most of my professional life, wherever I have lived, there has been a high-level Sweet Adelines chapter accessible to me for participation, not to mention many other singing groups I might have chosen to become involved in. But it was not until five years ago that I chose to do something for myself that was wholly personal—something that was not for my job, not for my career, not for my profession; not for my family nor for my friends. Just a choice for my own pleasure and enjoyment. That choice has ended up requiring an incredible amount of time and energy, effort, attention, and just plain work, but I get a very deep satisfaction and validation from developing my singing ability and performing with the Chorus. That it has been an occasion for learning that has helped me professionally is a serendipity.

I acknowledge that it is easier for me to join the Chorus now, at this point in my career, than it might have been earlier in my professional life. I know that for someone still in graduate school or pretenure it is far more difficult to find the time for a "hobby" or something just for oneself, and not for work or family. There are so many time demands for a pretenure young mother that taking time for a hobby may seem (or even be) impossible. I also recognize that openly pursuing a passion like singing, or gardening, cooking, or needlework—especially if the activity is making something that is feminized or identified with leisure—can seem dangerous to one's career. It can feel risky to acknowledge not working every minute of every hour, and I think it is reasonable to be concerned that if others know time is being spent on a "hobby," the hobbyist will be seen as cavalier about work or not invested enough in professional concerns. There may also be concern over revealing a pastime that might be considered nonintellectual. After all, it's one thing to read "good" literary fiction in one's spare time and quite another to read genre fiction. It's one thing to love listening to opera and quite another to sing barbershop songs. These kinds of concerns, while valid for others, don't matter to me now. I am in what Doug Hesse referred to in his 2014 WPA Conference plenary talk as "the last quarter" of a career as an academic scholar, but what I like to think of as singing the "last verse" of my academic song. All of the themes introduced in the preceding stanzas are finally fully integrated and articulated in the final stanza. I like to compare this to a barbershop "up-tune" in which the key continues to rise as the excitement expressed in the song progressively rises throughout, ending with a well-rung barbershop chord that brings the audience to its feet.

When I describe how singing with the Chorus has changed my life, I know some readers will wonder if I overstate the importance of that decision to attend a few rehearsals five years ago. I think it's natural to assert cause and effect relationships upon past experiences in order to make sense of them and to be able to narrate our lives in a coherent fashion. In fact, I have come to know that the personal and the professional are exceedingly difficult to untangle and that personal decisions are often inseparable from professional circumstances and expectations, just as professional opportunities and choices are determined by personal relationships and hopes and dreams. And I know that things could have turned out differently for me. But, thanks to my recent barbershop singing experience, I also know that singing this last verse of my professional work can be the most exciting, rewarding, and joyous time of my whole career, as I sing after decades of experience and years of disciplined practice.

WORKS CITED

Elbow, Peter. *Vernacular Eloquence: What Speech Can Bring to Writing.* New York: Oxford UP, 2012. Print.

Murray, Donald. *A Writer Teaches Writing.* 2nd ed. Boston, MA: Cengage, 2003. (First published by Houghton Mifflin in 1968). Print.

Rose, Shirley K. "The Voice of Authority: Developing a Fully Rhetorical Definition of Voice in Writing." *Writing Instructor* 8.3 (Spring 1989): 111–18. Print.

CONTRIBUTORS

ABOUT THE EDITORS

ELIZABETH A. FLYNN is Professor Emerita of Reading and Composition in the Department of Humanities at Michigan Technological University. She chaired her department, directed the graduate program in Rhetoric and Technical Communication, the undergraduate program in Liberal Arts, and Phase II of the Writing-Across-the-Curriculum Program. Phase II focused on writing in engineering and was supported by grants from the Whirlpool Foundation and the National Science Foundation. She is author of *Feminism Beyond Modernism* (2002) and coeditor with Patrocinio P. Schweickart of *Gender and Reading* (1986) and *Reading Sites* (2004), and of *Feminist Rhetorical Resilience* (2012) with Patty Sotirin and Ann Brady. Her essay "Feminist Perspectives on Postcolonial Rhetorical Practices: Spivak's Cosmopolitan Erudition and Nazer's Surveilled Silence" was published recently in *Rhetoric and Writing in the New Century*, edited by Cheryl Glenn and Roxanne Mountford.

TIFFANY BOURELLE is an Assistant Professor at the University of New Mexico where she teaches first-year writing and technical communication in face-to-face and online environments. Her work has been published in *Computers and Composition, Kairos: A Journal of Rhetoric, Technology, and Pedagogy,* and *Technical Communication Quarterly*. She designed and currently runs eComp (short for Electronic Composition), a fully online program that utilizes a multimodal pedagogy, helping distance education students acquire twenty-first-century literacies. She has a PhD in Rhetoric and Composition from the University of Nevada Reno, an MA in Rhetoric and Composition from Northern Arizona University, and a BA in Technical Communication from the University of Tennessee. She lives in Albuquerque with her husband, Andy, and her two children, Benjamin and Aubrey.

ABOUT THE CONTRIBUTORS

LINDA ADLER-KASSNER is cointerim Dean of Undergraduate Education and Professor of Writing Studies at the University of California Santa Barbara. Her research focuses on how writing and literacy are defined, taught, and assessed and with what consequences. She is author, coauthor, or coeditor of nine books as well as many articles and book chapters. Her most recent book, coedited with Elizabeth Wardle, is *Naming What We Know: Threshold Concepts of Writing Studies*. She is currently chair of the Conference on College Composition and Communication and is past president of the Council of Writing Program Administrators.

LYNN Z. BLOOM is Board of Trustees Distinguished Professor Emerita and Aetna Chair of Writing at the University of Connecticut. She learned the essentials of writing from: Dr. Seuss, fun; Dr. Strunk and E. B. White, elegant simplicity; University of Michigan professor Art Eastman, nitpicking revision; and Benjamin Spock, during interviews for *Doctor Spock: Biography of a Conservative Radical* (1972), "If you don't write clearly, someone could die." These precepts inform the heart, soul, and human voice of her teaching and writing, including *Writers Without Borders* and *The Seven Deadly Virtues and Other Lively Essays* (both 2008), and her current work on creative nonfiction—memoirs, essays, writing about food, travel, and medicine—that people love to read and write, also the subjects of her 2013 Fulbright in New Zealand.

M. ANN BRADY is Professor of Rhetoric, Scientific, and Technical Communication at Michigan Technological University. Her research and teaching interests focus on the intersections of interdisciplinary theory, feminist epistemologies, and science and technology studies. She has published widely in academic journals, such as *Technical Communication Quarterly* and *Rhetoric Review*. Along with Elizabeth A. Flynn and Patricia Sotirin, she coedited *Feminist Rhetorical Resilience*.

SUELLYNN DUFFEY'S career began during the late twentieth-century resurgence of composition and rhetoric studies. Thus her professional life reveals traces of the discipline's history. Currently, she is WPA at the University of Missouri-St. Louis and held similar positions at Georgia Southern, Ohio State University, and the University of Wisconsin-Eau Claire. She has published in *CCC, Writing on the Edge, Rhetoric Review, The Journal of Public Scholarship in Higher Education,* and *Writing Program Administration: Journal of the Council of Writing Program Administrators,* and has contributed chapters to several books. Her publications range from pedagogy to WPA work, from silence and listening to ethics and institutional cultures. Her current project is a study of place and literacy.

LISA EDE is Professor of English, Emerita at Oregon State University, where for thirty years she directed the Center for Writing and Learning. Ede is the author, coauthor, editor, or coeditor of nine books. Her most recent studies include *Writing Together: Collaboration in Theory and Practice* (2012), coedited with her frequent collaborator Andrea Lunsford, *The Academic Writer: A Brief Guide* (2008, 2011, 2014, 2017), and *Everyone's An Author* (2013, 2016), coauthored with Andrea Lunsford, Michal Brody, Beverly Moss, Carole Clark Papper, and Keith Walters. Ede's single and collaboratively authored scholarly work has been recognized by awards from the Modern Language Association, the Conference on College Composition and Communication, and the International Writing Center Association.

ANNE RUGGLES GERE is Arthur F. Thurnau Professor and Gertrude Buck Collegiate Professor at the University of Michigan where she directs the Sweetland Center for Writing and serves as chair of the Joint PhD Program in English and Education. A former chair of CCC and a former president of NCTE, she is the second vice president of the Modern Language Association and will become president in 2018. She has written a dozen books and more than one hundred articles. A current project is a longitudinal study of undergraduates' development as writers, looking at minors in writing and nonminors, both from a wide variety of disciplines. She is also engaged in a large-scale project of integrating writing-to-learn into gateway STEM courses.

IKLIM GOKSEL received her PhD in Language, Literacy, and Rhetoric from the University of Illinois at Chicago. She serves as an adjunct faculty member in the Women's Studies program at Indiana University Purdue University Fort Wayne in Northern Indiana. She was a monthly opinion columnist for 2016 in *Anthropology News of the American Anthropological Association*. In her column, titled *Pearls à la Turca*, she writes about issues related to gender and sexuality in the Middle East and North Africa (MENA) region. One of her recent publication titles is "Third Space Masculinities: Unnamed Sexualities in Turkey," which is forthcoming in the *Journal of Middle East Women's Studies*. She has native proficiency in Turkish and full professional proficiency in Swedish and German.

BETH L. HEWETT is a leading researcher and scholar in online writing and online literacy education at the postsecondary level. She is the President of the Global Society of Online Literacy Educators (GSOLE) The author of several academic books, she also is the editor/coeditor of books, journal issues, book chapters, and journal articles. Beth is the owner and lead writing coach at Defend & Publish, a company that teaches and assists dissertation and academic writers in completing their goals. She is a Certified Thanatologist (CT) and author of grief-related books, as well as a grief facilitation speaker, trainer, and coach.

LIBBY FALK JONES teaches creative, critical, and professional writing at Berea College where she is Professor of English and holds the Chester D. Tripp Chair in Humanities. Her poems have been published in regional and national journals and anthologies, including *Connecticut Review, Ruminate*, and *Low Explosions: Writings on the Body*. Jones is the Founding Director of Berea College's Center for Learning, Teaching, Communication, and Research. Her creative nonfiction has appeared in *The Little Norton Reader, The Art of College Teaching: 28 Takes*, and *I To I: Life Writing by Kentucky Feminists*. She is coeditor of *Feminism, Utopia, and Narrative* (1990).

NATASHA N. JONES'S research interests include activism, social justice, narrative, and rhetoric in technical communication and technical communication pedagogy. Her work has been published in *Technical Communication Quarterly,* the *Journal of Technical Writing and Communication,* and other academic venues. She is a graduate of the University of Washington's Human Centered Design and Engineering Department (2012), winner of the 2014 Conference on College Composition and Communication (CCCC) Outstanding Dissertation in Technical Communication Award, and of the 2017 Nell Ann Pickett Award for a coauthored article in *Technical Communication Quarterly*. She is chair of the Diversity Committee of the Council for Programs in Technical and Scientific Communication (CPTSC) and is currently an assistant professor at the University of Central Florida in Orlando.

IRENE PAPOULIS is a Principal Lecturer in the A. K. Smith Center for Writing and Rhetoric at Trinity College, where she teaches all levels of college writing. With Michelle Tokarczyk, she is coeditor of a collection of essays: *Teaching Composition/Teaching Literature: Crossing Great Divides*. She also leads workshops for teachers as a faculty associate of the Institute for Writing and Thinking at Bard College.

MALEA POWELL is Professor and Chair of the Department of Writing, Rhetoric, and American Cultures at Michigan State University as well as a faculty member in American Indian Studies. She is lead researcher for the Digital Publishing Lab at MSU, director of the Cultural Rhetorics Consortiom, editor in chief of *Constellations: A Journal of Cultural Rhetorics*, past chair of the CCCC, and editor emerita of *SAIL: Studies in American Indian Literatures*. A widely published scholar and poet, her current book project, *This Is A Story*, examines the continuum of indigenous rhetorical production in North America, from beadwork to alphabetic writing. Powell is a mixed-blood of Indiana Miami, Eastern Shawnee, and Euro-American ancestry. In her spare time, she hangs out with eccentric Native women artists and poets and does beadwork.

JACQUELINE RHODES is Professor of Writing, Rhetoric, and American Cultures at Michigan State University. Her scholarly work focuses on intersections of rhetoric, materiality, and technology and has been published in a variety of venues including *College Composition and Communication*, *JAC: A Journal of Composition Theory*, *Computers and Composition*, *Enculturation*, *Reader*, and *Rhetoric Review*. Along with Jonathan Alexander, she is the recipient of the 2014 Computers and Composition Distinguished Book Award and the 2015 CCCC Outstanding Book Award (for *On Multimodality*), and the 2016 CCCC Lavender Rhetorics Award for Excellence in Queer Scholarship (for *Techne*). Website: http://www.jacquelinerhodes.com.

SHIRLEY ROSE is a Professor and Director of Writing Programs in the Department of English of the College of Liberal Arts and Sciences at Arizona State University. She is a Past President of the Council of Writing Program Administrators and she is the Director of the WPA Consultant-Evaluator Service. She has served as a peer reviewer for the Higher Learning Commission of the North Central Association of Schools and Colleges for the past decade. She regularly teaches graduate courses in writing program administration and has published articles on writing pedagogy and on issues in archival research and practice. With Irwin Weiser, she has edited three collections on the intellectual work of writing program administration, including *The WPA as Researcher*, *The Writing Program Administrator as Theorist*, and *Going Public: What Writing Programs Learn from Engagement*.

INDEX

Aberdeen Proving Ground Job Assistance Center (JAC), Maryland, 159
"About" (Jones), 87
"Absent Director, The" (Jones), 84
accidental sagacity, 5, 27
Adams, Peter, 99
Adichie, Chimamanda Ngozi, ix
Adler-Kassner, Linda, 108–23
administrative responsibilities: Duffey, 98; Flynn, 42; L. Jones, 81; women and longer hours of, 46n3. *See also* writing centers; writing programs
adolegogical learning, 160–62
African Americans: jeremiad, African American, 117–18; professors, scarcity of, 220–21; *Telling Stories* (White), 9. *See also* Jones, Natasha N.
agency: accidental sagacity and, 5; Adler-Kassner and, 113–14, 119; chance and, 5; choice, intersection with, 4–5, 112–14, 119; definitions of, 4–5; Duffey and, 96–97; interruption and, 151; kairos and, 6; N. Jones and, 219, 225–26; rhetorical resilience and, 4, 83, 144. *See also* choice; empowerment
Ahmed, Sara, 142–43
Aisenberg, Nadya, 9
Albrecht, Lisa, 26
Alcoff, Linda, 28
Alexander, Jonathan, 148, 151
Allen, Jeanie K., 10, 38
America's Black Holocaust Museum, 138n10

Anderson, Benedict, 116–17
andragogy, 160
Anne Arundel Community College, 158–59
Anson, Chris, 116–18
Antifeminism in the Academy (Clark et al.), 8
Antioch College, 37, 46
Anzaldúa, Gloria, 9, 195
archetypal criticism, 35–36
Aristotle, 184
Arizona State University: Bourelle, 182–85; Rose, 235, 237, 239, 241–42
Ashton-Jones, Evelyn, 146–48
Atatürk, Mustafa Kemal, 192, 196
Auburn University, 223–28

Baker, Russell and Dorothy, 125, 132, 138n6
Baker, Sheridan, 156
Balancing Act, The (Bracken, Allen, and Dean), 10
Ballif, Michelle, 2–3, 97, 105n1
Barber, Elinor, 59–60
Bard College, 212, 213
Bartholomae, David, 18, 27, 97, 98–100, 209
Bateson, Mary Catherine, 74, 75, 77, 80, 86
Baudelaire, Charles-Pierre, 143, 144
Bay Area Writing Project (BAWP), 51
beadwork as metaphor. *See* Powell, Malea
Beauvoir, Simone de, 207
Beck, Charles, 175–76
Beckett, Gulbahar H., 9

249

Beckwith, Gladys, 41
Beja, Murray, 31, 34–35
Belenky, Mary Field, 178–79
Bennett, Dennis, 26
Bercovitch, Sacvan, 117
Berea College, 74–75, 76, 79, 81, 83–84, 86
Berger, John, 209
Berger, Linda, 175
Berkenkotter, Carol, 39
Berlin, Jim, 22, 28
Beyer, Werner, 68
"Beyond Anti-Foundationalism to Rhetorical Authority" (Bizzell), 211
Big Miami Reserve, 125, 138n5
Binghamton University, 204
biography and autobiography writing. *See* Bloom, Lynn Z.
Bizzaro, Patrick, 26–27
Bizzell, Patricia, 2, 5, 209–10, 211
Blackbird, Andrew, 136
Blackburn, William, 76
Blau, Sheridan, 208
Bloom, Lynn Z., 58–73; *Bear, Man, and God* (Utley, Bloom, and Kinney), 62; *Doctor Spock: Biography of a Conservative Radical*, 63–65, 69; *Forbidden Diary* (Crouter; ed. Bloom), 65–67, 69, 70; "How Literary Biographers Use Their Subjects' Works" (dissertation), 63; *The New Assertive Woman*, 69; *Symposium* (Kinney, Kuiper, and Bloom), 62, 68; "Why Don't We Write What We Teach? And Publish It?," 170
Blotner, Joseph, 50, 56
Booth, Wayne, 33
Borderlands (Anzaldúa), 9
Bourelle, Tiffany, 173–90
Bracken, Susan J., 10, 38
Brady, Ann, 4, 44, 82–83, 90, 144, 192, 196
Bridwell-Bowles, Lillian, 26
Britton, James, 37
Brodkey, Linda, 97
Brody, Michal, 25
Brosh, Allie, 151–52
Bruffee, Ken, 206
Buber, Martin, 164
Buck, Gertrude, 56
Burke, Kenneth, 33

Butler University, 72n10; Bloom, 68

Cameron, James, 138n10
Cannon, Walter, 60
Carey, James, 112–13
Case Western Reserve, 63
Catholic University of America, 160–61, 170
Celebration of Student Writing (CSW), 120–21
Central Texas College, 157–58
chance: choice and, 144; context and, x; Derrida on, 5; Duffey, 97; Ede, 21; Goksel, 201; "moral luck," 4–5
Cheever, Susan, 72n8
children. *See* family and childrearing; pregnancy and childbirth
Chiseri-Strater, Elizabeth, 198
choice: Adler-Kassner, 113–14, 118, 119; agency, intersection with, 4–5, 112–14, 119; Bloom, 58–59, 67, 71; Bourelle, 174–75, 184, 187; chance and, 144; context and, x; Duffey, 97; Flynn, 31, 40; Gere, 49, 51–52, 56; Goksel, 191–94, 199, 201; Hewett, 155, 168, 170; Powell, 124–36; queer families of choice, 144; resilience and, 4; Rhodes, 144, 148, 150, 152; Rose, 235, 236, 243–44. *See also* agency
Cintron, Ralph, 197, 198
City Colleges of Chicago, 158
Clark, VèVè, 8
class, socioeconomic, 33
Classroom Observation Reflections (CORs), 108–9
"Claudel" (Rhodes), 149–50
Clemenc, Annie, 41
Coe, Rick, 18
collaboration: Bloom, Kinney, and Utley, 62; Duffey, 102–3, 104; Ede and Lunsford, 23–26; Goksel, 196, 197; Hewett, 162–64; team-teaching, 99; *Virtual Collaborative Writing in the Workplace* (Hewett and Robidoux), 163–64
Collins, Terry, 114, 115, 118
Columbia College Chicago, 76, 78
Columbia University, 204
Coming of Age in Academe (Martin), 8
Committee for Effective Practices in OWI (CCCC), 169
commuting: Duffey, 101; Gere, 55; Hewett, 166

INDEX • 251

"Composing as a Woman" (Flynn), 42–43, 213
Comprone, Joe, 97
Conference on Basic Writing, 99–100
Conference on College Composition and Communication (CCCC): Committee for Effective Practices in OWI, 169; Deep Rewards and Serious Risks workshop, 196; Flynn, 44; Goksel, 195–96; Hewett, 162; "How to Get a Non-Academic Position" (Ede), 18, 19–20; N. Jones, 231; "On Literacy and the Kemalist Rhetorics of 1928" (Goksel), 196; Papoulis, 203, 213–14, 215, 216; "Resistance, Silence and Fear" (Goksel), 196; Rhodes, 148–49
Connors, Robert, 23, 28, 178
Cook, Kelli Cargile, 176
Cooper, Marilyn, 5
Corbett, Edward P. J., 19, 21, 23, 28, 31, 33–34, 36, 51, 96
Council of Writing Program Administrators, 237
Council on Basic Writing (CBW), 99
critical pedagogy, 183–84
Crouter, Natalie, 65–67, 70
Crowley, Sharon, 195–96
Culture as History (Susman), 116–17

Danielewicz, Jane, 213
Dautermann, Jennie, 139n24
Davis, Angela, 231
Davis, Diane, 2–3, 97, 105n1
Dean, Diane R., 10, 38
Deans, Thomas, 183
de Botton, Alain, 203–4
Deep Rewards and Serious Risks workshop (CCCC Globalization Committee), 196
Defend & Publish, LLC, 167
Dependent ID project (DID), 158
depression. *See* Rhodes, Jacqueline
Derrida, Jacques, 5
Dewey, John, 111, 113, 181
Dicken-Garcia, Hazel, 116–18, 122
Dillard, Annie, 59, 70
"Discovering Copper Country Women's Heritage," 40–41
Doctor Spock: Biography of a Conservative Radical (Bloom), 63–65

Doty, Mark, 143
Duffey, Suellynn, 19, 28, 89–107; "Come Sit at the Table," 101; "Conflict and Collaboration in Peer Teaching Groups" (Duffey et al.), 101; "Defining *Junior*," 98; "Student Silences in the Deep South," 102
Duhamel, Albert, 33
Duke University: L. Jones, 76, 78

Eastern Kentucky University, 77
Eastern Michigan University, 119–21
Eastman, Charles, 136
Ebert, Theresa, 150
eComp (Electronic Composition), 186
Ede, Lisa, 18–29; *The Academic Writer*, 26; "Border Crossings" (Ede, Glenn, and Lunsford), 25; *Essays on Classical Rhetoric and Modern Discourse* (Connors, Ede, and Lunsford), 23; *Everyone's an Author* (Lunsford et al.), 25; "How to Get a Non-Academic Position" (CCCC), 18, 19–20; "On Distinctions between Classical and Modern Rhetoric" (Ede and Lunsford), 23; *Singular Texts/Plural Authors* (Ede and Lunsford), 24; *Situating Composition*, 22, 28; *Writing Together* (Lunsford and Ede), 24–25
Elbow, Peter, 27, 34, 205–6, 209–15, 239
Emig, Janet, 51
empowerment: cultural, 228; expressivists and, 209–10; N. Jones and, 218–21, 226–30, 232; Papoulis and, 196, 209–10; relationality and, 83; Rumi on, 192; Shor on, 183, 184. *See also* agency
Emre, Yunus, 192–93
End of American History, The (Noble), 116–17
Enos, Rich, 50, 97
Enos, Theresa, 7
Estrem, Heidi, 119–20
eTC (Electronic Technical Communication), 186
ethics questions in rhet/comp, 28
"Experience One" method, 181
experiential learning, 181, 183
expressivist vs. social constructionist (Elbow vs. Bartholomae) debate, 208–10

Facts, Artifacts, and Counterfacts (Bartholomae and Petrosky), 98–99 family and ancestral connections. *See* Powell, Malea

family and childrearing: Adler-Kassner, 118; Bloom, 61; Bourelle, 174, 188; Duffey, 101; Flynn, 43, 45; Gere, 51–56; Goksel, 200; Hewett, 158, 166–67; L. Jones, 76, 81; N. Jones, 222–23, 224, 229; Papoulis, 214; single parenting, 41, 45, 222–23

Farr, Marcia, 197–98

feminism: academic resistance to, 8; Bloom and, 67; Bourelle and, 181; ethnography and feminist rhetorical scholarship, 197–99; Flynn and, 34–42, 43–45; intersectionality and, 2, 41; joy as feminist rhetorical response, 197; modern, antimodern, and postmodern, 43–44; resilience, feminist conception of, 4; rhetorics, intersection with, 25–26, 89

Feminism Beyond Modernism (Flynn), 42, 43–44

"Feminist Critical Theory: Three Models" (Flynn), 35–36

Feminist Rhetorical Resilience (Flynn, Sotirin, and Brady), 44, 82–83, 90, 144, 191–92, 196

Fetal Alcohol Syndrome (FAS), 52–53

Ffye, Paul, 187

Finnegan, Ruth, 50

Flannery, Clarinda, 120

Fleming, Alexander, 5–6, 60

Flower, Linda, 27

Flynn, Elizabeth A. (Beth), 4, 25, 28, 30–48; "Composing as a Woman," 42–43, 213; "Composing 'Composing as a Woman,'" 213; *Feminism Beyond Modernism*, 42, 43–44; "Feminist Critical Theory: Three Models" (dissertation), 35–36; *Feminist Rhetorical Resilience* (Flynn, Sotirin, and Brady), 44, 82–83, 90, 144, 191–92, 196; *Gender and Reading* (Flynn and Schweickart), 41–42, 43, 44; "Gender and Reading," 41; *Reading Sites* (Schweickart and Flynn), 44; "Reconsiderations," 42; Rhodes and, 148

Flynn, John, 32, 35–39, 43–45

Forbidden Diary (Crouter; ed. Bloom), 65–67, 69, 70

foundationalism, 211

Frank, Robert, 27

Friedan, Betty, 31, 181

"From Boundaries to Borderlands: Rhetoric(s) and Feminism(s)" conference, 25–26

Fulwiler, Toby, 27, 177

Gaines, William M., 122n2

Gardiner, Judith, 197

Garner, Shirley Nelson, 8

Garnes, Sara, 37

Gaskill, Dave, 129

Gay, Roxane, 1–2

gender and institutional structure of academia, 7

Gender and Reading (Flynn and Schweickart), 41–42, 43, 44

"Gender and Reading" (Flynn), 41

Gender Roles and Faculty Lives in Rhetoric and Composition (Enos), 7

Georgia Southern University, 102, 104

Gere, Anne Ruggles, 49–57; *Intimate Practices*, 54; *Writing Groups*, 52

Gillespie, Paula, 178

Giroux, Henry, 183

Glasser, Theodore (Ted), 112–13

Glassner, Barry, 10

Glenn, Cheryl, 25–26

Global Society of Online Literacy Educators (GSOLE), 169

Goksel, Iklim, 191–202

Goldblatt, Eli, 14

Gonzalez, Carmen G., 220

Goodburn, Amy, 2–3

Goodman, Kenneth, 36

Goodman, Yetta, 36

Goody, Jack, 50

Gopnik, Adam, 66–67

Gordon, Mary, 2

Goulden, Marc, 38

Great Lakes College Association, 37

Greer, Jane, 101

grief: Flynn, 43; Gere, 54; Hewett, 166, 169–70; Papoulis, 211–12; Powell, 128, 133; Rhodes, 149

Gunner, Jeanne, 99–100

Gutgold, Nichola D., 10, 46n3

Gypsy Academics and Mother-Teachers: Gender, Contingent Labor, and Writing Instruction (Schell), 8

Haas, Angela M., 226
Hairston, Maxine, 7
Halberstam, J. Jack, 143, 145
Hambidge Center for the Creative Arts and Sciences, 77
Hammond, Lynn, 212
Hanstedt, Paul, 101, 105n8
Harrington, Mona, 9
Harris, Angela P., 220
Harris, Joseph, 27
Hasselmo, Nils, 114
Hawhee, Debra, 90
Heath, Shirley Brice, 103
Hefling, Jim, 39
Heilman, Robert, 50
Herrera-Sobek, María, 9
Hertz, Rosana, 10
Hesse, Doug, 243
Hewett, Beth L., 154–72; *Good Words,* 170; *More Good Words,* 170; "Nathaniel Hawthorne" (Hewett and Singer), 166; *Reading to Learn and Writing to Teach,* 168–69; *Virtual Collaborative Writing in the Workplace* (Hewett and Robidoux), 163–64
Hewett, Russell J., 168
Higonnet, Margaret, 8
Holbrook, Sue Ellen, 8
Hollowell, John, 50
hooks, bell, 2, 181
Hopkins, Sarah Winnemucca, 134–35
Horner, Win, 7
Horowitz, Franklin Eugene, 178
Howard-Pitney, David, 118
Hull, Glynda A., 183–84
Hunt, Kellogg, 37

Imagined Communities (Anderson), 116–17
independent scholar path, 167–69
Indiana University at Kokomo, 129–31
Indiana University Purdue University Fort Wayne, 200
Indiana University Purdue University Indianapolis, 72n10
Innocence Project, 220, 227–28, 229–30
Institute for Writing and Thinking, 213, 214
Institutional Review Board (IRB), 198–99

intersectionality and feminism, 2, 41
intuition: accidental sagacity and, 5–6; Adler-Kassner, 112; Duffey, 91; Goksel, 193; Papoulis, 216
"invisible colleges," 179
Irmscher, William, 27

James, Henry, 67
James, William, 61
Jameson, Fredric, 36
Jarratt, Susan, 97, 148
job searches: Bloom, 67–68, 68–69; Bourelle, 180–81, 182, 185, 188; Duffey, 97–98; Ede, 19–20, 22; Flynn, 37; L. Jones, 83; Papoulis, 206
Jones, Libby Falk, 74–88; "About," 87; *Above the Eastern Treetops, Blue,* 77; "The Absent Director," 84; *Feminism, Utopia, and Narrative* (Jones and Goodwin), 79; "From the Darkroom," 76; "The Morning Light," 76; "Moving Toward the Center," 83; "On Cats, Children, Words, and Other Living Things," 76
Jones, Natasha N., 218–34; "Genetic Interfaces" (Sidler and Jones), 227–28
Julie, Timmermans, 110

kairos and kairotic opportunities: Bourelle, 174, 187–88; definitions of, 6, 174; Duffey, 96–97, 98; Ede, 27; Gere, 56; Goksel, 192, 199
Kallet, Marilyn, 76
Kansas State University, 157
Katrak, Ketu H., 8
Kennedy, X. J., 71n6
Kennelly, Ivy, 222
Kentucky State Poetry Society, 77
Khayyam, Omar, 192, 196
Kincaid, James, 31, 35
King, Martin Luther, Jr., 64, 232
Kinneavy, James, 6
Kinney, Arthur, 62
Kirkpatrick, Carolyn, 99
Kirsch, Gesa, 5
kismet, 62, 191–95, 199, 201
Kneupper, Charles, 22
knowledge: academic hierarchies of, 28; alternative modes of knowledge production, 14; Atatürk and knowledge-

making, 192; received, imagination to transcend, 63; scientific, 227; "taking teachings" in Native traditions, 138n13; troublesome, 110–12, 121–22; women's alternative forms, recognizing, 191; *Women's Ways of Knowing* (Belenky et al.), 178–79
Kroll, Barry, 97
Kustra, Erika, 186

Land, Ray, 108, 110
Lanham, Richard, 97
Larson, Russ, 120
Lauer, Claire, 184
law and rhetoric, 175
LeCourt, Donna, 2–3
Lee, Charlotte, 230
Leighninger, Anna Wolfe, 132–33
Lenape peoples, 132, 139n20
Lerner, Neal, 178
Let Your Life Speak (Palmer), 80
Leverenz, Carrie, 2–3, 101
Li, Guofang, 9
Lila, 142, 152
Lim, Shirley Geok-Lin, 9
Lindemann, Erika, 18, 27
Linse, Angela R., 10, 46n3
literacy crisis, 22
literary criticism, feminism introduced to, 43
Lives on the Boundary (LOB) (Rose), 114–16
Logan, Shirley Wilson, 2
Logic and Rhetoric of Exposition, The (Martin and Ohmann), 33
luck, 4–5, 60
Lunsford, Andrea, 2, 18, 19, 23–26, 28, 178; "Border Crossings" (Ede, Glenn, and Lunsford), 25; *Essays on Classical Rhetoric and Modern Discourse* (Connors, Ede, and Lunsford), 23; *Everyone's an Author* (Lunsford et al.), 25; "On Distinctions between Classical and Modern Rhetoric" (Ede and Lunsford), 23; *Singular Texts/Plural Authors* (Ede and Lunsford), 24; *Writing Together* (Lunsford and Ede), 24–25

Macalester College, 111
Macrorie, Ken, 34, 206
Markels, Julian, 93–94

marriage and spouse/partner's work: Bloom, 58–59, 65, 69–71; Bourelle, 174, 180–81, 188; Ede, 29n2; Flynn, 31–32, 38; Gere, 51, 53–54; Goksel, 199–200; Hewett, 157–60, 166; L. Jones, 81, 85–86; Papoulis, 212–13, 214; women making the accommodations, 38
Marshak, Robert, 160
Martin, Harold C., 33
Martin, Jane Roland, 8
Marxist criticism, 35–36
Mason, Mary Ann, 38
Mattson, Kyle, 231
Medicine, Bea, 40
Merton, Robert, 59–60
mêtis, 4, 83, 90, 97, 104
Meyer, Jan, 108, 110
Meyers, Morton, 174
Miami tribes, 131, 138n14
Miami University, 131, 133–34, 139n15
Michigan Humanities Council (Michigan Council for the Humanities), 40
Michigan Technological University, 37–42, 44–46
Michigan Women's Hall of Fame, 41
Michigan Women's Studies Association, 41
Middle East Technical University, Ankara, 193
Midwest Modern Language Association (MMLA), 41–42
Miller, Carolyn, 6, 174
Miller, Susan: challenges faced by, 7; Ede and, 18–19, 27, 28; as OSU Writing Program Administrator, 18–19, 95–96; Rhodes and, 148–49; study group of, 36–37; "textual subjectivity," 144
Modern Language Association (MLA), 8, 44, 50, 56
Moller, Marilyn, 25
Monson, Connie, 149, 151
"moral luck," 4–5
Moss, Beverly, 25, 198
Moss, Jean Dietz, 161
Moss, Thylias, 76, 86
Mountford, Roxanne, 2–3, 97, 105n1
multimodal composition, 183–84
Muñoz, Jose Esteban, 144
Murray, Donald, 51, 61–62, 206, 239

Nagel, Thomas, 4–5
National Writing Project (NWP), 51–52, 212
Native rhetorics and theory, 128, 134. *See also* Powell, Malea
NEH seminar, Carnegie Mellon (1978–79), 22
Neidermeyer, Presha E., 10
Nelson, Mark Evan, 183–84
neo-Aristotelian criticism, 35–36
Newburgh Free Academy, 33
Newkirk,Tom, 206
Newman, Samuel P., 156, 161–62, 166
New York Military Academy (NYMA), 33
Noble, David W., 116–17
normalization of women's challenges, ix–x
Northern Arizona University, 176–77
Northwestern University, 41

Ohio State University: Bloom, 62, 71n5; Duffey, 93–101, 102–4, 105n3; Ede, 18–19, 21; Flynn, 33–37, 46; Writing Workshop, 37
Ohmann, Richard, 33
Ojibwa tribal community, 40
Oliver, Mary, 74
Olson, David R., 50
Olson, Jon, 26
Ong, Walter, 33, 50
online writing centers (OWLs), 167
online writing instruction (OWI), 163, 165–69
Oregon State University, 22–23, 26, 27
Other Moms, 52–53
Ottenstein, Richard, 170
Our Studies, Ourselves: Sociologists' Lives and Work (Glassner and Hertz), 10

Pace University, 32–33
Palmer, Parker, 80, 82, 85, 86
Paludi, Michele A., 10
Panofsky, Erwin, 6
Papoulis, Irene, 203–17
Papper, Carole Clark, 25
Parks, Steve, 14
Pennsylvania State University, 166
Perkins, David, 110
Perl, Sondra, 206
Personal History Project (PHP), 111, 112
Petrosky, Anthony, 98–99

peyote stitch, 124–25, 126
Pfarr, Greg, 29n2
Phegley, Jennifer, 101
Photiades, John, 145
Picotte, Susan LaFlesche, 136
pilgrimage metaphor, 154–55, 170
Pimentel, Octavio, 231
plagiarism, 163
poetry writing. *See* Jones, Libby Falk
postmodernism, resistance vs. ludic, 150
Potter, Michael, 186
Powell, Malea, 124–41
Power, Race, and Gender in Academe (Lim and Herrera-Sobek), 9
Practical System of Rhetoric, A (Newman), 161–62
pragmatism, American, 113
pregnancy and childbirth: Bloom, 61; Bourelle, 188; Flynn, 42–43; L. Jones, 81; N. Jones, 222–23; Papoulis, 214. *See also* family and childrearing
Price, Reynolds, 76, 79, 85
Princeton High School, 49
promotion. *See* tenure
Puget Sound Writing Project, 51

queerness, queer time, and queer theory, 142–45, 149–51

rational model and nonrational lived experience, 89–91
Reading Sites (Schweickart and Flynn), 44
relationality, in rhetorical resilience, 4, 83, 91, 197
resilience: Adler-Kassner, 116; empowerment, transformation, and, 218–19; feminist conception of, 4; feminist rhetorical resilience, 82–86, 91; *Feminist Rhetorical Resilience* (Flynn, Sotirin, and Brady), 4, 44, 82–83, 90, 144, 191–92, 196; Goksel, 192, 194–96, 199; as interactive process, 96; N. Jones, 218–19, 221, 232; relationality, in rhetorical resilience, 4, 83, 91, 197; "resilient rhetorical action," 192; Rhodes, 147, 149; Rumi on, 192
Rewriting Success in Rhetoric and Composition Careers (Goodburn, LeCourt, and Leverenz), 2–3
Reynolds, Nedra, 150–51

rhetoric and composition (rhet/comp), field of: challenging circumstances in, 7–8; Ede and, 21–22; ethical questions in, 28; expressivist vs. social constructionist (Elbow vs. Bartholomae) debate, 208–10; feminism introduced to, 43; Flynn and, 36; important historical moment in, 15; intersection of feminism and rhetorics, 25–26; law and rhetoric, 175; multimodal composition, 183–84; stigmatization of writing and, 208; technical communication and rhetoric, 175–76. *See also specific topics, such as* job searches

Rhodes, Jacqueline, 142–53; "Claudel," 149–50; *On Multimodality* (Rhodes and Alexander), 151; "Risking Queer" (Monson and Rhodes), 149; *Techne* (Rhodes and Alexander), 145, 151, 152

Rich, Adrienne, 2

Richards, I. A., 33

risk: Adler-Kassner, 118; agency and, 15; Bloom, 59, 61–64, 68–69, 70–71; Bourelle, 183; Celebration of Student Writing (CSW) and, 120; Goksel, 193, 199, 201; Hewett, 156, 160, 164; Rose, 241, 243

Robertson, Wayne, 26

Robidoux, Charlotte, 163–64

Robinson, Marilynne, 146

Roen, Duane, 184

Rohan, Liz, 5

Rose, Mike, 97, 114–16

Rose, Shirley, 235–44

Rosenblatt, Louise, 41–42

Rosenmann, Martin, 5–6

Royster, Jacqueline Jones, 2

Rude, Carolyn D., 226

Rumi, 192–93, 197

Runciman, Lex, 26

Rycenga, John A., 33

Ryu, Mikyung, 220

Safire, William, 64

sagacity, accidental, 5, 27

Sams, Margaret, 67

Sarton, May, 80, 85

Savage, Gerald, 231

Schell, Eileen, 8

Schmidt, Jan Zlotnik, 2–3

scholarly teaching vs. scholarship of teaching, 186–87

Scholes, Robert, 62, 63

Schwartz, Joseph, 33

Schweickart, Patrocinio P. (Patsy), 41–42, 43, 44

Scott, Fred Newton, 56

Scottsdale Chorus, 235–44

Seegal, David, 60

Selfe, Cynthia L., 148, 183–84

semantic integrity theory, 167–68

serendipity: Adler-Kassner, 111, 113–14, 118, 121; Bloom, 58–65, 67–71; Bourelle, 174, 187; context and, x; Duffey, 93, 96–97, 101; Ede, 20, 26, 27, 28; Flynn, 33, 36; Gere, 50, 52, 55–56; Goksel, 192, 194–96, 201; L. Jones, 74, 77, 85–86; luck vs., 60; origin and meanings of term, 5–6, 59–61; Papoulis, 204; Rose, 236–37, 243; "Technologies of Serendipity" (Ffye), 187; *The Travels and Adventures of Serendipity* (Merton and Barber), 59–60

service-learning projects, 183

shame, 203–4, 207–10, 213–16

Shaughnessy, Mina, 70, 97

Shor, Ira, 182–83, 184

Shuck, Kim, 124, 137, 137n1

Shull, Lemuel, 126–27

single parenting: Flynn, 41, 45; N. Jones, 222–23

Sirc, Geoffrey, 118

Smarthinking, Inc., 166

Smith, Frank, 36

social constructionist vs. expressivist (Elbow vs. Bartholomae) debate, 208–10

Solomon, Andrew, 147, 152

Sotirin, Patricia, 4, 44, 82–83, 90, 144, 191–92, 196

Spock, Benjamin, 63–65, 72n8

Spyridakis, Jan, 229

Stafford, William, 74

Steinem, Gloria, 76

STEM courses, integrating writing into, 55–56

Stewart, Donald, 157

Stony Brook University (SUNY Stony Brook): L. Jones, 75, 76, 80; Papoulis, 204–6

Street, Brian, 50

subjectivity, textual, 144
Suleiman, Susan, 41
SUNY Brockport, 22, 26
Susman, Warren, 116–17
Sweetland Center for Writing, 55

Takayoshi, Pamela, 183–84
team-teaching, 99
technical communication: N. Jones, 223–24, 226–29, 231; rhetoric and, 175–76
"Technologies of Serendipity" (Ffye), 187
Telling Stories (White), 9
Temple University, 158
tenure: Bloom, 68; Bourelle, 173, 187; collaboration and, 23–24; Duffey, 97; Ede, 23–24; feminism and, 41; Flynn, 41; Gere, 53
Textual Carnivals (Miller), 7
textual subjectivity, 144
threshold concepts, 108–10, 121
Todorov, Tveztan, 41
Tokarczyk, Michelle, 215
Tompkins, Jane, 41–42
Trinity College, Hartford, 203, 214–16
troublesome knowledge, 110–12, 121–22
Trump, Donald, 33
Tuve, Rosemond, 33

University of California, Santa Barbara: Adler-Kassner, 121; Papoulis, 206–11
University of Connecticut, 71
University of Idaho, 146
University of Illinois at Chicago, 195–99
University of Louisville, 147
University of Maryland, 158
University of Maryland University College, 167
University of Massachusetts, 213
University of Michigan: Bloom, 58, 62, 71n5; Gere, 49–50, 54–56; L. Jones, 76, 79, 86; sex-discrimination in GPA requirements, 71n5
University of Minnesota, 112–19, 122
University of Missouri-St. Louis: Bloom, 69; Duffey, 102–4
University of Montana, 145–46
University of Montana Western, 181–82

University of Nevada, Reno, 177–80
University of New Mexico: Bloom, 69–71; Bourelle, 173, 185–88
University of Southern Mississippi, 146–48
University of Tennessee: Bourelle, 174–76; L. Jones, 76, 78, 86
University of Washington: Gere, 50–51; N. Jones, 228–30
University of Wisconsin, Eau Claire, 101–2
University of Wisconsin, Madison, 20–21
"Usable Past: CCC at 50, A," *College Composition and Communication* (CCC) special issue, 27
Utley, Francis L., 62

Valian, Virginia, 8
Virginia Center for the Creative Arts, 77
Virtual Collaborative Writing in the Workplace (Hewett and Robidoux), 163–64
Vitanza, Victor, 22, 28
voice, 239, 242

Waldo, Mark, 178
Wall, Beverly, 214
Walpole, Horace, 5, 60
Walters, Keith, 25
Washington University, 69
Watson, Sam, 22
Weaver, Richard, 33, 162
Webber, Joan, 34, 95–96
Webster University, 69
Western Maryland College (McDaniel College), 155
Western New England College, 213
White, Deborah Gray, 9
White, E. B., 58
White, Ed, 50, 97
White, Richard, 139n19
White Eyes (*Koquethagechton*), 132, 139n21
White's Institute, 128, 138n11
Why So Slow? (Valian), 8
Williams, Bernard, 4–5
Williams, Gareth, 5
Williams, Miriam F., 226, 231
Wolfinger, Nicholas H., 38
Women in the Academy (Gutgold and Linse), 10

Women of Academe (Aisenberg and Harrington), 9
Women's Caucus for the Modern Languages, 44
Women's History Month, 44
Women's Ways of Knowing (Belenky et al.), 178–79
Women's Ways of Making It in Rhetoric and Composition (Ballif, Davis, and Mountford), 2–3, 90, 105n1
Women/Writing/Teaching (Schmidt), 2–3
Work, Life, and Family Imbalance (Paludi and Neidermeyer), 10
work–life balance, 10, 61–62. *See also* family and childrearing; marriage and spouse/partner's work
Wright, Mindy, 99–100
Writing-Across-the-Curriculum (WAC) program and workshops, 37, 39, 177
"writing as," prison house of, 128
writing centers: Auburn University, 224–25; Berea College, 74–75; Oregon State University, 26; Sweetland Center for Writing, 55; University of Nevada, Reno, 178–79
writing programs: Arizona State University, 184–85, 235, 237, 239, 241–42; Baltimore community college, 165; early "classic patriarchal construction," 7; Eastern Michigan University, 119–21; Georgia Southern University, 102; Ohio State University, 18, 22–23, 95–96, 98–101; Smarthinking, Inc., 166; Stony Brook, 205–6; Trinity College, Hartford, 214–15; University of California, Santa Barbara, 121; University of New Mexico, 69–70, 186
Writing Together (Lunsford and Ede), 24–25

Young, Art, 27, 38, 177
Young, Richard, 22

Zachry, Mark, 229
Zoellner, Robert, 157, 167

www.ingramcontent.com/pod-product-compliance
Lightning Source LLC
Chambersburg PA
CBHW030132240426
43672CB00005B/111